AF711585

Perpetual Children

New Histories of Psychology
Michael Pettit, Series Editor

Associate Editors

Saulo Araujo	Alexandra Hui
Sunal Bhatia	Sarah Igo
Cathy Faye	Edward Jones-Imhotep
Peter Hegarty	Dana Simmons

Governed By Affect:
Hot Cognition and the End of Cold War Psychology
Michael Pettit

Perpetual Children: The Politics of Autism in France since 1950
Jonathyne Briggs

Perpetual Children

The Politics of Autism in France since 1950

JONATHYNE BRIGGS

OXFORD
UNIVERSITY PRESS

OXFORD
UNIVERSITY PRESS

Oxford University Press is a department of the University of Oxford.
It furthers the University's objective of excellence in research, scholarship,
and education by publishing worldwide. Oxford is a registered trade mark of
Oxford University Press in the UK and in certain other countries.

Published in the United States of America by Oxford University Press
198 Madison Avenue, New York, NY 10016, United States of America.

© Oxford University Press 2025

All rights reserved. No part of this publication may be reproduced, stored in a retrieval system, transmitted, used for text and data mining, or used for training artificial intelligence, in any form or by any means, without the prior permission in writing of Oxford University Press, or as expressly permitted by law, by license or under terms agreed with the appropriate reprographics rights organization. Inquiries concerning reproduction outside the scope of the above should be sent to the Rights Department, Oxford University Press, at the address above.

You must not circulate this work in any other form
and you must impose this same condition on any acquirer.

CIP data is on file at the Library of Congress

ISBN 9780197682975

DOI: 10.1093/9780197683002.001.0001

Printed by Marquis, Canada

FSC www.fsc.org MIX Paper | Supporting responsible forestry FSC® C103567

For Sean

CONTENTS

ACKNOWLEDGMENTS

In 2009, my youngest child was diagnosed with autism spectrum disorder (then called autistic disorder in the Diagnostic and Statistical Manual of Mental Disorder IV). While it was not my first experience with autism, it certainly changed the trajectory of my life and, as an academic, led me to read as much as I could about it. Even as my son's challenges became more apparent as he aged, I still hoped that he might share experiences with his siblings, especially in my hopes of having them travel with me on a research trip to France. However, this dream led to my realization of how different the experience of autistic peopleand their families were in France, which was the genesis of this project. As a historian of modern France, I hoped to understand more about how this difference developed and what it suggested about my beloved object of study. As that project became this book, I learned about the importance of having a team to help, something that has been crucial to both my son's growth and maturity and my own as a parent of an autistic person. Without this team, none of this would have been possible and so I want to recognize their contributions.

My scholarly community has been a bedrock as I have found my way through the project. They listened to countless presentations, read drafts, and shared ideas in ways that have strengthened this book. I want to recognize Roxanne Panchasi, Rebecca Scales, Sarah Fishman, Jessie Hewitt, Keith Rathbone, Catherine Kudlick, Nick Underwood, Richard I. Jobs, Bonnie Evans, and Richard Bates for their support, encouragement, and contributions as the "autism project" became the "autism book." At IU Northwest, I appreciate the support of my colleagues in my home department and throughout the institution, especially David Parnell, Nicole Anslover, Diana Chen-Lin, Gianluca Dimuzio, Debi Qualls, Mark Baer, Kate Gustafson, Mark Hoyert, David Klamen, Vicki Romàn-Lagunas, and Amy Diaz. Extra special thanks to my writing group partner Maureen Rutherford for helping me commit to putting in the hours to get this book to completion.

Elements of this book have been presented at the meetings of the Western Society for French History, the Society for French Historical Studies, the Western Michigan University Medical Humanities Conference, the IU European Studies Workshop, and the Globalisation of Autism Workshop. I want to thank the organizers and participants for their questions and input to improve the manuscript.

Also, I want to recognize the contributions of all my students at IU Northwest in my H303 History of Disability classes.

At Oxford University Press, I thank the support and belief of my editors Sarah Harrington and Michael Petit, as well as my production crew of Emily Benitez and Sarah Abel.

My family, of course, has been central to this book on families and disability, so I want to recognize their love and support during this endeavor. My wife Jamie lived with me talking about this book for over a decade, while Regan and Graham kept asking when I would be finally done with the book. Sean just wanted to show me a video on his phone, which always reminded me what this is all about. Also, Ray Dominguez is a pretty great brother. My closest friends Robbie and Kristi St. John and Chuck Armburst-Kohler are the emotional support machines who have been part of my team for decades, while Julian and Olivia St. John have provided their own contributions to my work. I could not have gotten to the end without them.

The team of specialists at Great Strides Rehabilitation has been as much a part of my son's life as his family and their work has helped him with his struggles to find his way. I cannot thank them enough especially Kaitlin Sparks, Josh Breeden, Makayla Earl, Megan Lester, Amber Short, Lauren Pierce, and the countless others who have contributed to my son's well-being and happiness. Also, much gratitude to David Cook and his team at Sugar Valley for providing my son with a place where he feels free to be himself as he approaches adulthood. I am also grateful to Bob and Wendi at the Courtyards for providing a home away from home for my family.

Elements of this manuscript have previously appeared in articles in *Modern Intellectual History*; *French Politics, Culture & Society*; *Historical Reflections/Réflexions Historiques*; and *Contemporary European History*. Research has been partly supported by an IU New Frontiers in Arts and Humanities grant and an International Research Grant from the IU Office of the Vice President for International Affairs.

ABBREVIATIONS

ABA	applied behavioral analysis
ADAPEI	Association départementale de parents et d'amis des personnes handicapées mentales
AIDERA	Association Ile-de-France pour le développement de l'éducation et la recherche sur l'autisme
ARAPI	Association pour la Recherche sur l'Autisme et les Psychoses Infantiles (after 1983) Association pour la Recherche sur l'Autisme et la Prévention des Inadaptations
ASF	Autistes sans frontières
ASITP	Association au Service des Inadaptés ayant des Troubles de la Personalité
CAT	Centre d'aide par le travail
CCNE	Comité consultative national d'ethique
CEREDA	Centre d'Etudes et de Recherche sur l'Enfant dans le Discours Analytique
CFTMEA	Classification française des troubles mentaux de l'enfant et de l'adolescent
CLE Autistes	Collectif pour la Liberté d'Expression des autistes
CTRA	Comité technique regional sur l'autisme
DSM	Diagnostic and Statistical Manual of Mental Disorders
ECSR	European Committee of Social Rights
EPICEA	Enseignement Pratique et Information sur la Communication chez l'Enfant Autistique
FC	Facilitated Communication
ICD	International Classification of Diseases
IGAS	Inspection générale des affaires sociales
ILSMH	International League of Societies for the Mentally Handicapped
IMP	Instituts medico-pédagogiques
INSERM	Institut national de la santé et de la recherche médicale
PREAUT	Programme de recherches et d'études sur l'autisme
SATEDI	Spectre autistique, troubles envahissants du développement, international

TEACCH	Treatment and Education of Autistic and Related Communication Handicapped Children
UNAFAM	Union nationale des familles de malades mentaux et de leurs associations
UNAPEI	Union nationale des associations de parents et amis de personnes handicapées mentales

INTRODUCTION

The French Divergence

In 2012, the French Ministry of Health announced a national plan to grapple with the challenges faced by autistic persons and their families as part of the government's choice of the *grande cause nationale* for that year. The French state and its response to autism had been the subject of increased scrutiny from domestic and international advocacy groups who argued that the French model, which remained tied to psychoanalysis as part of the treatment of autistic patients, had resulted in harm to the population and distanced French practices from other forms of intervention that had broad support outside France. Despite an ever-increasing budget allocation for the treatment and education of this disabled population and growing public awareness of the challenges it faced, the outcomes for many autistic individuals remained bleak because of a lack of both coordination among agencies and state support for models developed outside France. The understanding of autism had achieved a relatively stable global consensus across national boundaries by the beginning of the twenty-first century with a few exceptions, France being the major one. Although autism was recognized as a developmental and behavioral disorder, it had been a subject of great consternation concerning its rapidly expanding numbers throughout the world beginning in the 1990s. The word *epidemic* had been used to frame these discussions, often originating from parents' groups seeking to elevate both increased government intervention and social awareness.[1] In many cases, states responded to concerns about autism with increased funding toward programs and efforts to raise parental and medical awareness through improved diagnoses. However, in France, the quest for greater state support for autistic persons and the efforts for awareness were complicated by the French divergence from the rest of the Western world in the political and medical realm of autism.

The French divergence concerning autism reveals several important aspects about the meaning of psychology in a global age, the assumed values of childhood and family that framed psychological interventions, and the challenges of adapting within a shifting set of ideas about what autism is without the full inclusion of all voices in the conversation. One of the confluences of these various strands of divergence is the question of the ontology of autism, which remained a

Perpetual Children. Jonathyne Briggs, Oxford University Press. © Oxford University Press (2025).
DOI: 10.1093/9780197683002.003.0001

primary focus for French professionals since the initial acknowledgment of autism in the postwar era. The need to understand the origins of autism ultimately lent a great deal of weight to psychoanalytic theory, which purported to explain how and why the disorder developed among children and accumulated a great deal of cultural capital in France in the second half of the twentieth century. Building on ideas advanced in the 1930s and rooted in the developing field of child psychoanalysis, psychological professionals emphasized the explanatory and therapeutic value of analysis to treat autistic behaviors and allow for proper development in troubled children, as well as its flexible nature that allowed for a variety of individual treatments. Intervention was both individual and collective; autistic children were recognized as a byproduct of a disrupted emotional ecosystem within the family, and analysis of the parents, with a primary focus on the mother, was suggested as a component of proper treatment. However, the focus on origin obscured the experiences of autism as a disability that impacted people throughout their lives. This approach was reflective of the state of psychoanalysis in France during this period, since inroads in the psychological profession were not made there until much later than in other Western countries due to the presence of a rich domestic tradition of psychology. Once the French developed their own celebrated ambassador of Freudian thought with Jacques Lacan, the number of analysts working in France grew and its credibility in society increased.[2] One area where this acceleration was most evident was child psychology; interest in the development of children increased in the postwar era because of concerns about social hygiene and the traumas of the war impacting family life, although psychoanalysis became common throughout all areas of French medicine.[3] Psychoanalysts were positioned to help guide and assess psychological norms using a method focused on the impact of development on mental wellness, allowing them to develop influence in the French medical field, especially in interventions directed at children.

In the immediate period after the Second World War, psychoanalysis was an international culture that connected thinkers in France, the United Kingdom, and the United States, among other places. The transatlantic nature of psychology allowed for ideas to cross national boundaries and develop in conversation with myriad thinkers while permitting some national specificity.[4] Dagmar Herzog observed the unique position of psychoanalysis in the postwar period as a "language for thinking about the changes in what counted as truth about how human beings are, and what could and should be done about it," amplifying its impact on intellectual thinking in the Western world.[5] She also noted the cultural specificity of practices of psychoanalysis that helped to establish a variety of interpretations, typically indicative of notions of sexuality that dominated individual societies. The preeminent historian of psychoanalysis in France, Élisabeth Roudinesco, saw the emergence of a new psychoanalytic interest following the end of the war, one that diverged from the international model of psychoanalysis that was highly influenced by the United States, in which politics and philosophy influenced the development of techniques and concepts.[6] Significant figures in philosophy, including Michel Foucault, Gilles Deleuze, and Frantz Fanon, engaged with the implications of psychoanalytic ideas and logics in their own assessments and interrogations of cultural norms that introduced psychoanalytic concepts to a broader public, especially in France. While the practice of psychoanalysis had deep fractures within French circles, as a culture it proved influential within the medical profession as a framework to connect numerous strands of intellectual traditions. The philosophical nature of psychoanalysis allowed contemplation of the origins of conditions within the language of French politics.[7]

As psychoanalysis became more influential in French thinking, it brought French practitioners into alignment with strands of thought concerning the development of children that emphasized the importance of the family as a catalyst for healthy upbringing. The emphasis on mothers and their centrality to childrearing was not new in the postwar period, but the changes in the experiences of women politically, socially, and economically complicated the social ideal of the mother, especially when combined with the theories of psychoanalysis. For example, in her classic *The Reproduction of Mothering* (1978), Nancy Chodorow argues that the transformation of Western society with wage labor and compulsory education has led to a parallel transformation in the meaning of mothering, charging it with an emotional intensity that psychoanalysis reified.[8] There was also a proliferation of parenting experts that signaled an era of anxiety concerning proper childrearing, with that anxiety often directed at and manifest in mothers, and the expansion of child psychology added another field of experts offering advice.[9] Much of this advice emphasized new roles for fathers in rhetorical terms that highlighted the value of their emotional investment in their children, but the shift away from paternal authority led some observers to warn against permissiveness and its corrosive effect on children.[10] Additionally, there was a continued natalist approach operant in France that stressed the importance of motherhood as a social good necessary for the growth of society; it reinforced mothering as a natural function that warranted focused attention and surveillance to encourage healthy children.[11] In this context, analysts scrutinized the role of mothers in cases of autism through concepts that pathologized maternal anxieties as a pathway to establishing disabling behaviors in children.

The most extreme example of these anxieties was the "refrigerator mother," a concept that has been embedded in the history of autism since the 1940s thanks to Leo Kanner's cursory observations of his patients' mothers' demeanors. A refrigerator mother was emotionally unavailable to her children, and Kanner postulated that this unavailability influenced the development of autistic behaviors in response to mechanical and passive dispositions of mothers.[12] According to many analysts, the refrigerator mother concept symbolized how poor parenting disabled children through emotional trauma in early childhood, causing a deliberate retreat from reality that required the intervention of analysts to repair the psychological damage. Autistic children, sensing their parents' anxieties, withdrew to protect themselves from the emotional turmoil of their parents' desires. Because of its focus on the mental states of infants and toddlers, child psychoanalysis became the accepted method for the treatment of autism during the 1950s, establishing norms that would prove durable in the French context but at the time were not unique to it. Throughout the Western world, the threat of the refrigerator mother led professionals and experts to provide advice on childrearing that was targeted at women, while emphasizing the need to provide analysis directly to mothers as part of the treatment of autism.

The threat of the refrigerator mother illustrates the transformation of the ideal of motherhood during the modern period and its subsequent entrenchment within medicine as normative and healthy. The image of the emotionally committed and connected mother as a nurturing figure developed as a type from the work of Enlightenment thinkers who argued for the specific need for child development as a method of enrichment and education. As Claire Duchen argues, by the twentieth century, motherhood was "a profoundly political question in France," given the greater interest in child development as an element of public health.[13] The assumed material instinct of women reified their position as the primary caretaker within the family, which itself was changing as a result of increased female labor outside the household and greater political and social independence for women in French society. In turn, such assumptions enhanced the role of the mother within the family while failing to elevate her authority to the level of the father; this type of thinking echoed psychoanalytic philosophy concerning the healthy structure of the family that allows for the proper development of children. As Élisabeth Badinter observed, this social paradox informed the modern notion of mother love that went on to influence the cultural understanding of normative motherhood and its significance as an inherent part of Western society.[14] Jordynn Jack understood this emotional ideal as part of the construction of the enduring archetype of the refrigerator mother who became central to the story of autism beginning in the 1950s, revealing the pervasive nature of the acceptance of maternal emotional norms within medicine and gendered understandings of autism in general.[15] Although they did not use the same terminology, many French psychological theorists and practitioners embraced elements of the refrigerator mother theory, which conformed to their own assumptions about motherhood and its emotional role in establishing healthy domiciles and could be understood within the logics of psychoanalysis.

In conjunction with the tensions between the changes in the lives of women in postwar France, the role of parents as advocates for their children accelerated in the context of disability rights. With the increased diagnosis and recognition of developmentally disabled children, mothers and fathers became interlocuters for this population and its need to navigate educational, social, and medical worlds. The disruptions to the family as it engaged with these systems have historically characterized the relationship between disability and family because the disruptions reified the definition of family in a symbolic manner that assumed ability.[16] Thus, the children in these families operated socially as different from other children, reinforcing the alleged abnormality that justified their separation during the twentieth century.[17] Disabled children challenged the notion of families by the otherness imposed on them by professionals, and cultural understandings of families were bound to ableist notions of childhood that segregated the children, despite the medical attention they attracted.[18] With these children remaining socially and culturally isolated from the population of abled children, their parents organized and pressed for change through a series of approaches that required parents to become political and medical advocates, often asserting their own expertise in the field of developmental disability based on their experiences raising their children. This phenomenon was certainly not unique to France: parents in the United States and Europe were important agents of change in terms of pressing for increased state intervention and support in the field of child disability.[19] Their efforts put them in conflict at times with psychology professionals and at other times with disabled populations, but nevertheless, in France parents were crucial to developing a coordinated response to the treatment of its autistic population and the increased awareness of the population itself.[20] Mothers and fathers occupied vital roles in associations dedicated to improving the lives of autistic children, with some of the organizations increasingly recognizing that those children grew into adults who remained segregated from French society. Through advocacy, mothers had many opportunities to engage in a new form of militancy that still often rested on their emotional role in families.

While rooted in domestic notions of family, advocacy efforts brought these issues into the public view with awareness campaigns and lobbying efforts that attempted to engage the French in recognizing the social challenges of disability. Often, these efforts relied heavily on emotional arguments that reified existing parental stereotypes, but in the fifties and sixties these organizations were primarily run by fathers, which suggested the limits to changing parental roles. By the seventies, mothers had been elevated in the discourse, especially in the wake of biographical accounts that emphasized parents' experience to challenge stereotypes concerning autism among the French population.[21] Afterward, mothers played leadership roles in organizations at a greater rate, bringing them directly into the political conflicts about the proper treatment of autism. By the turn of the century, mother blaming had lost its valence as an explanation for the origin of autism, but the effects of decades of that idea continued to influence therapeutic interventions despite evidence to the contrary from many vectors outside France. Motherhood remained central in the discussion of autism, especially given the issues emphasized by parents' associations that stressed the challenges faced by caregivers.

The emphasis on motherhood and the emergence of child psychoanalysis in France also framed normative notions of childhood, including the proper development of children, their behavioral expectations, and the importance of intervention to ensure their rightful place in French society. Given anxieties about natalism that fixated the French population during the nineteenth and twentieth centuries, normative childhood was emphasized as an element of the continuing social hygiene movement that aimed to direct French families through concepts and ideas that had grown in stature following the Second World War.[22] In child psychoanalysis, the emphasis on discourse was challenged by the less developed verbal expressiveness of some autistic children, leading to questions about how subjects might engage in analytic work. Yet theorists such as Anna Freud, Melanie Klein, and Françoise Dolto offered theoretical frameworks that applied psychoanalytic theory to explain the emotional lives of children, including infants, that established normative behaviors within the family. Understood as an example of child psychotherapy, child psychoanalysis provided a space for children to operate unconditionally so that the analyst could observe and develop a relationship to the child, which led analysts to embrace forms of play and art therapy as pathways to understanding the child's inner world. These expressions were interpreted through a psychoanalytic lens to elucidate the triggers of behaviors that led parents to bring the child to therapy, at times in response to additional prompting from medical professionals and social workers.

Often, child analysts focused on the relationship between children and their mothers (although fathers had a defined role as well) to try to understand the actions of children who did not conform to social norms or displayed problematic behaviors that led to their marginalization. Analysts interpreted children's actions in the clinical setting within the narratives of psychoanalysis, especially their focus on the importance of separation from their mothers through the natural resolution of the Oedipal complex, which led analysts to often require the parallel analysis of mothers as part of treatment. Klein, for example, postulated that passing through the stages of the Oedipal complex beginning around the age of three led to a child's wish to destroy the object of desire (their mother), which she thought explained some violent behavior in children.[23] Klein's subsequent analysis of an autistic child in 1930 revealed how she applied her ideas in cases where the child did not speak in a coherent or organized manner, reinforcing her assumptions about the desire to destroy and disengage with the mother as an object of desire.[24] Klein's influence on French child psychology solidified the influence of psychoanalysis on that field and its practitioners, who had their own influence on French society, including Dolto, Maud Mannoni, and Serge Lebovici. Klein's ideas also reflected the social ideal of the emotional mother as important to the proper development of children's independence and social belonging.

The growing influence of child psychoanalysis also speaks to the changing contours of childhood normativity in the postwar period, with parents remaining responsible for the healthy upbringing of children but accompanied by a growing interest from the state and medicine in providing guidance on achieving this social good. The postwar era saw the emergence of organizations dedicated to educating parents on the most recent developments in child psychology to give them the best information available. Organizations such as École des parents, which had established itself in the 1930s, expanded their influence on parents through conferences, seminars, and publications designed to guide and support parents through challenges they faced to ensure they had the knowledge to raise proper children. These efforts did much to reinforce the idea of disabled children as being somehow separate from the population of abled children, and attitudes within medicine and psychology did little to undermine it. The psychological classification of children as developmentally disabled often led professionals to suggest their segregation as the most effective response if analytical interventions did not work, a response with a long history of implementation dating back to the nineteenth century.[25]

The emphasis on understanding autism through familial relationships and the psychoanalytic models established a tendency to link autism and childhood, a relationship often fostered by parents of disabled children to stress the vulnerability of this population. Part of this pattern was influenced by the increased value of emotional connection assumed from mothers, but an additional factor was the transformation of the meaning of childhood at the beginning of the twentieth century, based on legal and educational reforms in France. The increased protection afforded children by the French government led experts and professionals to advocate for engagement with parents to help develop new parental behaviors that aligned with psychological norms. Accompanying this trend was an increase in state surveillance of children, which contributed to the identification and isolation of disabled children.[26] In that context, the development of children who were outside the norm was couched in the rhetoric to better protect this population, although what that protection looked like varied based on the influence of professionals and parents (and eventually autistic persons themselves). Although disabled children did not conform to the definitions of normative children, they were also often understood as being caught in a pattern of perpetual childhood, unable to develop.[27] This paradox was most evident in the history of autism in France, where the confluence of psychoanalysis, parental activism, and the failure to recognize the voices of autistic persons created a pattern that kept this population both apart from and tethered to childhood for decades.

In situating autism in childhood, parents retained an important voice in debates and remained an obvious target of therapeutic efforts from analysts, both of which shifted focus away from the experiences of autistic individuals and kept them sidelined in discussions. This phenomenon was not unique to autism in comparison to other forms of disability, but because of their invisibility and the influence of parents' groups on the discourse, the infantilization of the autistic population remains an issue in contemporary France.[28] The conflation of disability and childhood justified a form of intervention that was at times emotive and at other times scientific in nature, but in both cases it sought to subjugate the autistic person to reinforce normative behaviors. With this approach, the assumed subservience of children permitted a longer period of control of autistic individuals, especially with the durability of psychoanalysis and its continued emphasis on childhood dynamics as an explanation for autistic behaviors. As objects of state and medical concern, disabled children continued to elicit attention in terms of institutional care in the postwar period, but coupled with this was their increased visibility in Western society and the growing pressure to recognize the limits placed on their inclusion. Again, in this case, the centrality of parents in advocating for autistic rights in the twentieth century dovetailed with cultural assumptions concerning disability and childhood, even as autistic children were classified outside the latter (and even, at times, outside the former). The durability of the figure of the child as representative of autism speaks to a stability of notions of childhood normativity during the postwar era despite the demographic, cultural, and social shifts at work in France.

The confluence of the rise of psychoanalysis, the change in parenting expectations, and the emergence of a diagnostic definition of autism in the United States impacted how that definition would be received in France. With the recognition of autism as a distinct disorder, professionals were keen to find interventions that worked within the social norms of a society. Roy Richard Grinker has observed the powerful influence of culture in defining autism and its treatment across national boundaries, even with broadly influential consensus concerning its diagnosis during the 1950s. Childhood and parenting norms were certainly part of this culture, influencing the reception of scientific and psychological ideas in France. Grinker noted that there was a correlation in the United States between the decline of psychoanalysis and the increase in autism diagnoses, which also speaks to the French divergence.[29] However, it was not just parenting norms that were part of the context of the French divergence but also interpretations of behaviors, which were the primary form of diagnosis for autism. With autism being defined by observable actions, the definition of those actions varied across different societies, leaving some differences in the rates of autism diagnosis. In France, rates were much lower for much of the twentieth century in comparison to the United States; to this day, France has a significantly lower rate of diagnosis despite efforts by parents and autistic persons to increase access to diagnostic clinics as part of increased public health funding in the twenty-first century.

While these factors are significant in understanding how a specific culture concerning autism developed in France, they do not illuminate what autism is, a question that still challenges researchers and professionals despite the voluminous amount of scholarship on the subject. At the time of this writing, the World Health Organization defines autism as "a diverse group of conditions . . . characterized by some degree of difficulty with social interaction and communication," which can also include sensory disorders and atypical behaviors.[30] Since the 1980s, autism has been conceptualized as a spectrum to include various disorders that have a social component, although the medical definition of autism has been revised dramatically since the first diagnoses in 1943 thanks to the global influence of the *Diagnostic and Statistical Manual of Mental Disorders* (*DSM*), a handbook developed by the American Psychological Association in 1952.[31] Much of the literature on autism has focused on issues of its diagnosis and etiology, revealing the shifts in the history of psychology in the latter half of the twentieth century and particularly the decline of psychoanalysis within clinical practice. Nevertheless, the initial diagnostic developed by Kanner in 1943 was based on his observations of children in his clinic, again linking autism and childhood from the outset. As Mitzi Waltz noted in her social history of autism, Kanner's "semantic choice, his selective use of case studies, and the Freudian dominance of psychology and psychiatry during this period set the direction for the next forty years of research and treatment," which undoubtedly was felt in France as well.[32] From the moment of identification, the treatment of autism was characterized by controversies and disagreements concerning efficacy and harm, which often led to new ideas and understandings but also established a tradition of factionalism that explains how new methods were introduced through debate and conflict.[33]

The concept of autism had been introduced to French professionals through the work of Eugen Bleuler and his French acolytes in the 1930s; it was defined as a form of childhood schizophrenia to explain the linguistic and behavioral traits exhibited in children. Bleuler's work in Switzerland provided a language to identify these patients—he developed the term *autism* that Kanner later used—and the blaming of parents was inherent in his formulations as well.[34] Kanner was not the only researcher following Bleuler's work in a clinical setting; Hans Asperger also engaged in research in Austria on children with social impairments who nevertheless showed high cognitive function. His work was introduced broadly in the 1990s in the West through the efforts of British researchers Lorna Wing and Uta Frith and his name became synonymous with a subset of autistic individuals who did not exhibit the classic symptoms of Kanner's diagnostic. More recently, the work of Edith Sheffer on Asperger's links with the Nazi Party has put his research in a new context that emphasizes the influence of eugenics in his clinical formulations.[35] Nevertheless, in France there was an increased awareness of autism in the postwar period thanks to the international exchange of ideas in child psychology. The diagnostics that Kanner and Asperger developed remained influential on the professional understanding of autism, wherein the only treatment for the condition required intervention from psychologists. Initially in France, autistic persons were grouped with other populations that exhibited deviations from social norms, such as delinquents, since their behavioral responses were coded as intentional by psychological professionals who sought to eliminate these behaviors.[36]

One of the reasons that autism remains difficult to define is that its meaning continued to change with developments in research that suggested the limitations of psychoanalytic understandings and the potential value of behavioral psychology in providing support for autistic persons. With radical shifts in the definition and diagnosis of autism in the *DSM-III* in 1980 that detached it from childhood schizophrenia, French professionals developed their own manual in 1987, the *Classification française des troubles mentaux de l'enfant et de l'adolescent* (*CFTMEA*), to align with psychoanalytically oriented practices more common in France.[37] Compiled by a team of medical professionals and analysts, the *CFTMEA* affirmed the link between autism and psychosis from which many other countries had moved away. In Lacanian thought, psychosis offered an example of the crisis of the symbolic in a subject's relationship to the world, and the analyst can begin from this position to help the subject establish stabilization and develop a healthy sense of self.[38] The *CFTMEA*'s emphasis on disorders of childhood also cemented the linkage between autism and childhood well into the twenty-first century for French professionals. Revised several times since its initial appearance, the *CFTMEA* has become a part of the so-called *bataille de l'autisme* that has defined much of the public debate concerning autism since the 1990s, especially given its radical difference in defining autism in comparison to the World Health Organization and the *DSM*, as well as other European states.

The medicalization of autism reveals an important aspect of the history of autism, namely, its conceptualization as an illness that needed to be extinguished to permit the continued development of a normal child. Until the mid-twentieth century, most disabilities were understood as medical issues, meaning that disability was defined as a physical deficiency or impairment that required medical intervention to re-establish normativity in the individual.[39] This tendency helped to justify the intervention of professionals within the family dynamic to advocate (from their perspective) for the child's emotional and behavioral health. The symptoms of autism were understood as signals of parental failure, a failure that created a form of psychosis. In this sense, autism, although it was a disability, was classified by French professionals as an illness through a continued reliance on the medical model of disability, further marking this population as separate from other disabled children whose condition was considered chronic and therefore in need of long-term social intervention. As a result, much of the literature on autism in the 1950s and 1960s was written from a medical perspective that emphasized autism as a temporary psychological condition that could be treated. Yet the method of treatment that was popular in the West—institutionalization—often required housing these young people with other disabled groups, including those with Down syndrome and epilepsy, to provide them treatment to eliminate the symptoms once they were removed from the caustic conditions of their households. The belief in this practice was that children would develop through a healthy relationship established with medical professionals and be cured of their condition. The reliance on institutionalization in many cases suggested that those who did not respond to treatment could remain separated from society in the long term as a form of protection to keep their condition from worsening or to prevent them returning to a traumatic environment.

However, the tendency to institutionalize developmentally disabled individuals came under question during the 1960s and 1970s throughout the Western world, especially with emergence of the civil rights movement in the United States and the archipelago of student protest movements in Europe. The question of the treatment of the disabled population hinged on the emergence of the social model of disability, whereby the disability developed from the treatment of the individual by society and not from an inherent condition. The growing awareness of the social model challenged the assumptions about developmental disabilities and their medicalization by professionals.[40] The question of rights for disabled persons had already been taken up by parents' associations in France during the 1960s, but with little success in achieving those goals in the recognition of their equality and increased funding for public health programs.[41] Yet the continued re-evaluation of the meaning of autism led to new interventions and a shift away from a medical understanding to one that implied the need for educational support in order to integrate autistic children with neurotypical children so that they could be a part of society. This shift to a new context first happened in the United States but was emulated in many other places thanks to informational exchanges and the efforts of parents to find new solutions outside the existing orthodoxy. Deinstitutionalization was a product of these trends, leading more autistic persons to be integrated into communities and, as some argue, creating a larger awareness of the extent of this population by the 1990s.[42] In conjunction with increased awareness, concerns regarding the growing number of autistic individuals suggested the emergence of an epidemic at the end of the twentieth century, with parents and professionals offering a variety of theories to explain this trend. With the tapering off from institutionalization, autistic persons and their families sought access to services through the process of diagnosis, which was a challenge in France well into the twenty-first century.

One of the primary reasons for this lacuna was the continued conflation of autism and mental illness—in essence, the ongoing conceptualization of autism as a deliberate emotional response to parental emotional abuse thanks to the continued influence of psychoanalysis in France that suggested autism was a medical condition and therefore treatable. Even as the practice declined in popularity and endorsement outside France after the 1970s, psychoanalysis became an entrenched culture in the psychological world within France and grew in stature among the broader public. And nowhere was its influence more evident than in the history of autism, which illustrates the French divergence in a clear manner. With their continued reliance on the concepts of psychoanalysis, French professionals found little merit in diagnostics built on ideas and observations from behavioral and cognitive psychologists in the United States, especially because those disciplines did little to explain the origins of the disorder and continued to rely on their own diagnostic tools and practices. Considered a form of psychosis, autism did not conform to the concept of disability that suggested a lifelong condition, keeping autistic individuals separate from other disabled populations. As an element of this tendency, narratives of cures remained commonplace in works that detailed professional interventions that helped psychotic children come out of their shell. In some cases, the belief in curing autism allowed for harmful practices, such as packing–the wrapping of the body in cold wet cloths–to have a level of acceptance from parents and professionals seeking to find an effective way of treating psychosis. This element of the divergence contributed to the continued privileged position of psychoanalysis in France and hindered the development of an autistic self-advocacy movement there for years, especially when coupled with the tendency to locate autism in childhood despite the number of autistic adults.

Still, a movement did emerge in the twenty-first century, buttressed by the French media and autistic militants who expressed frustration with how the disorder was categorized and the ongoing challenges for diagnosis and resources available for autistic individuals. This movement was broadly conceived and lacked cohesion; at times, it was critical of the influence of psychoanalysis, while at other times it celebrated its recognition of individuals. French autistic persons took up these ideas thanks to the growing visibility of this movement in the United States and Great Britain, but within the specific context of the French divergence. The neurodiversity movement bloomed in the late 1990s in North America thanks to connections made through the expansion of the Internet and the emergence of new online communities that allowed autistic persons to communicate directly with each other.[43] In France, both the efforts of autistic individuals such as Hugo Horiot, Daniel Tammet, and Julie Dachez and the advocacy of associations led by autistic persons transformed the conversation that had been dominated to this point by parents and professionals and challenged the stereotypes that linked autism and childhood. Horiot's 2018 *Autisme: j'accuse* offered his perspective on the failures of French efforts to understand and support autistic persons because of the persistence of psychoanalytic ideas and the emphasis on parental perspectives, arguing for the need to understand autism as a new form of human intelligence.[44] These efforts speak to the growth of the neurodiversity movement, in which autistic individuals became involved self-advocates to establish a new way of thinking about autism that called for their acceptance and inclusion within society. The neurodivergent movement rejected the notion of illness so pervasive in the history of autism, asserting that the condition was a natural variation of human cognition rather than an illness requiring a cure and that the autistic population deserved an equal place in society. Neurodivergent advocates critiqued the notion of cognitive norms as incomplete and questioned the nature of both psychoanalytic and behavioral interventions as harmful to autistic persons and psychology's involvement in treatment.[45]

Given the inspiration that came from the neurodivergent community in the United States, the narrative of the French divergence also serves as a reminder of the relationship between the two nations, which was often strained in terms of cultural exchange.[46] The period in which autism was increasingly identified and recognized coincided with French efforts to resist American popular culture in some manner, although individuals were keen consumers of this culture.[47] Often, this situation added another level of tension in the history of autism, especially as parents and autistic persons looked to ideas in the United States as possibilities to transform the treatment of autism in France. Given the influence of Lacan in French psychoanalysis, the disagreements concerning autism often reified the cultural assumptions that questioned the appropriateness of behavioral ideas working in France, with some French professionals seeing resistance to these ideas as protecting patients. While in the immediate postwar period there was a transatlantic interchange between professionals, by the 1960s the ascendence of influential French thinkers such as Maud Mannoni and Françoise Dolto helped establish an internal system of interpretation that proved resistant to research developments outside France. As this phenomenon continued, parents' associations increasingly sought the implementation of methods from the United States to treat their children, arguing for the need for professionals to engage with more foreign research as part of their advocacy work. The divergence ultimately created issues for the French state with the appearance of supranational organizations such as the European Union, which condemned the French treatment of autistic persons by the early 2000s. Yet, professionals remained committed to their approaches as necessary to aid French autistic individuals in the most effective manner. The nationalist nature of the French divergence suggests an element of French exceptionalism in the history of autism, especially given the influence of intellectuals within the discussion and their cultural prominence in postwar France.[48] It also speaks to the tensions between the universalist approach of French cultural ideas and the experiences of disabled populations that did not fit that category.[49]

More recently, French professionals have postulated that the divergence affords the French greater insights on autism in the wake of criticism of behavioral methods such as applied behavioral analysis from autistic advocates. Autistic persons argue that these interventions do little to help their quality of life and are reliant on behaviors being benchmarked against neurotypical concepts of normality, creating stigmatization and anxiety among the population.[50] The leading historian of autism in France, Jacques Hochmann, notes that psychoanalytically oriented professionals historically had been champions of new ideas and movements but remained critical of the determinism of diagnostic criteria in understanding the experience and meaning of autism. Rejecting the notion that autism was reducible to a constellation of observable behaviors, analysts asserted that they were alone in their efforts to defend autistic individuals against the incursion of behavioralist approaches.[51] This understanding of the value of analysis to understand autism in a more profound and less harmful way became a method of understanding the need for French divergence and its importance in offering a vital alternative to the regimentation of behavioral methods. This conceptualization of French resistance to global models of psychology suggests that the struggles of autistic persons remain framed within the established dynamics of conceptions of autism that have continually ignored the experiences of the autistic population while claiming to speak for them.

The chapters that follow outline the conflicts over the meaning of autism along a chronological path, detailing the rationales and actions of professionals, parents, and ultimately autistic persons themselves as they navigated the contested landscape of diagnosis, treatment, and acceptance in the latter half of the twentieth and the beginning of the twenty-first centuries. Chapter 1 focuses on the case of Sammy Y., a nine-year-old autistic child whose treatment became the subject of a popular book that helped introduce autism to the French public. The case study illustrates several significant points about the history of autism in France, particularly the early transatlantic engagement between child psychologists, the assumptions about childhood shared between different nations, and the questions concerning the appropriate treatment of disabled children. Chapter 1 examines these elements as well as the history of child psychology as a distinct discipline in France to illuminate how autism treatment developed there in a divergent manner. It foregrounds the work of child psychologists such as Serge Lebovici, Maud Mannoni, and Françoise Dolto, noting their significant influence in the interpretation of autism as their work reached wider professional and eventually general audiences. The chapter also examines the growing acceptance of psychoanalysis in French psychology and how its rise was connected with larger trends in postwar French intellectual life.

Chapter 2 pivots away from the activities of professionals to those of parents' associations, which dramatically expanded in size and number in the postwar period; by the 1960s, through local and national efforts, they were established throughout France. These associations formed to connect parents of disabled children and help them advocate for services and share their stories with each other. The tension between parents and medical professionals developed as a result of the acceptance of the psychogenic origins of autism, which blamed parents for their children's disability. Organizations sought to develop methods of assisting their children, engaging with professionals, and spreading information to the public to ameliorate the treatment and education of their children. They became important in drawing attention to the challenges facing autistic children in France, especially after a series of tragic events in the 1960s.

Chapter 3 focuses on the impact of the antipsychiatry movement in the wake of the events of 1968, the continued ascendance of psychoanalysis as a part of French intellectual life, and its impact on the actions of parents' associations. During this period, new types of institutions developed that took increasingly experimental approaches to treatment, while ideas concerning the origins of autism were reinforced in a manner that challenged parents' participation in therapy. The French interpretation of autism as a psychological disorder was solidified during this period, even as parents learned of new ideas and approaches developed outside France. Associations sought increased interventions from the French state to protect the rights of their children, but the state delegated these questions to the professionals. The growing French divergence led to the paradox of removal as a form of treatment just as many social critics were questioning the need for institutions to house disabled children in the 1970s.

Chapter 4 highlights the reaction of parents to this situation during the 1980s, with many associations attempting to understand the research on autism developed abroad and introduce those methods domestically. French parents increasingly became advocates for new interventions outside the accepted norms in French psychology, forming new associations that directly challenged professionals and questioned psychoanalysis. Parents positioned themselves as the experts on the issue of autism and found some allies within French medicine and abroad. In this period, there was also an increased awareness in the French public of the psychogenic interpretation of autism, fueled by several significant media events despite public campaigns by associations and parents' biographies that rejected the assumptions of parent blaming.

Chapter 5 examines the renewed advocacy of parents' associations in the 1990s, as many other countries abandoned the psychogenic assumptions about autism. Although these new efforts to change treatment strategies did not meet with sustained success, they did lead to greater international cooperation. The creation of the European Union added another layer of authority that advocates used to challenge the situation in France, and many families sought treatment outside France. These efforts contributed to important legal reforms during the 1990s specifically addressing the educational needs of autistic children. At the same time, the prominence of these groups marginalized the voices of autistic people and kept the focus on autism as a disorder of childhood rather than a lifelong disability.

Chapter 6 details the continued challenges facing autistic persons in France in the twenty-first century as well as the recent development of advocacy groups run by autistic people that counter the entrenched stereotypes of autism in France. The diagnosis and treatment of autism has become the center of a cultural war in France between autistic individuals, caregivers, and medical professionals, with social, political, and legal ramifications. Psychoanalysts were put on the defensive thanks to a new generation of advocates who directly challenged their authority and position. With the continued rise in numbers elsewhere, the definition of autism in France diverged further from that of other countries. This difference led the French government to take a greater interest in autism in the form of identifying it as a national cause in 2012, even as medical professionals remained entrenched in their methods of treatment. The emergence of prominent autistic self-advocates suggested a powerful shift in the framework of the debate, which had to this point been dominated by the viewpoints of professionals.

The conclusion reveals how the tensions created by the French divergence calcified despite numerous efforts from parents, professionals, politicians, and self-advocates to address the challenges facing autistic persons in France. With the end of yet another autism plan in 2023, the divisions between the various factions showed how the continuities of the divergence continued to define solutions and kept the focus on autism firmly placed in childhood.

NOTES

1. See, for example, Mark Roithmayr, "The United States Is Experiencing an Autism Epidemic," *Phi Delta Kappan* 94, no. 4 (2012): 12. Roithmayr was the president of the largest advocacy organization in the United States, Autism Speaks, in 2012. Although Autism Speaks operates in the United States, it has become an influential organization in connecting with parent-led organizations throughout the world.
2. Sherry Turkle, *Psychoanalytic Politics: Jacques Lacan and Freud's French Revolution* (New York: Basic Books, 1978).
3. Michel Botbol and Adeline Gourbil, "The Place of Psychoanalysis in French Psychiatry," *BJPsych International* 15, no. 1 (February 2018): 3–5.
4. Robert Kugelmann and Jacob A. Belzen, "Historical Intersections of Psychology, Religion, and Politics in National Contexts," *History of Psychology* 12, no. 3 (2009): 125–31.
5. Dagmar Herzog, *Cold War Freud: Psychoanalysis in the Age of Catastrophe* (New York: Cambridge University Press, 2017), 2.
6. Élisabeth Roudinesco, *Jacques Lacan & Co.: A History of Psychoanalysis in France, 1925–1985* (Chicago: University of Chicago Press, 1990), 163–64.
7. Botbol and Gourbil, "Place of Psychoanalysis," 4; and Jean Menechal, *Psychanalyse et politique: Le complexe de thésée* (Paris: Erès, 2008).
8. Nancy Chodorow, *The Reproduction of Mothering: Psychoanalysis and the Sociology of Gender* (Berkeley: University of California Press, 1978), 6.
9. See, for example, Rima Dombrow Apple, *Perfect Motherhood: Science and Childrearing in America* (New Brunswick, NJ: Rutgers University Press, 2006). The conflict over parental versus scientific expertise has defined other aspects of parenting, such as questions concerning breastfeeding, as part of the expansion of the meaning of motherhood and the value judgments that attend that expansion. The maternal identity that Charlotte Faircloth observed in her fieldwork on members of La Leche League in twenty-first-century France has analogues in both the judgment put on mothers of autistic children and their self-identification as "autism mothers" as a method of redefining motherhood against professional expertise; see Charlotte Faircloth, *Militant Lactivism? Attachment Parenting and Intensive Motherhood in the UK and France* (New York: Berghahn Books, 2013).
10. Sarah Fishman, *From Vichy to the Sexual Revolution: Gender and Family Life in Postwar France* (New York: Oxford University Press, 2017), 70–71.
11. Richard Togman, *Nationalizing Sex: Fertility, Fear, and Power* (New York: Oxford University Press, 2019), chap. 5.
12. Leo Kanner, "Problems of Nosology and Psychodynamics of Early Infantile Autism," *American Journal of Orthopsychiatry* 19, no. 3 (July 1949): 416–26.
13. Claire Duchen, *Women's Rights and Women's Lives in France, 1944–1968* (New York: Routledge, 2003), 97.
14. Élisabeth Badinter, *Mother Love: Myth and Reality, Motherhood in Modern History* (New York: Macmillan, 1981).

15. Jordynn Jack, *Autism and Gender: From Refrigerator Mothers to Computer Geeks* (Urbana: University of Illinois Press, 2014).
16. Aude Béliard and Jean-Sébastien Eideliman, "Familles et handicaps mentaux ou psychiques," *Savoir/Agir* 47, no. 1 (2019): 73–82.
17. Laura Middleton, *Disabled Children: Challenging Social Exclusion* (New York: Wiley, 1999).
18. Sandra M. Sufian, *Familial Fitness: Disability, Adoption, and Family in Modern America* (Chicago: University of Chicago Press, 2022).
19. Bonnie Evans, *The Metamorphosis of Autism: A History of Child Development in Britain* (Manchester, UK: Manchester University Press, 2017), 201–5; and Chloe Silverman, *Understanding Autism: Parents, Doctors, and the History of a Disorder* (Princeton, NJ: Princeton University Press, 2012).
20. Brigitte Chamak, "Autism and Social Movements: French Parents' Associations and International Autistic Individuals' Organisations," *Sociology of Health & Illness* 30, no. 1 (2008): 76–96.
21. Jonathyne Briggs, "From Collaboration to Resistance: The Family Dynamic in Autism Literature in Contemporary France," *Contemporary European History* 32, no. 2 (2023): 254–69.
22. Elinor Ann Accampo, Rachel G. Fuchs, and Mary Lynn Stewart, *Gender and the Politics of Social Reform in France, 1870–1914* (Baltimore: Johns Hopkins University Press, 1995).
23. Melanie Klein, "Early Stages of the Oedipus Conflict (1928)," in *The Selected Melanie Klein*, ed. Juliet Mitchell (New York: Free Press, 1987), 71.
24. Frances Tustin, "Thoughts on Autism with Special Reference to a Paper by Melanie Klein," *Journal of Child Psychotherapy* 9 (1983): 119.
25. Jessie Hewitt, *Institutionalizing Gender: Madness, the Family, and Psychiatric Power in Nineteenth-Century France* (Ithaca, NY: Cornell University Press, 2020).
26. Anne Borsay and Pamela Dale, "Introduction: Disabled Children—Contested Caring," in *Disabled Children: Contested Caring, 1850–1979*, ed. Anne Borsay and Pamela Dale (New York: Routledge, 2016), 2.
27. Janice McLaughlin, Edmund Coleman-Fountain, and Emma Claverling, *Disabled Childhoods: Monitoring Differences and Emerging Identities* (New York: Routledge, 2016), 4–5.
28. For a snapshot of this trend in the United States, see Jennifer L. Stevenson, Bev Harp, and Morton Ann Gernsbacher, "Infantilizing Autism," *Disability Studies Quarterly* 31, no. 3 (2011): 1–17.
29. Roy Richard Grinker, *Unstrange Minds: Remapping the Worlds of Autism* (New York: Basic Books, 2008), 4.
30. World Health Organization, "Autism," accessed June 29, 2023, https://www.who.int/news-room/fact-sheets/detail/autism-spectrum-disorders.
31. Ethan Watters, Crazy Like Us: The Globalization of the American Psyche (New York: Free Press, 2010), 4-6.
32. Mitzi Waltz, *Autism: A Social and Medical History* (New York: Palgrave Macmillan, 2013), 40.
33. Laura Schreibman, *The Science and Fiction of Autism* (Cambridge, MA: Harvard University Press, 2005).
34. Hans Asperger, "Autistic Psychopathy in Childhood," in *Autism and Asperger's Syndrome*, ed. Uta Frith (New York: Cambridge University Press, 1991), 41.

35. Edith Sheffer, *Asperger's Children: The Origins of Autism in Nazi Vienna* (New York: W. W. Norton, 2018).
36. Lucien Malson, *Les enfants sauvages: Mythe et réalité* (Paris: 10/18, 1964).
37. Roger Misès, J. Fortineau, P. Jeammet, et al., "Une classification française des troubles mentaux de l'enfant et de l'adolescent," *La psychiatrie de l'enfant* 31, no. 1 (1988): 67–134.
38. Stijn Vanheule, *The Subject of Psychosis: A Lacanian Perspective* (New York: Palgrave Macmillan, 2011), chap. 3.
39. The literature on the contrast between the medical and social models of disability is vast, especially in the realm of disability activism. The development of the social model during the 1960s fit with the push for independent living and disabled rights, with the awareness of the social context of medical experiences and how that defined disability. See, among others, Simon Brisenden, "Independent Living and the Medical Model of Disability," *Disability, Handicap & Society* 1, no. 2 (1986): 173–78.
40. Tom Shakespeare, "The Social Model of Disability," *The Disability Studies Reader* 2, no. 3 (2006): 197–204.
41. Jonathyne Briggs, "Les enfants perdus: Asylum Reform, Parents' Groups, and Disability Rights in France, 1968–1975," *French Politics, Culture & Society* 39, no. 3 (2021): 26–45.
42. Gil Eyal et al., *The Autism Matrix: The Social Origins of the Autism Epidemic* (New York: Polity Books, 2010).
43. Steve Silberman, *NeuroTribes: The Legacy of Autism and the Future of Neurodiversity* (New York: Avery Books, 2015).
44. Hugo Horiot, *Autisme: j'accuse* (Paris: L'Iconoclaste, 2018).
45. Steven K. Kapp, "Introduction," in *Autistic Community and the Neurodiversity Movement: Stories from the Frontline*, ed. Steven K. Kapp (New York: Palgrave Macmillan, 2020), 1–19.
46. The literature on the specter of Americanization in France includes Richard Kuisel's classic *Seducing the French: The Dilemma of Americanization* (Berkeley: University of California Press, 1993); and Kristin Ross's *Fast Cars, Clean Bodies: Decolonization and the Reordering of French Culture* (Cambridge, MA: MIT Press, 1996).
47. See, for example, Jonathyne Briggs, *Sounds French: Globalization, Cultural Communities, and Pop Music, 1958–1980* (New York: Oxford University Press, 2015).
48. Michael Kelly, "French Intellectuals: The Legendary Exception," in *The French Exception*, ed. Emmanuel Godin and Tony Chafer (New York: Berghahn Books, 2005), 193–94.
49. Myriam Winance, Isabelle Ville, and Jean-François Ravaud, "Disability Policies in France: Changes and Tensions between the Category-Based, Universalist and Personalized Approaches," *Scandinavian Journal of Disability Research*, 9 (2007): 160–81.
50. Abraham Graber and Jessica Graber, "Applied Behavior Analysis and the Abolitionist Neurodiversity Critique: An Ethical Analysis," *Behavior Analysis in Practice* 2 (March 2023): 1–17.
51. Jacques Hochmann, "Autism in the Neoliberal Age: Some Reflections," in *Treating Autism Today: Lacanian Perspectives*, ed. Laura Tarsia and Kristina Valendinova (New York: Routledge, 2022), 17.

1

The Transatlantic Era of Autism

In the summer of 1954, nine-year-old Sammy Y. visited the Paris office of Dr. Joyce McDougall, a young therapist who specialized in the treatment of child "psychotics." Sammy had been previously diagnosed with infantile psychosis and had received therapy when his family lived in New York. However, their relocation to Paris meant that he would need to continue with a new therapist in a new country, certainly a challenge for any family. Given that therapy for psychosis was heavily reliant on talking with patients and that Sammy and his family spoke English, most French therapists were not able to treat him; McDougall had been recommended to the family primarily based on her ability to conduct sessions in English.[1] However, Sammy's case attracted the attention of French therapists, especially that of Serge Lebovici, a pioneering child analyst who collaborated with McDougall on Sammy's case and helped her to assemble her reflections on Sammy's therapy into a book that captured the attention of French readers in the early 1960s. Sammy's treatment plan consisted of a combination of play therapy and psychoanalysis. In her analysis, McDougall pointed to issues of sexual repression and anxiety revealed in their sessions as the catalyst for Sammy's autistic behaviors, indicating that these behaviors were tied to issues within the relationship dynamics of his family. Her approach to addressing these issues emphasized the importance of storytelling and narrative as a part of normal childhood, underscoring the central nature of verbal exchange as part of his analysis. She offered Sammy explanations in hopes of transforming his behaviors, but his therapy ended prematurely with his return to the United States in 1955. The book generated from her session notes, *Un cas de psychose infantile* (1960), cultivated greater awareness of the challenges facing autistic children in the postwar period in France, while emphasizing the critical role that parents played in their children's maladaptive behaviors and the power of psychoanalysis to ameliorate damage caused by poor parenting.

The public interest in Sammy's case revealed that psychoanalysis was becoming more accepted in the emerging realm of child psychology in postwar France, especially with the efforts of Lebovici, Françoise Dolto, and other prominent figures. Psychoanalysis had become a dominant force in psychology in the anglophone world, especially in the United States, but in France it remained relatively

Perpetual Children. Jonathyne Briggs, Oxford University Press. © Oxford University Press (2025).
DOI: 10.1093/9780197683002.003.0002

marginalized in practice prior to 1945.[2] Even after the war, psychoanalysis operated primarily on the margins of French medicine but was drawing greater attention thanks to the work in the 1950s of Jacques Lacan, who engaged with Sigmund Freud's work through the intellectual currents of structuralism, which was then a dominant paradigm in French thinking; Lacan's work energized debates concerning the interpretation of Freud and provided new insights into applications of his ideas. Lacan formulated a combination of Freudian analysis and linguistic theory that became popular through his standing room–only lectures at the Sorbonne and his growing number of acolytes in the realm of psychology.[3] The connection between psychoanalysis and childhood developmental disabilities had already attracted attention in the interwar period, but Lacan's influence touched numerous thinkers, including Dolto, who became a towering figure in the realm of parenting in postwar France, and Lebovici.[4] In the wake of the cohesion between psychoanalysis and therapy for disabled children, child therapists such as Maud Mannoni emerged as important advocates for the value of psychoanalysis to treat forms of developmental disability by the end of the 1950s. At the same time, Fernand Deligny continued his work with developmentally disabled children within the framework of institutions, honing approaches that were influenced by psychoanalysis, although not exclusively or distinctively psychoanalytic in praxis.[5] Other important developments in psychology were operant in France during the 1950s, with the ongoing work at the La Borde clinic and the appearance of critical publications by Frantz Fanon and Michel Foucault challenging the position and purpose of psychology and psychoanalysis in French society.[6] The combination of publications and the emergence of experts appearing by the end of the 1950s reveal how educators, psychologists, and therapists developed a framework to understand and treat autistic children in a new manner, increasingly and exclusively informed by psychoanalysis. This framework was built on prominent French interpretations of Freudian thought during the middle part of the twentieth century based on shared ideas about the natural role of the family in children's mental health. This combination established an enduring foundation for how autism would be defined well into the twenty-first century as a disorder distinctly located in childhood.

Moreover, psychoanalysis provided a conversion narrative for developmentally disabled children that emphasized analysts' ability to treat behaviors effectively and "cure" autism, marking it as an illness rather than a disability. When conceived as an illness, autism represented a form of deviance to be eliminated through the actions of an analyst to bring the child into normativity.[7] According to James T. Fisher, conversion narratives were "a record of the quest for a transformed or redeemed self" and could be found in early texts of 1960s American literature on autism.[8] McDougall's *Dialogue with Sammy*, the English translation of *Un cas*, followed a similar pattern, albeit with a less heroic conclusion, and other examples in this chapter will show how the French case had its share of conversion narratives rooted in psychoanalysis. The narrative structure of analysis is a form of storytelling that provides meaning to the experiences and recollections of the patient, as directed by the analyst.[9] In the 1950s, psychoanalysts, experts, and doctors dominated the narratives of infantile schizophrenia, thus linking its origins to failures to achieve normative developmental milestones due to disrupted family dynamics while establishing pathways to recovery and redemption through forms of analysis. The monopoly of expert publications and professionals' public engagement in this period meant that this was the story of autism that was told at the time, with analysts often operating in a savior-type role that confronted "bad" parents in an effort to provide these children with an escape from their situation that would allow them to develop their own selfhood free of their parents' caustic desires.

AUTISM, PSYCHOSIS, AND DISABILITY ANXIETIES

The centering of psychoanalysis countered some of the predominant assumptions concerning autistic children in the 1950s, namely, the notion that these children were noncommunicative and unable to receive effective treatment, thus requiring institutionalization. The initial work of Leo Kanner in the United States and Hans Asperger in Austria during the 1940s established a series of diagnostic norms concerning autistic children that would become the basis of the definition of autism for decades in much of the Western world, although their works were not translated into French until 1983 and 1998, respectively.[10] Trained as physicians, Kanner and Asperger each took a rigid and clinical approach in their formulations of diagnoses, which differed from the more speculative and pathological interests of the French theorists; Kanner in particular attempted to orient understandings of autism away from psychopathology and later questioned the link between autism and schizophrenia after his initial emphasis on psychogenic origins.[11] Much of the French thinking on autism reinforced its perceived connection to infantile schizophrenia, suggesting that the breakdown in communication and retreat into interior life could be treated through analysis. The early-twentieth-century observations of Eugen Bleuler, Eugène Minkowski, and Henri Ey informed this interpretation, which was easily reconciled with Kanner's and Asperger's conclusions about the behaviors of their patients. Minkowski defined autism in the 1920s as a profound expression of schizophrenia that caused a child to retreat from the world as a defense mechanism in favor of an inner life. His definition proved durable and influential to the group of French thinkers who appeared in the postwar period, who developed their ideas from the logic of withdrawal as an engine for autistic behavior.

A Polish émigré who arrived in France during the First World War, Minkowski manifested an early French propensity to combine elements of psychology and philosophy. He was instrumental in introducing Bleuler's concept of schizophrenia into the French psychological lexicon, all while operating from a distinctly clinical perspective. Bleuler had coined the term *autism* in 1911 to identify a subset of schizophrenic patients who had presented nonsocial behaviors and did not verbally communicate in treatment sessions. For Bleuler, however, autism was a condition found in adult patients.[12] Minkowski, who was a student of Bleuler, expanded on his definition of autism as an expression of schizophrenic detachment from reality as a deliberate reaction to negative stimuli. Minkowski saw autism as symptomatic of a child's troubled engagement with the external world in the form of deficits in communication, sociability, and pragmatic thinking. He also differentiated between autistic thought and action, noting that the latter could serve as a marker for schizophrenia since access to the inner world of schizophrenics was often difficult.[13] For him, autism, like schizophrenia, was an expression of disordered thinking and lack of connection with the world.[14] The implication of Minkowski's theories was that they established the interpretations that the actions of autistic children were indicative of their willful disconnection from reality and that their withdrawal from reality was defensive in nature, suggesting treatability. Since the world of children was primarily based on their interactions with parents, the likely source of conflict was within the family, establishing a fertile ground for psychoanalysis as an obvious intervention. Minkowski's conception of autism as an example of schizophrenia helped to frame understandings of the psychic experience of autism for French psychologists seeking to explain the disturbed communication of autistic children and placed the disorder firmly within childhood.

Like Minkowski, Henri Ey was a pivotal interlocutor for bringing Bleuler's ideas to French psychologists in the period before the Second World War. As a neurologist, Ey understood autism as an expression of both biological and psychological factors, helping to reposition understandings of the origins of schizophrenia away from purely biological factors and toward considerations of psychogenic ones. Bleuler's theories were influential in this shift as well because his conception of autism was informed by psychoanalysis and set the important precedent of situating autism as something understood through psychoanalysis.[15] Bleuler's notion of autism as an expression of detachment from reality certainly was a primary aspect of this equation. However, Bleuler's work on autism remained largely marginalized in France, only circulating through the scholarship influenced by him, which often did not completely engage with the complexity of his theories.[16] Ey had been deeply interested in Bleuler's reformulation of schizophrenia and its possible connection with autism. Psychoanalysis was a revolutionary way of thinking about clinical treatment for Ey, but he saw it exclusively as another expression of medicine rather than something distinct from it.[17] This position, however, would not hold because many of the childrearing experts and analysts were not practicing doctors and gained their expertise from their knowledge of and experience with psychoanalysis rather than formal medical training.

Outside the influence of Bleuler, child psychology in France in the early twentieth century also developed within the context of what David Mitchell and Sharon Snyder have termed the eugenic Atlantic: a shared intellectual world that defined disability as a threat to the wellness of the social body.[18] For Mitchell and Snyder, eugenics was a "primary catalyst for international collaboration" of systemic medical ideas, which included psychology.[19] While the primary driver of much of the eugenic discourse was racial in nature, Mitchell and Snyder noted that these ideas also formulated the establishment of criteria in the United States and the empires of western Europe to identify biologically deficient populations through shared forms of scientific research. The circulation of normative notions of intelligence and behavior colored perceptions of developmental disabilities such as autism in the immediate postwar period in France, especially with autism linked to familial psychogenic origins. The continued influence of eugenics in France led to a more subtle approach focused on hygiene and promoting more valuable elements of French society, exemplified in the continued operation of Ungemach Gardens in Strasbourg into the 1980s or the social discourse of regeneration and youth during postwar reconstruction. The case of Ungemach Gardens reveals how different forms of eugenics thrived after the Second World War thanks to support from municipal government and the belief in the validity of the project in creating a form of "soft eugenics" that maintained support among the French populace.[20] The actions of autistic children threw into question their ability to conform to French universalism and highlighted the need to discipline them and their families to produce healthy and productive citizens through therapy or to remove them from society through institutionalization.[21] The rhetoric of youth and regeneration certainly has a long history in France, but the strong emphasis on youth during the postwar period dovetailed with the anxieties inherent in the appearance of new organizations and government bodies focused on guiding youth and controlling delinquency.[22] The concerns over hereditary disability continued after the Second World War through notions of fitness, including mental fitness, which influenced social perceptions of families with autistic children and the treatment they received.

The durability of the etiology of autism as a reaction to parental influence was also reinforced by the social origins of many of the families studied in the early French autism literature. The children who attracted the interest of the analysts tended to come from the urban middle class, with professional fathers and homemaking mothers as a common trait. The question of parenting had long been a concern for French society, even in those cases where parents mirrored the social ideal of the nuclear family with a strict gendered division of labor.[23] Parents, especially mothers, were perceived as critical to the success of French recovery from the Second World War, centering their efforts within the home as vital to the creation of a healthy society. The notion of a child's behavior as reflective of the nature of their home life was a common assumption among postwar psychologists and experts.[24] This assumption dovetailed with the belief that the mental behavior of autistic children was a defensive reaction to bad parenting. While this assumption was tied to larger historical ideas about delinquency, the issue here was how delinquency and autism were interpreted as antisocial behaviors rooted in similar experiences linked to parenting. Concerns about proper parenting continued in the postwar period, and the recognition of autism exemplified the potential dangers of poor parenting as disabling and thus detrimental to society within the broader eugenic context.

With the end of the Second World War, French authorities were deeply troubled by the emergence of youth crime and delinquency as potent social problems that required their intervention. Sarah Fishman notes the persistent belief in the structured roles within families as a method of understanding the rise in delinquency given the perceived loss of paternal authority and the assumed inability of mothers to discipline their children because of their more emotional relationship with them.[25] The need to address juvenile crime in a more humane way led to the rise of the juvenile court system in 1945, with psychologists playing a role in its operation.

Much like the treatment of autistic children, the disciplining of delinquents spoke to the need to regulate and reduce the influence of irregular families through psychology, which led to the emergence of *instituts médico-psycho-pédagogiques* in the postwar period as a method of intervention and education for children and families. These institutions became significant sites for the treatment of autism in France and will be discussed in greater detail in the next chapter. However, their origins in concerns about regulating and eliminating antisocial behavior led to the conflation of treatment in some cases.[26]

The intersection of psychology, parenting, and autism established a strong foundation for how autism was understood in postwar France and explicitly tied the interventions in treating autism to treating the family, again primarily the child and the mother, to abate abnormal behaviors. In making this connection, French experts established precedents that would firmly place autism in the realm of child psychology (and autism in childhood) and put parents on the defensive. At this juncture, the French approach, however, was not radically different from ideas circulating in the Western world and often informed by medical developments and political ideas outside France. As Michal Shapira has argued in the case of postwar Great Britain, "the understanding of children and the mother–child relationship [were] key to the successful creation of social democracy."[27]

CHILDREARING EXPERTS

After the Second World War, the uneven transformation of marriage and gender roles amplified rooted perceptions of the central importance of mothers in the rearing of healthy children in France. In reaction to the conservative and restrictive ideology of the Vichy regime, French women expected and to some degree found greater political and social freedoms in the postwar period, even if the inherent expectation of marriage and childrearing remained durable.[28] However, the idea of motherhood as a natural expression of sacrifice was tempered in the postwar era by the recognition of other ideals for women, as well as the reality of transformation of families in the wake of the war. In this context, childrearing experts, rooted in psychology and psychoanalysis, became more prevalent in France to help guide families (but primarily women) through changing expectations of parenting along the paths supported by research, also making them a target of efforts to shape the ideals of normative childhood and the treatment of developmental disability. The development of experts as a public voice helped to both shift and reinforce expectations of childrearing, with the specter of disability as an inherent example of the importance of this work. While Françoise Dolto occupied a dominant space in this discourse, multiple experts had notions of how to effectively raise children to mitigate developmental disability and promote happy childhoods for the betterment of French society.

Dolto emerged as a critical voice on parenting during the 1950s, largely because of her expertise in pediatrics and child psychology. Dolto had studied pediatrics but had been deeply interested in psychoanalysis since her youth and pivoted to child psychology during the 1930s. She built her private practice around the treatment of psychotic children, who she saw as attempting to communicate despite their mutism or incoherent speech. Her assessment was that these psychotic children were attempting to communicate through other means, and analysis offered a method of interpretation. In combination with her conservative politics, Dolto was deeply invested in the notion of the nuclear family as the social ideal, which dovetailed with broader French anxieties about the erosion of families in the postwar period and the attendant social ills associated with that erosion. While she was an ally of Lacan, she did not engage with his work directly and instead developed her own techniques of play therapy and familial analysis that emphasized an approach based on her personal connection with the child. She was open to any method she felt could serve as a method of communication for her patients, including music therapy.[29] Her relationship with Lacan elevated her standing within the psychology world despite her conservative positions and her less developed clinical work. Dolto's ideas about the importance of two involved parents and the significant developmental importance of the mother–child relationship were established during her work in the 1950s, helping to popularize many psychoanalytic ideals about the nature of families.

Dolto's expertise had potent influence over the acceptance of psychoanalysis in the treatment of psychotic children, especially given her reported successes in treating their behaviors. Her engagement with parents was part of the broader acceptance of psychoanalysis in French society as a way of understanding the nature of the family.[30] Rather than participating in an internal conversation with her colleagues, she instead chose to engage with the public through presentations and publication aimed at a lay audience to address mothers and fathers directly about their role in transmitting values to their children.[31] This equivocation was a basic tenet of psychoanalysis, which inherently places children's behavioral and mental health as a maternal responsibility.[32] Dolto occupied a central role in the cathexis of parenting and mental disability in postwar France, eventually becoming an even more significant media figure in parenting by the 1970s. Well before she took to the airwaves for her famed advice show, she had become profoundly influential by introducing psychoanalytic concepts into the lexicon of parenting and motherhood for many French people.

Motherhood had long been a political question in France, and the demographic anxieties of the postwar era exacerbated the need to promote certain ideals of motherhood as a method of restoring French society. In 1945, a heroic discourse in media aimed at women emerged in which mothers were characterized for their sacrifice for their children through constant nurturing and love, with little thought of their own career or desires. Authors such as Laurence Pernoud emphasized the need for specific gender roles within the family that stressed the dominant "natural" role of women in effective child care.[33] Pernoud's book *J'attends un enfant* first appeared in 1956 and has been a staple of the childrearing experience in France ever since, establishing important norms of French motherhood. Her second book, *J'élève mon enfant*, arrived in 1965, and these two books have remained in print. More than just attending to children, the need for love was critical in this postwar formulation of the mother.[34] As Kelly Colvin observes, the postwar reconstitution of marriage was reliant on a notion of femininity that the French press scaffolded for women as the source of love in society, which, of course, included her family.[35] An expectation of a mother was self-abnegation, and those women who did not follow such a pattern courted social instability and potentially disability in their children. Thus, parental love was expressed in highly gendered terms and primary represented the influence of the mother on the health of the family and the proper development of children.[36] This ideal of the loving, sacrificial mother mapped well onto assumptions about the relationship between mothers and children present in psychological theories, but did not reflect the changing social dynamics of women's suffrage and the ongoing presence of women in the labor force and the political realm.

The experts of the postwar period continued to emphasize the need for women to remain in the home to raise their children in a proper and healthy manner. The overarching concern about delinquency in the postwar moment positioned motherhood as an important tool in the stable development of French society, yet motherhood needed to follow a particular path to prevent delinquency from undermining the determined efforts to rebuild France following the Vichy interregnum.[37] Similarly, in the context of more subtle expressions of eugenics in this era, a particular type of motherhood was emphasized as a bulwark against disabling children. Inherent in the immediate postwar period was the conflation of delinquency with developmental disability, often leading to similar concepts of treatment such as psychoanalysis. The notion of proper child care had inherent connections to notions of social welfare, but specific programs such as the Ungemach Gardens illustrate how eugenic policies echoed notions of proper upbringing and useful children within a government-sponsored program.[38] This idea emphasized that, with proper support and direction, parents were pivotal in serving the social need of healthy citizens beyond a mere biological role. Within this context, proper parenting had an important social function of stabilizing French society, and the foundation of a family rested on the position of the mother as the loving center.

The ideal mother was both informed by scientific breakthroughs in child care and rooted in an emotional foundation that provided nurturing for her children. The need to inform mothers became of high importance in the postwar period, leading to the expansion of parenting literature aimed at women to communicate to them their duties and responsibilities as parents. The ideal mother, of course, was coupled with the ideal child, who properly responded to parental guidance by developing the necessary manners and actions that would allow them to thrive in society. Disabled children did not conform to this ideal, making their place in the world unclear. As Amanda Apgar observes, the figure of the disabled child does not fit within "the discourses of childhood" because their impairment places them outside normalcy.[39] It was hoped that the emergence of a new regime of parental experts would help parents alleviate any potential impairments by offering guidance on the newest developments in parenting that reinforced notions of normalcy that displaced disabled children in the social landscape.

As a method of connecting experts with parents, an existing association, L'école des parents, became more prominent in disseminating vital ideas about proper child care in the postwar era. The association's bulletin began publication in 1949 and featured articles and editorials from professionals whose perspective was informed by psychoanalysis. Established by Marguerite Vérine-Lebrun in 1929, L'école des parents was created in response to the need to inform parents about development and education to help them guide their children, with numerous regional branches appearing by the 1950s. Despite Vérine-Lebrun's conservatism, the well-established national organization had a major voice in public discussions of child care.[40] After her death in 1946, new leadership emerged at L'école des parents under the guidance of Georges Heuyer, whose influence on child psychoanalysis was evident in his practice at La Salpêtrière; Heuyer transformed the previously religiously oriented organization into something more secular and guided by scientific research.[41] As a conduit between child psychologists and parents, the association connected psychoanalytic concepts and norms to the notion of the proper family, with mothers as the primary target audience. Articles by Dolto and Hélène Brulé were examples of how L'école des parents engaged with the emerging ideas of child psychology and the critical nature of maternal nurturing in this new approach. This was not to say that no experts were concerned about the role that fathers should play in child care; Alexis Néret, in his *Guide du chef de famille* (1950), noted the importance of fathers learning about the ideas present in child psychology.[42] Nevertheless, the figure of the mother, so critical to psychoanalysis, was at the heart of these efforts.

Dolto also gave a series of lectures at L'école des parents beginning in 1950, amplifying her ideas about the role of proper families and childrearing and reinforcing her position as an expert. Her concern about the makeup of a proper family was evident in lectures on parents of only children, on parents who were separated, and even on the place of grandparents in childrearing.[43] In his book on Dolto's profound influence on French thinking in the twentieth century, Richard Bates underscores the importance of L'école des parents in giving Dolto an opportunity to introduce psychoanalytic concepts to an audience of parents in a manner that made the concepts more relevant to their experiences; Dolto conducted at least six lectures at the organization between 1950 and 1954.[44] She also participated in clinical work at the Centre Claude Bertrand in Paris, a pioneering French child guidance clinic, in this same period, and her work there illustrates her continued emphasis on the role of unconscious conflict in the family as a driver for a diverse set of maladaptive behaviors in children. Although Dolto was not exclusively treating autistic children in this period, her centering of the Freudian family romance in interpreting childhood behaviors was both influential in popularizing the idea and indicative of the shift in defining effective interventions.

The connection of parenting experts with child psychology shows how ideas informed by Freud and psychoanalysis became common elements of discourse concerning parenting in the immediate postwar era, especially given lingering concerns about both unfit parents and unfit children. The broader interplay of these ideas certainly focused on behavioral issues in children and the larger meaning of those issues in the potential treatment of their behaviors. More importantly, child psychology was emerging as a more formalized and clinical field in this era, with the development of specialists as influential thinkers within the psychological profession and as resources for parents to seek out. At the same time, the conclusions of professionals dovetailed with the broader assumptions about the ideals of parenting in the postwar period, adding additional relevance to their efforts to educate parents. In this sense, the constellation of social workers, advice columnists, and other childhood experts who shaped the engagement and acceptance of child psychoanalysis in France as a critical tool in the making of healthy, normal children had allies within the medical field who were increasingly embracing the therapeutic potential of analysis.

CHILD PSYCHOLOGY

Although Dolto is often the chief symbolic figure of child psychology among the French public, informing her work was the pioneer of child psychoanalysis in France: Sophie Morgenstern. Morgenstern, Dolto's mentor, worked in Paris at the Hopîtal Vaugiraud during the 1920s, and her practice and approaches were vital influences. She recognized the value of psychoanalysis to help understand and treat the psychological challenges of disabled children and introduced many important Freudian concepts into early discussions of child psychology. Morgenstern, a Polish émigré, had studied at Zürich University and previously worked in the Burghölzli Clinic in Switzerland. The director at that time, Eugen Bleuler, developed his ideas concerning infantile schizophrenia there. Burghölzli had been established in the 1860s as an institution for the humane treatment of the developmentally disabled population, and when Bleuler became its director in 1898, he continued that mission. Bleuler's work revolutionized the understanding of schizophrenia as a distinct disorder and identified autism as one of its variations.[45] At the clinic, Morgenstern also worked alongside Minkowski; she was connected to researchers engaged with autism during her brief career. When she came to France in 1924, she was interested in introducing psychoanalysis into the nascent field of child psychology after her sessions with Eugénie Sokolnicka.[46] Establishing herself as Heuyer's assistant at La Salpêtrière, Morgenstern worked in its outpatient clinic with a population of developmentally disabled children. Her practice introduced several techniques to the French context for psychoanalytic work with children, including dream interpretation, play therapy, and art therapy, the latter of which were used by later therapists in interventions with autistic children, including McDougall's intervention with Sammy Y. For her, these approaches were substitutes for free association, which was more common in adult analysis and difficult to elicit among disabled children. An active researcher, Morgenstern published fifteen articles and a book, *Psychanalyse infantile* in 1938, before her death in 1940, but her work was primarily directed at fellow analysts and medical professionals, unlike Dolto's more populist approach after the war. Although she did not focus on autistic children as a specific population, her ideas influenced the approach of subsequent child psychologists because she argued that psychoanalysis should have a privileged position in the treatment of childhood behavioral disorders.

In her practice, Morgenstern asserted that the purpose of analysis was to ameliorate family conflicts, which themselves were part of her treatment of disorders. Working from Bleuler's assumptions about the defensive nature of behaviors in autistic children, Morgenstern sought to understand the negative family element that must be present in the home environments of her patients. Her article "Un cas de mutisme psychogène" (1927) highlighted the story of Jacques R., a nine-year-old mute who stopped talking to his father and for several months would only say one word. Morgenstern understood mutism to be within the spectrum of Bleuler's notion of schizophrenia as an expression of retreat to an interior world. Jacques, however, did continue to draw, so Morgenstern used his drawings as a way of interpreting his reactions to external stimuli and his preference for his interior life. Morgenstern first encountered Jacques in October 1927, when he was admitted to her clinic, and she learned of Jacques's anxieties surrounding his mother's health and his loss of interaction with her. After a series of sessions with him, Morgenstern ameliorated much of Jacques's mutism, and he began speaking again by January 1928. Informed by Freudian concepts, she noted the centrality of transference of his loss of connection with his mother (with herself as the object) in the effective treatment of Jacques, another technique that many other child therapists later employed within an analytic framework to treat autism.[47]

In her "La psychanalyse infantile et son rôle dans l'hygiène mentale" from 1930, Morgenstern emphasized how the failure of normative libidinal development led to a fixation that was a potential trigger for antisocial behavior in response to perceived traumatic events, including discord among the parents.[48] The emphasis on the critical role played by parents in proper development was counterbalanced by the need of professionals to help children resolve their conflict within the family dynamic. For Morgenstern, the centering of the Oedipal complex was key to resolving this conflict and making the child healthy again because it highlighted how parents created the conflict, and the complex could serve as a map to understand the behaviors of the child. Through psychoanalysis, she believed that the conscious and subconscious actions of parents could be discovered and the discord resolved. In terms of autism, Morgenstern believed the condition to be rooted in a trauma that was exacerbated through additional traumas in the family.[49] This conclusion put analysis at the heart of the emerging child psychology field. Morgenstern's untimely death in 1940 did not diminish her influence on the field of child psychology, especially given her attention to the specific challenges in treating children through psychoanalysis despite its origins in adult psychology. The case of Jacques also stressed the inherent anxiety in children losing connection with their mothers as a driver for the emotional retreat of developmentally disabled children.

Françoise Dolto, having worked with Morgenstern, followed her path in the application of psychoanalysis in children with the analyst as a crucial mediator for disabled children, but others who were equally influential in child psychology in France saw value in further developing Morgenstern's techniques to develop child psychoanalysis into a more rigorous approach. Serge Lebovici, who began his residency at La Salpêtrière with Heuyer in 1951, shared many of the same beliefs that Morgenstern had championed about the use of psychoanalysis in the treatment of developmentally disabled children, even as he questioned the extent to which her work qualified as true psychoanalysis.[50] While Lebovici did not have the same broad popularity that Dolto had, he was central in solidifying the place of psychoanalysis in French pediatrics, establishing a clinical foundation for child psychology, and mentoring the next generation of child psychologists. Like Morgenstern's, his work was influenced by Melanie Klein's notion of the mother–child dyad, and Lebovici emphasized the centrality of mothers in the development of the child and the inherent anxieties already present in infants. Perhaps most important, Lebovici was critical in the development of connections between child analysts in France and abroad and acted as a diplomat for many of the ideas developed in Britain during the 1940s and 1950s on child psychology, introducing the work of many British theorists to the French context, which often ignored the localized ideological conflicts in the psychoanalytic world.

While Lebovici often agreed with Dolto about the importance of the maternal relationship in the mental health of a child, he approached the issue from a different philosophical stance in comparison to the conservative, Catholic background informing her concepts of family. Lebovici assisted the Resistance during the Second World War, providing aid as a medic, and briefly joined the French Communist Party. After the war, he moved from pediatrics into child psychology, following a path similar to Dolto's, and by 1947, Lebovici had become interested in the specific subset of autistic children, as both a therapist and an advocate. His centering of the mother in the treatment of the child illustrates his profound interest in how the disruptions in the emotional bond between mother and child catalyzed behavioral disorders that psychoanalysis could mitigate. Much like his fellow analysts, Lebovici surmised that autism was a retreat into a fantasy life, often something that could be ascertained through techniques of psychodrama and the use of filming patients to help them understand their unconscious actions in order to change them. At the same time, he was interested in interrogating the methods of psychoanalysis and their application within a clinical setting, throwing into question the role of the analyst as a neutral interlocuter and the nature of fantasy in developmentally disabled children.

Lebovici's 1949 article "Contribution à l'étude nosologique et psychopathologique de la schizphrenie infantile" engaged with the concept of infantile schizophrenia and its differences compared to adult schizophrenia. Lebovici noted that several American researchers were deeply engaged with studying the phenomenon but that it had not attracted the same interest among European scholars, which he was hoping to change to make the diagnosis more effective. He was concerned with how broadly it was being diagnosed and that treatment was based on those diagnoses without a clear set of criteria.[51] The article details his experience in treating Roger, a nine-year-old boy who had been hospitalized over two years for mutism and had experienced a range of treatments—including psychotherapy and electroshocks—without any real change to his condition, and André, a seven-year-old boy whose intellectual and social development had plateaued. In each case, Lebovici was interested in the role of fantasy, as expressed by Roger's role playing as a lion and through André's drawings, in articulating the primordial anxieties of these children concerning their connections with their mothers. Again, the techniques of art and play therapy were determined to be the most effective tools to help young psychotics.

Lebovici interpreted these children's fantasies as examples of internalized frustration with their mothers that had been left unresolved since their infancy. Rooted in Klein's work on object relations and unconscious fantasy, his analysis of the boys' behavior emphasized how the aggressive nature of the relationship between mothers and children could lead to frustration and anguish, manifested in the appearance of infantile schizophrenia as a defense mechanism. Klein believed that infants had an inherent and rich unconscious that colored their perception of their interactions with the most important object in their life: their mother. The primordial moment of this interaction occurred during breastfeeding, when infants made a value judgment about the object (the mother) that could persist and lead to negative emotions linked to the object. For child psychoanalysts, disturbances caused by negative object relations allowed children to understand better the differences between the internal fantasy and the external reality without the baggage of the negative value judgment. In "Contribution," Lebovici linked Klein's assertions of the role of fantasy in infant psychology to Lacan's broader assessments of the role of the maternal body in defining desire and the process of understanding one's independent body.[52] Furthermore, he surmised that a child learned the value of emotional expression from their mother, a key element of normative development that was disturbed among infantile psychotics.[53] This type of work reveals how Lebovici combined different elements of psychoanalytic theory together and how French child psychology was germinating in a manner that incorporated intellectual developments elsewhere.

Although Lebovici continued to develop his theories throughout his long career, he was a critical contributor at an important moment of child psychology (and child psychoanalysis) in the early 1950s, bringing together the strands of thought from Bleuler, Minkowski, and Lacan with the clinical praxis of Morgenstern, as well as the work being published in Great Britain and the United States. His emphasis on the role of the mother in the development of infantile schizophrenia, however, showed no real difference from that of his colleagues, revealing that the consensus on the psychogenic origins of autism was readily accepted in this intellectual context. With mothers playing the vital role, medical professionals had placed the focus on assessing parenting in cases of autism, pointing to the behaviors of the mother in instigating the condition.

INFANTILE PSYCHOSIS AND THE CASE OF SAMMY

When McDougall began her sessions with Sammy Y. in October 1954, all these influences were evident in her diagnosis of his behaviors. Sammy had been referred to her by Lebovici, who also worked with her to develop her diagnoses, but McDougall was concerned about her own lack of experience. Nevertheless, she took the case and proceeded to meet with Sammy weekly, eventually expanding her session work to include working with Sammy's parents to redirect his behaviors to more socially acceptable ones, but also to discover the driving force behind his behaviors. Her work with Sammy's mother reinforces how motherhood and autism were explicitly linked in France, even without the influence of Kanner's famed phrase "refrigerator mothers," underscoring the influence of parenting experts during a period of social change with the enfranchisement of women. Sammy's diagnosis—as prepsychotic—was related to his inability to differentiate reality and fantasy and to his acting out, behaviors that would likely elicit a diagnosis of autism according to current diagnostics. Unsurprisingly, McDougall interpreted his behavior as a defensive response to the anxieties stemming from the distortion of the mother–child bond, leading her to analyze not only Sammy but also his mother as part of her treatment plan. Sammy's case served as a nexus that brought together the assumptions at play in child psychoanalysis and introduced them to a broader French audience that was increasingly informed by its concepts and ideas.

McDougall emerged from an international context in which psychoanalysis drew together divergent thinkers and practitioners. She had worked with several important clinicians in London, especially during her tenure at Maudsley—a child guidance clinic had been established there by the 1930s to treat the increasing number of developmentally disabled children—but attempted to avoid the doctrinal conflicts that characterized psychoanalytic societies at that time.[54] At the clinic, she developed her techniques and conclusions about how patients' actions could be understood through the metaphor of the theater, noting that their activities were subconscious but were believed in the moment. Her encounters with Anna Freud and D. W. Winnicott shaped McDougall's desires to work with children and the application of psychoanalysis in clinical work with them in France, where the type of work that characterized British child psychoanalysis was less developed. Freud recommended she relocate across the English Channel to help train new analysts, and once she arrived in France in 1953, McDougall entered an intellectual landscape dominated by the ideas of Lacan and his acolytes.[55]

In Paris, McDougall found allies in her efforts to develop a form of analysis rooted in the work of British clinicians, but she also engaged with the robust discourse happening in the capital. Her associations with Marie Bonaparte and Lebovici were particularly important in her ability to make connections within the more fractured psychoanalytic societies of France and to secure placement at the Centre Claude Bernard, which gave her the opportunity to practice analysis with children. There, she also engaged with the work of René Diatkine, the director of the Hôpital Necker, and other French professionals informed by the work of Lacan. These professional networks helped McDougall to develop her practice in France, despite her early struggles with integrating into the psychological world there. Élisabeth Roudinesco's magisterial history of psychoanalysis in France details the profound intellectual divisions among analysts, based largely on reactions to Lacan and his acolytes and their efforts to establish a return to the intent of Sigmund Freud in the postwar era.[56] McDougall ultimately found her place in France, and her first public case was crucial to her integration. When Lebovici reached out to her in 1954 to help with the treatment of a young schizophrenic, the case established a career that spanned several decades and gave her methodology and conclusions a powerful influence in France.

Un cas provides an epistolary narrative of Sammy's treatment for his childhood schizophrenia, for which he had been receiving psychotherapy in the United States during the previous year. His reported behaviors included stereotyped movements, eating issues, and social isolation from children his own age, which McDougall and Lebovici connected to Bleuler's notions of childhood schizophrenia in the original French introduction to their book.[57] For Lebovici, the unique role of psychoanalysis was to establish a new set of relations between the mother and the child based on information coming from the child through nonverbal means.[58] Recognizing the new research from the United States, including Kanner's diagnostic categories for infantile autism, Lebovici insisted on the use of psychoanalysis to repair the distorted relations that impact the behaviors of children, with Sammy serving as a *ne plus ultra* example of childhood psychosis.

When Sammy arrived in McDougall's office in the fall of 1954, he was highly verbal but struggled in school and at home because of his tendency to express inappropriate comments to his family and teachers. The two met multiple times a week. In their initial session, Sammy painted several pictures for McDougall, and the content of the pictures—mainly anthropomorphic animals in domestic scenes—led her to interpret them as evidence of transference as the explanation of his abnormal behaviors. This approach of art therapy continued for several subsequent sessions, with McDougall encouraging Sammy to provide his own narrative for his pictures. Afterward, Sammy's stories took up more of the session time than his artwork, providing McDougall and Lebovici with a more discursive set of observations to draw on for their interpretations. By December, Sammy had developed a wide menagerie of characters in his ongoing stories, while also growing more wary of his visits to the office. Sammy questioned the differences in McDougall's approach in comparison to that of other therapists he had previously seen, leading McDougall to try to emulate their play therapy approach with games and toys by her twenty-fifth session.[59]

McDougall encouraged Sammy to create stories with the dolls in her office and Sammy obliged, speaking to the narrative aspects of psychoanalysis and the role of storytelling. These stories—fantastical tales of cows and horses often leavened with bawdy humor—provided McDougall with insights into Sammy's internal world, which she interpreted as driven by the anxiety of his inability to develop an independent identity from his mother.[60] She worked within a framework that emphasized the importance of the Oedipal conflict as a primary aspect of child development, and she surmised that Sammy suffered from the lack of resolution of issues stemming from the disruption of this development. Many of the sessions between December 1954 and January 1955 were dominated by Sammy's overt inquiries about McDougall's body, which she saw as further evidence of Sammy's unresolved sexual longing, in this case transferred to the analyst as a result of the perceived emotional detachment of Sammy's mother, Mrs. Y.

By February 1955, McDougall had encouraged Sammy to move from storytelling back to drawing. With this shift, the role of the parents became much more prominent in her analysis, especially as the possibility emerged of Sammy returning to America to attend a residential school—the Orthogenic School at the University of Chicago led by Bruno Bettelheim. McDougall believed that Sammy was making real progress in dealing with his anxiety and stress but felt that his mother was increasingly resentful of Sammy's independence and that perhaps the boarding school was to be used as a form of punishment.[61] Sammy's own stress about ending McDougall's sessions somewhat confirmed this interpretation for her. With his eventual move looming, Sammy continued to visit McDougall's office multiple times a week to talk about his fantasies, frustrations, and anxieties.

McDougall's recounting of her therapy sessions with Sammy provides insight into how vital the novel intervention of the analyst was to correcting autistic behaviors; the sessions helped to re-establish the dialogue that had been broken within the family, preventing Sammy from developing a healthy sense of reality. For McDougall, this situation required analysis of the parents, particularly Sammy's mother, to help Sammy develop appropriate behaviors. Mrs. Y. agreed to meet with McDougall a month after Sammy's departure for the Orthogenic School for a series of sessions that lasted nearly a year. In these sessions, Mrs. Y. shared her anxieties about losing her son to the school permanently, especially given Bettelheim's suggestion that Mrs. Y. was also psychotic. A recovering alcoholic, Mrs. Y. had undergone analysis prior to her sessions with McDougall, who concluded that Mrs. Y. had a deeply troubled relationship with her own mother and that the anxieties of that relationship had been transferred to Sammy.[62] McDougall's deep and genuine interest in Mrs. Y.'s maternal relationship contrasted sharply with her experience with Sammy's father, Mr. Y. Her lone interview with him in May 1958 reveals that the expectations of the father and his role in Sammy's behavior were markedly different; the interview focused on Mr. Y.'s complaints about the Orthogenic School and the lack of progress concerning Sammy's behavior. There was no analysis of the father's position, again reinforcing the psychological centering of the mother as the primary emotional foundation of the family and the key player in proper child development, as well as the lesser expectations of paternal emotional connection.

Mrs. Y.'s role in Sammy's disability was evident for McDougall—Sammy's sexual anxieties stemmed from his awareness that, from his mother's perspective, he was an unwanted object of desire: an incomplete resolution of the Oedipal complex. Her diagnosis fit neatly into the psychoanalytic understanding of autism as an expression of childhood schizophrenia rooted in deliberate defensive actions against emotional violence rendered within the family. Whether intentionally or not, McDougall's conclusions linked the actions of mothers to the potential of disability while reinforcing the definition of autism as an expression of childhood psychosis for a broader audience through the publication of *Un cas*. This coupling remained steadfast among mental health professionals and the French public for decades following, linking concerns about autism to parental behavior and notions of development and limiting the broader conceptualization of autism as a lifelong condition by locating it in childhood. Her conclusions suggested the power of analysis to ameliorate the primary causes of autistic behavior and allow the child to live a healthy, normative life. In 2001, McDougall observed in an interview that "Sammy is no longer psychotic, he is doing very well now," while remarking that his mother died many years after his treatment at the Orthogenic School and his father remarried.[63] The redemption of Sammy, both from his mother and from childhood psychosis, reinforced the conversion aspect of *Un cas* as an example of an autistic child made whole through the efforts of analysts.

Another significant aspect of McDougall's treatment of Sammy is her place in the transatlantic psychological world, especially through the different experts who appear in Sammy's broader story. He had been treated by Margaret Mahler while in New York, Lebovici has assisted McDougall in her analysis, and Bettelheim accepted Sammy at the Orthogenic School when Sammy returned to the United States in 1955. Jacques Hochmann also notes the influence of Klein in McDougall's work, especially in her centering of object relations theory as critical to the healthy development of a child, although McDougall was not as rigid in her understanding of the mother–child dyad as other French scholars.[64] McDougall followed the same international vectors that interested Lebovici, revealing his influence on her practice. The intersection of these different thinkers and practitioners points to the interconnectedness of psychology in this immediate postwar era, especially with the growing acceptance of psychoanalysis in the West, and McDougall's own experience of working in both Britain and France during a period of great intellectual activity shows that these ideas were in motion across national boundaries. As perhaps another signal of the international nature of this period, *Un cas* was eventually translated into several languages, with D. W. Winnicott providing the introduction for the English translation. *Un cas* presaged the appearance of other autism conversion narratives such as *Dibs: In Search of Self* and *The Empty Fortress*, each of which made a significant impact in the framing of the disorder for general audiences in the 1960s.[65] McDougall's work bridged the English and French elements of child psychology while revealing that French psychologists in this era were in line with broader trends concerning the treatment and definition of autism. This connection underscores that the French divergence concerning autism developed much later, in contrast to the more harmonic and collaborative era of the 1950s.

BUILDING ON THE CONSENSUS

By the end of the 1950s, the consensus on the role of psychoanalysis in the treatment of infantile schizophrenia was clear, and a new cluster of practitioners began to publish on their experiences working with autistic children. These works followed much of the pattern established by Dolto, Lebovici, and McDougall, namely, the singular role of the mother in the origins of autistic behaviors and the pivotal role of the analyst as the communicator for the child. However, their interventions became much more focused on parental analysis as the central focus of treatment, with the child needing protection from their parents' behaviors. This approach was the culmination of the psychogenic theory of autism, now mainstreamed in French child psychology, that recognized the patient's silence as a signal for the analyst to speak for them. Perhaps the most prominent and notable analyst to emerge in response to Dolto's and Lebovici's innovations in child psychology was Maud Mannoni, who became another advocate of the important relationship between autism and psychoanalysis that proved so durable in France.

Maud Mannoni arrived in Paris in 1949 and quickly came into the orbits of both Dolto and Lacan, becoming an active participant in the Société parisienne psychanalytique. She later followed Lacan in his split from the group in 1953. Mannoni was deeply influenced by Lacan's thinking about the role of language in shaping the self and saw the possibilities of using his ideas to better understand the thinking of autistic children. Rather than just seeing their lack of verbal communication as evidence of retreat into an interior life, Mannoni believed that their disordered speech itself signified the nature of the child's relationship with their mother. She saw the mother as the central figure, in line with the conclusions of Dolto and Lebovici, and believed that treatment of autistic behaviors needed to bring mothers directly into the analysis. Additionally, she noted the failure of these children to develop a distinct ego as another element in the development of autism. Although her published works did not appear until the 1960s, Mannoni was already developing and practicing her techniques in the 1950s in Paris within the broader psychoanalytic context.

Mannoni's formulations of *parole pleine* and *parole vide* illustrate Lacan's influence on how she interpreted the silences and echolalia of autistic children as evidence of an overbearing parent (likely the mother) in preventing the free expression of the child's desires. *Parole pleine* was the healthy form of communication, in which the child had access to their own desires separate from those of their parents and expressed them verbally. *Parole vide* was the disrupted communication, likely rooted in the parent's conscious or unconscious desire for the "imaginary child." This led to disrupted speech because the "actual child" had not developed the ability to articulate their own desires. The maternal persistence of the desire for the imaginary child led to behaviors in the actual child, which required analysis to unmask this dynamic.[66] Mannoni centered psychoanalysis in the treatment of autistic children and was less interested in the play therapy that informed the interventions of Dolto and Lebovici. Only through a shared analysis of the child and the mother could this desire for the imaginary child be made manifest to help to understand the child's alienation from its mother. The analyst helps to mediate the mother's acceptance of the loss of the imaginary child so that she can accept the actual child, which would then allow the child to speak in *parole plein*.

Lacan's influence over Mannoni marked his strongest presence in the realm of child psychology in France, and her lasting contributions led to the continued use of psychoanalysis as a tool to treat autism well into the twenty-first century. While Dolto and Lebovici were certainly responding to Lacan's interpretations of Freudian theory, Mannoni was directly building on it and applying those ideas in her analyses and conclusions. Lacan did not specifically address autism until much later, in 1975, in his account of the relationship between language, the Other, and psychoanalysis, with autistic children being present within language despite not being "speaking beings."[67] He had been supportive of Mannoni's scholarship, lauding her *L'enfant arriéré et sa mère* as a vital work in understanding childhood psychosis.[68] His concept of *cut*, in which the subject achieves psychic separation from the Other, was arguably based on his interactions with her work with disabled children and illustrates how Mannoni's clinical practice reinforced her equivocation of developmental disability and psychosis.[69]

In Mannoni's estimation, the analyst plays a necessary role in struggling against the parents' desires to prevent the child from completely succumbing to the emotional structures established by the parents, another example of a conversion narrative. Mannoni suggested that analysts might be challenged by parents during their treatment of autistic children since they are the progenitors of the disturbed relations.[70] As an example, Mannoni details her sessions with Mireille, an eight-year-old girl diagnosed with "schizophrenia against a background of mental retardation," who did not speak much in the presence of her parents.[71] By working with Mannoni, Mireille showed signs of improved behavior in a few months, which subsequently caused anxiety in her mother. Mannoni saw that her success with Mireille was creating new tension from the parents, who sought to end psychotherapy for their daughter. She ultimately diagnosed the mother's desire for Mireille to remain sick because of her own neuroses and anxieties, which disturbed the inherent harmony of the family. Yet, in her recounting, Mannoni pressed the parents even after they ceased sending Mireille to analysis. For Mannoni, the solution was to make the child aware of the limitations imposed by the family through analysis, which would allow them to become aware of their own subjectivity and the negative environment: "The case of Mireille raises in a particularly acute form a problem commonly encountered in child psychoanalysis. The analyst finds himself [*sic*] confronted from the outset with the importance, perversion, criminality, or madness of an adult whose words are disseminated through the family."[72] In this sense, psychoanalysis set the stage in the coming conflicts over autism by challenging the authority of parents of disabled children to dictate the proper treatment for their children's disability, which in many ways ran counter to the traditions of the family in French society.

Sympathetic to the position of these children and recognizing their individual struggle, Mannoni reiterated a paradigm that cements parent blaming as the basis for autism while reinforcing its connection to infantile psychosis. Within the context of 1950s France, the parent in question remained the mother, an assumption shared across political and theoretical spectrums in French child psychology, whether rooted in Dolto's conservative notion of family, Lebovici's notion of social ills, or Mannoni's conception of Lacanian theory. Overall, analysts questioned the tendency to seek institutionalization, seeing autistic children as belonging in the home, albeit one that needed to change. The ascent of child psychoanalysis led to the inscribing of autism distinctly in childhood as a form of childhood psychosis and positioned psychoanalysis as the logical and effective response to the challenges presented by these children. The greater challenge, however, was not to their parents, who had contributed to their behavioral state, or their authority, but rather to French society, which had remained concerned with the proper upbringing of children and the need for healthy children during a time of profound social change. A central tenet in achieving that goal was the assurance of mentally healthy mothers and, to a lesser degree, fathers through psychoanalysis, which would benefit all French society. Within the psychological world, the recognition of autism foregrounded the efforts of analysts to bring tranquility to troubled youth, although the reported number of cases remained small during the 1950s and the most publicized cases ended in the extinguishing of autistic behaviors. Psychoanalysis was considered an effective treatment.

Yet the consensus concerning the role of families in the origins of autism often put parents on the defensive, even as they sought assistance in helping their children and advocated for their equality in a society that struggled to understand them. While parents were positioned as problematic and potentially caustic in their attitudes toward their disabled children, they continued to work with experts to try to improve their children's condition. They were willing to submit to the authority of professionals during the 1950s but began to increasingly question that position. In reaction to the centrality of psychoanalysis in the medical and scientific community in France, parents formed associations in increasing numbers by the beginning of the 1960s, suggesting a growing number of families impacted by autism in France and the need to address the shortcomings of existing treatments. The intervention of associations changed the tenor of how parents interacted with professionals and challenged the assumptions at the heart of the psychoanalytic response.

NOTES

1. Serge Lebovici and Joyce McDougall, *Un cas de psychose infantile: Étude psychanalytique* (Paris: Presses universitaires de France, 1960); published in English as Joyce McDougall and Serge Lebovici, *Dialogue with Sammy: A Psycho-analytical Contribution to the Understanding of Child Psychosis* (New York: Avon Books, 1969).
2. Sherry Turkle, *Psychoanalytic Politics: Jacques Lacan and Freud's French Revolution* (New York: Guilford Press, 1978), 49.
3. Annick Ohayon, *L'impossible rencontre: Psychologie et psychanalyse en France 1919–1969* (Paris: La découverte, 1999), 365–68.
4. Richard Bates, *Psychoanalysis and the Family in Twentieth-Century France* (Manchester, UK: Manchester University Press, 2022).
5. Jonathyne Briggs, "Reinventing Play: Autistic Children and the Normativity of Play in Postwar France," *Historical Reflections/Réflexions historiques* 45, no. 2 (2019): 47–64.
6. Camille Robcis, *Disalienation: Politics, Philosophy, and Radical Psychiatry in Postwar France* (Chicago: University of Chicago Press, 2021).
7. Carol Thomas, *Sociologies of Disability and Illness: Contested Ideas in Disability Studies and Medical Sociology* (New York: Palgrave Macmillan, 2017), chap. 2.
8. James T. Fisher, "No Search, No Subject? Autism and the American Conversion Narrative," in *Autism and Representation*, ed. Mark Osteen (New York: Routledge, 2008), 51.
9. Roy Schafer, "Narration in the Psychoanalytic Dialogue," *Critical Inquiry* 7, no. 1 (Autumn 1980): 29–53.
10. See Gérard Berquez, *L'autisme infantile: Introduction à une clinique relationnelle selon Kanner* (Paris: PUF, 1983); and Hans Asperger, *Les psychopathes autistiques*

pendant l'enfance (LePlessis-Robinson, France: Institut synthélabo pour le progrès de la connaissance, 1998).

11. Ibid., 39.
12. Mitzi Waltz, *Autism: A Social and Medical History* (New York: Palgrave Macmillan, 2013), 43.
13. Annick Urfer, "Phenomenology and Psychopathology of Schizophrenia: The Views of Eugene Minkowski," *Philosophy, Psychiatry, and Psychology* 8, no. 4 (December 2001): 284–85.
14. Josef Parnas, Pierre Bovet, and Dan Zahavi, "Schizophrenic Autism: Clinical Phenomenology and Pathogenic Implications," *World Psychiatry: Official Journal of the World Psychiatric Association* 1, no. 3 (October 2002): 133–34.
15. Majia Holmer Nadesan, *Constructing Autism: Unraveling the "Truth" and Understanding the Social* (New York: Routledge, 2005), 39.
16. Julian Bourg, "You Can't Always Get What You Want: The Psychoanalytic Ambivalence of Michel Foucault," in *The Politics of Desire: Foucault, Deleuze, and Psychoanalysis*, ed. Agustin Colombo, Edward McGushin, and Geoff Pfeifer (Lanham, MD: Rowman & Littlefield, 2022), 127.
17. Élisabeth Roudinesco, *Jacques Lacan & Co.: A History of Psychoanalysis in France, 1925–1985*, trans. Jeffrey Mehlman (Chicago: University of Chicago Press, 1990), 132.
18. David Mitchell and Sharon Snyder, "The Eugenic Atlantic: Race, Disability, and the Making of an International Eugenic Science, 1800–1945," *Disability and Society* 18, no. 7 (2003): 843–64.
19. David Mitchell and Sharon Snyder, *Cultural Locations of Disability* (Chicago: University of Chicago Press, 2006), 103.
20. Paul-André Rosental, *A Human Garden: French Policy and the Transatlantic Legacies of Eugenic Experimentation*, trans. Carolyn Avery (New York: Berghahn Books, 2020).
21. Joy C. Schaefer, "Truffaut's *L'enfant sauvage* (The Wild Child, 1970): Evoking Autism and the Nascent 'Eugenic Atlantic,'" *Ought: The Journal of Autistic Culture* 1 (2019): 34–35.
22. Richard I. Jobs, *Riding the New Wave: Youth and the Rejuvenation of France after the Second World War* (Stanford, CA: Stanford University Press, 2007), 27. See also Kristin Ross, *Fast Cars, Clean Bodies: Decolonization and the Reordering of French Culture* (Cambridge, MA: MIT Press, 1995); and Jonathyne Briggs, *Sounds French: Globalization, Cultural Communities and Pop Music, 1958–1980* (New York: Oxford University Press, 2015), chap. 1.
23. Jan Windebank, "Family," in *Encyclopedia of Contemporary French Culture*, ed. Alex Hughes, Alexandra Hughes, and Keith A. Reader (New York: Routledge, 1998), 198.
24. Jobs, *Riding the New Wave*, 161.
25. Sarah Fishman, *The Battle for Children: World War II, Youth Crime, and Juvenile Justice in Twentieth-Century France* (Cambridge, MA: Havard University Press, 2002), 2–3.
26. See Lucien Malson, *Les enfants sauvages: Mythe et réalité* (Paris: 10/18, 1964), for a narrative example of different populations put together in treatment centers.
27. Michal Shapira: *The War Inside: Psychoanalysis, Total War, and the Making of the Democratic Self in Postwar Britain* (Cambridge: Cambridge University Press, 2013), 1.

28. Sarah Fishman, *From Vichy to the Sexual Revolution: Gender and Family Life in Postwar France* (New York: Oxford University Press, 2016), 57–58.
29. Françoise Dolto, *Séminaire de psychanalyse d'enfants* (Paris: Seuil, 1982), 20.
30. Camille Robcis, *The Law of Kinship: Anthropology, Psychoanalysis, and the Family in France* (Ithaca, NY: Cornell University Press, 2013), 120.
31. Bates, *Psychoanalysis and the Family*, 132.
32. Beverly Birns and Niza Ben-Ner, "Psychoanalysis Constructs Motherhood," in *The Different Faces of Motherhood*, ed. Beverly Birns and D. F. Hay (Boston: Springer, 1988), 48.
33. Claire Duchen, *Women's Rights and Women's Lives in France, 1944–1968* (New York: Routledge, 1994), 103–4.
34. Laurence Pernoud, J'attends un enfant (Paris: P. Horay, 1956); and Laurence Pernoud, J'élève mon enfant, de la naissance à l'école (Paris: P. Horay, 1965).
35. Kelly Colvin, *Gender and French Identity after the Second World War: Engendering Frenchness* (New York: Bloomsbury, 2017), 186.
36. Yvonne Knibiehler, *La révolution maternelle: Femmes, maternité, citoyenneté depuis 1945* (Paris: Perrin, 1997).
37. Fishman, *Battle for Children*, 138–39.
38. Paul-André Rosental, *Human Garden*; and Jonathyne Briggs, "From Collaboration to Resistance: The Family Dynamic in Autism Literature in Contemporary France," *Contemporary European History* 32, no. 2 (2023): 254–69.
39. Amanda Apgar, *The Disabled Child: Memoirs of a Normal Future* (Ann Arbor: University of Michigan Press, 2023), 14.
40. Fishman, *From Vichy*, 45.
41. Bates, *Psychoanalysis and the Family*, 127. The phenomenon of the emergence of scientific motherhood was not limited to France; it was part of a larger shift in Western understandings of motherhood during the twentieth century. See, for example, Rima D. Apple, *Perfect Motherhood: Science and Childrearing in America* (New Brunswick, NJ: Rutgers University Press, 2006).
42. Fishman, *From Vichy*, 87.
43. Camille Robcis, *Law of Kinship*, 126.
44. Bates, *Psychoanalysis and the Family*, 127.
45. Roy Abraham Kallivayalil, "The Burgholzli Hospital: Its History and Legacy," *Indian Journal of Psychiatry* 58, no. 2 (Spring 2016): 226–27.
46. Dominique Fessaguet, "De Sophie Morgenstern l'oubliée à Françoise Dolto la tapageuse," *Topique* 2, no. 115 (2011): 79.
47. Sophie Morgenstern, "Un cas de mutisme psychogène," *Revue française de psychanalyse* 1, no. 3 (1927): 492–504.
48. Sophie Morgenstern, "La psychanalyse infantile et son rôle dans l'hygiène mentale," *Revue française de psychanalyse* 4, no. 1 (1930): 136–37.
49. Jean Losserand, "La psychanalyse d'enfant: L'histoire de la psychanalyse d'enfants en France," *Le coq-héron* 119 (February 1991): 45.
50. Claudine Geissmann and Pierre Geissmann, *A History of Child Psychoanalysis* (New York: Routledge, 1998), 288–89.
51. Serge Lebovici, "Contribution à l'étude nosologique et psychopathologique de la schizphrenie infantile," *Evolution psychiatrique* 1949:331.
52. Ibid., 339.

53. Françoise Coblence, *Serge Lebovici* (Paris: Presses universitaires de France, 1996), 61.
54. Ruth Mehahem, *Joyce McDougall* (Paris: Presses universitaires de France, 1997), 11–12.
55. Philippe Porret, *Joyce McDougall: Une écoute lumineuse* (Clamency, France: Campagne Première, 2006), 101.
56. Élisabeth Roudinesco, *History of French Psychoanalysis*, 259.
57. Lebovici and McDougall, *Cas de psychose infantile*, 10–11.
58. Ibid., 54.
59. McDougall and Lebovici, *Dialogue with Sammy*, 79–80.
60. Ibid., 113.
61. Ibid., 164.
62. Ibid., 307.
63. Marie Rose Moro, "Entretien avec Joyce McDougall," *Le carnet PSY* 67 (July 2001): 22.
64. Jacques Hochmann, *L'histoire de l'autisme: De* L'enfant sauvage *aux troubles envahissants du développement* (Paris: Odile Jacob, 2009), 319.
65. Fisher, "No Search, No Subject," 53. Virginia Axeline's *Dibs* (1964) and Bruno Bettelheim's *The Empty Fortress* (1967) were major bestsellers in the United States and each eventually was translated into French, *Dibs* in 1977 and *The Empty Fortress* in 1971.
66. Maud Mannoni, *The Backward Child and His Mother: A Psychoanalytic Study*, trans. Alan Sheridan (New York: Pantheon Books, 1972), 62–63.
67. Quoted in Leon S. Breener, *The Autistic Subject: On the Threshold of Language* (New York: Springer, 2020), 219.
68. Silvia Elena Tendlarz, *Childhood Psychosis: A Lacanian Perspective* (Milton Park, UK: Karnac, 2003), 62.
69. Laure Razon, Olivier Putois, and Alain Vanier, "The Lacanian Concept of Cut in Light of Lacan's Interactions with Maud Mannoni," *Frontiers in Psychology* (December 2017): 4–5.
70. Mannoni, *Backward Child*, 78.
71. Maud Mannoni, *The Child, His "Illness," and the Others* (New York: Pantheon Books, 1970), 168–69.
72. Ibid., 184.

2

Parents as a United Front

In 1960, the first French national association of parents with disabled children, Union nationale des associations de parents et amis de personnes handicapées mentales (UNAPEI), formed in Paris to advocate for the rights of developmentally disabled children. Initially representing 126 regional associations and about 11,000 families, UNAPEI provided a forum for parents of disabled children to share their experiences, to advocate for their children's right to equality, and to press the French government for reforms to increase the education and inclusion of their children (some now adults) in society. UNAPEI included not only families of autistic children but also families whose children experienced other developmental disabilities, such as Down syndrome (trisomy 21), epilepsy, and other intellectual and developmental conditions. The association began publication of *Nos enfants inadaptés* in 1962, signaling its efforts to reframe developmental disability away from its link with psychosis and instead focus on methods that would help children and young adults to operate more independently with a lifelong condition. While they were not a wholesale rejection of the psychoanalytic regime that had formed in the 1950s, the efforts of this association pointed to the limits of what analysis provided for these families and instead hoped to create more opportunities for disabled children to interact with others and be able to work as adults in a way that would allow them to participate in society. Other associations that focused on autistic children followed, namely, the Association au service des inadaptés ayant des troubles de la personalité (ASITP) and the Union des familles de malades mentaux et de leurs associations (UNAFAM), both formed in 1963, but many of these groups formed alliances by the end of the 1960s.

The emergence of parents' associations marked the beginning of a long challenge to psychoanalysis from parents who were interested in developments in autism research outside France and in exploring new forms of treatment, but this challenge was not evident at the outset of these associations. Instead, these groups were figuring out ways of working with medical professionals and advocating for the social acceptance of their children, mainly by sharing their own experiences with each other to bolster solidarity among parents. The audience for the associational bulletins was primarily parents of developmentally disabled children, which

Perpetual Children. Jonathyne Briggs, Oxford University Press. © Oxford University Press (2025).
DOI: 10.1093/9780197683002.003.0003

was a growing audience during the 1960s. UNAPEI claimed over forty thousand families as part of its association by 1969, revealing that despite the interventions of analysts, the number of developmentally disabled children continued to climb in France.[1] As the 1960s came to a close, associations were increasingly concerned about the ability of psychoanalysis to treat autism effectively, especially given the increased interest in behavioral-based methods in the United States, and were seeking greater intervention from the French government to support their efforts to educate their children. Several events energized their efforts, but perhaps the most significant were a court decision in 1966 and a fire in a residential facility in 1968, which led to greater political activism from UNAPEI. In contrast to the assumptions of the psychoanalytic literature on autism of the 1950s, the bulletins and activities of the parents' associations in the 1960s centered the parental experience as a location of expertise and knowledge about disability and the contribution that parents could make to their children's well-being, not through analysis but through advocacy.

In the activities of parents' associations, both mothers and fathers played important roles in the education, treatment, and advocacy for their children on governing boards, as contributors to association publications, and in leading specific campaigns for legislative reform. In these cases, parents were highly engaged in understanding the need for improvement in terms of therapies and opportunities, especially as their children became adults. This attitude was in sharp contrast to how parents had been encouraged by some professionals to regard these children as "hopeless and to exclude them from society," primarily through institutionalization as the solution to their treatment.[2] However, much of the rhetoric of parents' associations emphasized the need to protect disabled children, playing on emotive stereotypes of innocent suffering. Parents eventually leaned on the concept of the poster child as a method of advocacy, which again emphasized the connection between autism and children.[3] The work of these associations also reveals how parents of developmentally disabled children were not indifferent or reticent to their own children as a cause of their disorder, going against the grain of many assumptions concerning such parents during the 1950s.

Parental advocacy took the form of informing members of the associations of efforts to seek the reform of existing services, to expand government support of education and vocational training of disabled children, and to alert association members about resources and new materials published about research on disabilities. The bulletins served as a place for parents to voice their concerns and speak about the challenges facing their children without the inherent issues of blaming that occurred within the typical treatment for autistic children. Bulletins introduced new approaches and techniques to help educated their disabled children, encouraging parents to take an active role in their medical care by learning new interventions. However, the centering of the parental experience was not without its challenges, especially in light of how parental activism, while still nominally focused on their children's needs, aligned with how parents envisioned what their children would say or do if they could (in this sense, replacing the role of the analyst as the cypher for their disabled child).[4] In these efforts, the shift to what Chloe Silverman has termed *parent-experts* contrasted with the previous dominance of professional experts in the 1950s.[5] This approach reified the idea of a disabled child as a child whose future is uncertain and whose future contributions to society are unclear, yet parents asserted the importance of their inclusion. As Amanda Apgar points out, the activism of parents "gesture[s] to a more political way to think about disability as a social experience" rather than a medical one.[6] This shift suggests a change in the narrative about how parents of autistic children were rethinking how disability impacted their children's ability to participate as equal citizens, making parental political activism more deliberate and direct.

Within these associations, fathers and mothers told the stories of their children to highlight the challenges they faced in their ostracism from French society and the need to protect them from prejudice and ignorance. These stories fueled awareness campaigns directed at the national government to increase accommodations to fulfill the promise of equality inherent in the French Constitution and the promises the government made as a signatory to several United Nations resolutions. Many of these associations also monitored the French press to find stories to highlight the need for greater acceptance of disabled people, but especially of their children who did not fit the ideal of normative children in France. For the most part, however, these associations did not truly engage in activism until the end of the 1960s, after a series of events brought greater public attention to the challenges facing disabled people and their families. By then, associations became much more combative about how to ameliorate the problems facing their families, and professionals were themselves questioning the medical regime and some of the assumptions underpinning it.

PARENTING IN THE AGE OF AUTISM

The equivocation of the onset of autism with poor parenting challenged the ability of parents to engage in activities to help their children in a broader social context. Autism was indicative of challenges within the home, and the need to address them meant that it was more of a domestic issue than a social one. Religion continued to play an important role within the family in France. The efforts of the Catholic Church to reorient after its profound association with the Vichy regime during the war softened an exodus from the church, and an overwhelming percentage of the French public continued to identify as Catholic in the immediate postwar period.[7] Moreover, the church played a key role in welfare and charity efforts in postwar France as an important intermediary between citizens and the state; this included a tradition of efforts to educate young people, including disabled youth, through funding from organizations such as Secours catholique.[8] As Richard Bates noted, the Catholic Church also proved receptive to the ideas of psychoanalysis as part of the postwar change, which impacted how some parents chose to engage with analysis and helped strengthen the position of thinkers such as Françoise Dolto.[9] The continued stress on the importance of the family within this new Catholic approach led to the development of literature informed by church teachings that addressed contemporary domestic issues for families. One of the more influential reviews was *Feuilles familiales*, a Belgian monthly publication that introduced and promoted values aligned with Catholicism and contained articles written by its readers. The purpose of the magazine was "to study the problems and achieve the fulfillment of the family through the diffusion of solutions."[10] *Feuilles familiales* had an audience in France, and the publishers were interested in the specific challenges facing the magazine's subscribers, which it gauged through annual questionnaires of readers. In 1954, readers responded to inquiries with their thoughts on disabled children, and the words of these parents led to the publication of a collection, *Nos enfants handicapés*, in 1962.

With commentary from the editors of *Feuilles familiales*, Gaston and Marie-Françoise Falisse, *Nos enfants handicapés* reflected on the letters sent to the magazine that detailed the domestic experiences of families with disabled children and how they challenged the magazine's purpose of uplifting families through faith-based solutions. The responses included many types of physical and developmental disabilities, but they often shared similar elements of confusion, exasperation, and frustration about the situation. As part of their stories, parents questioned their faith and the future of their children, but the Falisses countered in their words with encouragement as well as excerpts from psychology professionals about how to help parents care for their disabled children. The Falisses noted the tendency of these families to hope for a miracle cure, but stressed the importance of working with professionals to develop proper techniques for the education of disabled children and being loving toward them as part of their commitment to faith.[11] Although it was informed by religion, this approach nevertheless echoed some of the conclusions of analysts concerning the proper response toward developmentally disabled children.

Much of the collection attempted to encourage parents to remain engaged with their children and integrate them into family life, reinforcing the importance of the family as a place of comfort and grace. The Falisses asserted that acceptance was key in the process, especially in the context of the importance of suffering within the Catholic faith.[12] Moreover, they offered solutions based on the existing medical literature on disability, modeling an approach for parents to become experts in the treatment of their children despite the emphasis on spirituality. In their advice, the Falisses stressed the need for parents to treat disabled children as they would any other child, with a combination of love and discipline that would allow the child to develop a full emotional life.[13] In these exhortations, they stressed that there was a tendency for some parents of disabled children to despair about their child's condition and ultimately reject the child, dovetailing with the conclusions of psychoanalytic literature, but asked parents to reconsider this reaction and instead rely on their faith to help them cope with the stresses of their situation. Additionally, the pronatalist nature of *Feuilles familiales* encouraged parents with disabled children to have large families and integrate siblings into their care.[14]

Nos enfants handicapés marked the growing awareness of the ongoing challenges facing parents of disabled children, but *Feuilles familiales* did not have a particular political or social agenda beyond encouraging adherence to Catholic teachings. Nor were these responses solely about autistic children. Although the group's publications were informed by parents, it did not ultimately focus its energies on the issues of disability in francophone Europe and instead continued to operate as a source of advice for its readers that emphasized the ministerial role of the church. Even with its popularity in the late 1950s and early 1960s, *Feuilles familiales* did not offer any solutions outside the existing mainstream in terms of treatment or education. Furthermore, its advice for parents of developmentally disabled children offered little to specifically address the challenges in presenting concepts of faith and spirituality to these children. Religion was certainly important to these families, because they would later voice concerns to other parents about the challenges of raising their children to hold religious values. The responses in *Nos enfants handicapés* revealed that parents were struggling to navigate the existing system in France and limited by what they could hope to accomplish for their children within that framework. The editors pressed parents to become experts in their children's disability, which would become an important aspect of the parents' movement in the 1960s. It would take a different type of association, however, to push against the norms of the system and bring greater attention to the aspirations of parents to advocate for more services and options to help their children.

WHITE BUTTERFLIES AS EARLY ADVOCATES

Local parents' associations formed in the immediate postwar period in parallel to the introduction of psychoanalysis within the psychology profession as the response to autism. While at first the associations were interested in creating solidarity among parents of developmentally disabled children by sharing their stories, the mission changed as the dynamics concerning disability changed by the 1960s. Brigitte Chamak recognizes the pivotal role these associations played in the development of public interest, government policy, and importation of educational and behavioral methods pioneered outside France, but at the outset they were focused primarily on telling their children's stories to connect with other parents.[15] Early associations were organized around parents' challenges in working within the system and their understanding of the needs of their children. Governing boards were populated by parents, grandparents, and other family members, with medical professionals acting as consultants. These organizations operated in the social space between government bureaucracies and medical professionals but did not initially challenge the authority of either until the end of the 1960s.

The first parents' association for families with developmentally disabled children consisted of seven parents in Lyon in 1948 who worked together to lend support to each other and their children. Shortly thereafter, a group of seven families in Paris established Les papillons blancs, an association that quickly grew to one hundred families by 1951 and established a model that was duplicated throughout France. The Papillons blancs expanded throughout the 1950s (and continues to operate well into the twenty-first century) through the creation of other regional associations, culminating in the first national organization in 1958. One of the major tent poles that brought parents together was the issue of education because the French state was failing to provide educational resources for their children. Because compulsory education had a long history in France, one of the issues in the postwar period was the continued expansion of special education to better serve developmentally disabled students, with a population of over fifty-six thousand children in some type of special educational setting by 1958.[16] The development of educational psychology not only provided a method of assessment that led to the establishment of *instituts medico-pédagogiques* (IMPs) during this expansion, but also defined critical norms that could marginalize children who did not meet the goals. These institutions were the primary concern of the associations, which sought to help parents improve conditions and outcomes at these clinics.

IMPs were founded to address the educational gap for disabled children, especially those with developmental disabilities, in the late nineteenth century. The education of disabled people has a rich tradition in France, dating back to the establishment of important institutions for the deaf and blind and the treatment of the Wild Boy of Aveyron by Jean-Marc Gaspard Itard in the early nineteenth century.[17] Pioneers of educating developmentally disabled children such as Itard and Édouard Séguin established important social norms within France that influenced the creation of special education in the twentieth century. With the development of educational psychology and intelligence testing in France, the notion to create different types of education for developmentally disabled children appeared in the early twentieth century.[18] The creation of IMPs gave physicians and educators a location to develop treatment for some children who were not integrated into the existing educational system, but they were limited in scope and often centered in major urban areas. Within the residential asylum system, there were no institutions developed to treat specific developmental disorders in children, and that system was itself experiencing a period of reform in the immediate postwar period in response to the level of treatment there during the Second World War.[19] As alternative residential facilities to asylums, IMPs were adapted to serve the growing population of developmentally disabled children while providing resources to families in the various corners of the nation. However, the resources devoted to the different forms of disability were not equal, primarily because of pervasive beliefs about the educability of certain populations.[20] Another aspect was the understanding that autism was not defined as a form of disability like deafness, blindness, or even epilepsy and thus could be treated through psychoanalysis to allow integration of these children. Nevertheless, IMPs were vital to the care of autistic children in the immediate postwar period as sites of treatment and care attempting to address the specific needs of that population.

IMPs operated as private institutions with the support of the Ministry of Health and the Ministry of Education, but were increasingly connected to specific associations, which managed their functions in coordination with medical and educational professionals. They served developmentally disabled children between the ages of six and fourteen at the outset, although other facilities were later developed to provide for a broader age range. There was an interest in using IMPs to help develop physical skills in developmentally disabled children because experts believed that the lack of motor skills was part of their infantile nature.[21] Although IMPs combined elements of special education, psychoanalysis, and vocational training to help disabled children find social acceptance, the populations in IMPs grew because of the segregation of this population from mainstream schools. Run through private organizations and associations, IMPs received funding through the government, but this funding was often not enough and became a subject of debate in the National Assembly, with representatives seeking a commitment of support.[22]

Residential psychiatric hospitals were the other option for families—often the normative preference within the medical field—and the number of these institutions increased during the 1960s. The construction of new facilities expanded after 1960, with new hospitals opening in departments throughout mainland France to bring a greater equity of services available to patients outside Paris.[23] These state-run institutions differed from IMPs in their focus on medical interventions in contrast to the combination of special education and psychoanalysis used in the latter. Although the professional community championed the long-overdue expansion of psychiatric asylums due to their relative dearth prior to the war, there was also an awareness of the need to reform the operations of existing hospitals to bring them in line with developments in the psychological field concerning the treatment of developmentally disabled individuals, which included an awareness of the specific challenges facing disabled children. Nicolas Henkes notes that efforts to reform the operation of psychiatric facilities involved the profession lobbying the legislature, which included interventions from child psychologist Georges Heuyer, but that the 1960s marked the first new laws posted in the National Assembly that attempted to address the professionals' concerns.[24] Parents were not part of these discussions, even as the emergence of associations brought them increasingly into political and medical discussions.

The Papillons blancs were deeply committed to expanding the number and services of IMPs, especially outside Paris, to help educate their children and provide them with a place to socialize and grow. The IMPs that the association developed were collaborative with medical authorities, who used the facilities to conduct psychoanalysis as part of treatment, but also had a role for parents in the education of their children. Parents found opportunities to work with medical experts and did not challenge their authority at this time. The early organization of associations around a particular service was quite common throughout the Western world because these localized projects provided a way for parents to become involved in their children's care and to learn about the challenges of advocacy. The Papillons blancs certainly followed this model, organizing local educational centers and collaboration among parents to alleviate the difficulties of keeping their children at home rather than opting for institutionalization. The original organizations were focused on expanding services that parents believed would be most beneficial to their children, but these efforts functioned within the psychoanalytic norms of leaving treatment up to psychological professionals.

The work of these associations fell primarily on the parents, and both fathers and mothers shared duties within the organizations, although fathers more often played leadership roles in the first group of Papillons blancs. Léonce Malecot, who helped established the first Papillons blancs in Lyon, had a disabled daughter, while another important founder, Maître Perret-Gayet, had a disabled son. Michel

Garapin, a judge in Finistère, was the founder of the Papillons blancs in that city in 1961, although his wife also contributed to the group's efforts to establish an IMP there for twenty-five students, including their son.[25] Guy Corlay, president of the Papillons blancs in Côtes-du-Nord during the 1960s and the father of a developmentally disabled child, was important in the continued expansion of associations in Brittany during this period. Although he was not a member of an association, President Charles de Gaulle was perhaps the most famous parent of a disabled child in this period: his daughter Anne was born with Down syndrome. Parents occupied leadership positions in UNAPEI, ASITP, and UNAFAM, among others, and the associational literature reveals them to be highly engaged with their children's conditions, in stark contrast to how parents were characterized in the psychoanalytic literature of the 1950s. Corlay noted that the activities of the associations were "above all familial . . . the Association is certainly a practical and well positioned organization but never forget that it is also a spirit formed by the hundreds of families that make it up."[26] As a parents' association, the Papillons blancs was focused on the concerns of parents, including the role of religious education in the lives of developmentally disabled children, and worked with religious leaders to develop a specialized catechism for their children.[27] The Catholic Church lent its support in terms of encouragement from Pope Paul VI, who stated that these associations "brought honor to the human family," again suggesting that the association operated as an extension of the family.[28] The early purpose of these associations reinforced all efforts of parents to raise their children as they would a neurotypical child and offered examples to encourage parents to follow this path, even with the challenges they would face. Besides religious education, the Papillons blancs also emphasized the need for further vocational training in specialized workshops for their children, an acknowledgment of their looming adulthood. All these efforts reinforced the role of parents as primary advocates for their children in counterpoint to the attitudes of psychological professionals that developed in the 1950s.

Beyond the parents' associations, nongovernmental organizations such as the Red Cross were important in the expansion of IMPs in France. The Red Cross reported that in 1963, it contributed to the expansion of several existing IMPs to accommodate more patients, while also converting facilities that had been used to treat tuberculosis into new IMPs.[29] The organization recognized the growing issue facing disabled children and the continued lack of support despite the increase in their population. Supporting these children was central to the Red Cross's mission and the creation of more IMPs would contribute to that mission. In a 1965 issue of the organization's bulletin dedicated to the topic of developmentally disabled children, the Red Cross encouraged its supporters to see the value in contributing relief and aid to the creation of IMPs, offering insights into the activities within the centers, expert analysis of pedagogical approaches used there, and the statistical shortfall of availability for French children.[30] However, the Red Cross relied on the charity model for the support of these initiatives, and parents' associations did not see that approach as sustainable or equitable in the face of the shortage of facilities.

To coordinate efforts and share resources, UNAPEI formed in Paris to bring together parents across France in 1960. Initially, the organization continued the work of the Papillons blancs by emphasizing the need to grow the number of IMPs in France to better serve disabled children and their families and address the shortfall in educating disabled children. While the associations did not press for integration and mainstreaming of their children, they did stress that the children had a place in French society despite the prejudices and challenges they faced. Although the Papillons blancs and UNAPEI included families with autistic children, the first association that focused exclusively on autistic individuals, ASITP, formed in 1963. ASITP followed a model similar to that of the other disability-oriented associations—seeking increased government support for education, more facilities, and greater social acceptance of their children's condition—and helped to establish the Hôpital du jour Santos Dumont in Paris, which allowed autistic children to continue to reside with their parents while receiving treatment.[31] The initial medical consultant for the facility was Serge Lebovici, and the patients at Santos Dumont were exclusively children below the age of fifteen, although associations supported the development of a clinic there for people between the ages of fifteen and twenty-five in 1970.[32]

The expansion of IMPs and other clinics allowed parents to participate in their children's care in a manner that was different from analysis. While many parents discussed in the previous chapter acquiesced to undergoing psychoanalysis as part of their children's treatment, within the context of associations, parents found new avenues to work on their children's behalf and even grow their own expertise concerning their children's condition. Although the efforts of associations contributed to some important developments in terms of facilities and approaches concerning the treatment of mental disability, there was still a tendency to question the role of parents in their child's disability. For example, in a 1965 issue of the journal *Esprit* dedicated to the question of disability, a panel of experts weighed in on the issue of childhood disability in France. In his analysis of parent associations, Paul Vernon, then-president of UNAPEI, provided an imagined narrative of how parents react to the news of disability in their children, focusing on disabilities that appear after childbirth. In his telling, all parents experience a great trauma when learning of their child's condition, which typically leads to self-blaming and depression, with the disabled child representing an "intrusion in the home of a diminished, flawed, and incomplete life" that forces the parents to ask why their child is not like other children.[33] While the remainder of the article highlights the work done by parents' associations to change the situation and the need for more resources and services, Vernon illuminated the underlying assumptions concerning childhood normativity and the impact of disability on families, along with the implications that parents struggled to accept their disabled children in the context of an imagined child, a crucial bedrock of the emphasis on psychoanalysis. Even among the most active and activist parents, the struggle to accept their child's condition was part of their experience, which highlights the difficulties within these families. This tendency reveals that understandings of normative childhood were internalized among parents and that the failure of their children to conform to these norms caused anxiety, especially with regard to how these children were treated in society.

Vernon observed that even with IMPs and education, the social acceptance and integration of disabled children remained a significant problem, rooted in the concern for how these children would become disabled adults. Associations tended to focus their efforts on services for young children, undoubtedly based on their members' experiences, which again reinforced the association between autism and childhood. Questions of their future contributions to society, especially in terms of labor and social participation, meant that these children were not able to project their future as other children could. Again, in this sense, disabled children occupied an imagined space of perpetual childhood that emphasized their invalidity and their inability to participate in society as constructed, yet at the same time they were not exactly children since they did not conform to the norms of childhood. The work of parents' associations, while focused on helping their children develop knowledge and skills through special education, continued to intersect with these attitudes during the 1960s, forcing leaders to rethink their approach and reach out to new allies to help them challenge these assumptions.

CHAMBERY AND THE INTERNATIONAL POLITICIZATION OF ASSOCIATIONS

In November 1966 in Chambery, the mother of a disabled toddler was brought to trial, accused of murdering him with an overdose of phenobarbital. Three-year-old Fausto Gourand had had several disabilities since the age of six months, including epilepsy and developmental disability. Fausto had been receiving care from multiple doctors, but this experience had worn on his mother, who had lost hope and sought a more permanent solution. The mother, Mireille Gourand, was brought to the *cour d'assises* (criminal circuit court) for premeditated murder. During the trial at Savoie, the prosecution accused Gourand of premeditation and asked her to explain her actions. She argued that her son's life was too much of a struggle and that he was better off somewhere else. She emphasized her son's condition: "He was deaf and mute. His language was paralyzed, it took all my time [to care for him]."[34] She decided to pour a lethal dose of phenobarbital into Fausto's milk. She then told the judge that she had to choke her son to complete the act, information that had also been included in the police report. When asked if she would do it again, Gourand replied, "I believe yes . . . he's fine where he is."[35] Despite her confession to the crime, the defense was able to convince the jury to acquit Gourand after deliberating for thirty minutes. The acceptance of filicide among parents of disabled children has a long history, but this case occurred as parents' associations had asserted themselves as an authoritative voice for their children and showed how parents had influence on perceptions of their children.[36]

In reaction to the court's decision, the editorial staff of *Nos enfants inadaptés* sent a rallying cry to its readers, calling on the association to strengthen its efforts to advocate for disabled children in the wake of the failure of the state to protect their rights. The editorial notes that the death of Fausto Gourand was just one in a litany of examples of how the French state excused filicide by devaluing the lives of disabled people. In response, the editors offered to help families in similar situations to prevent future tragedies, but noted the limitations of such efforts in the context of more pervasive attitudes about developmental disability and youth. "What is [French] society trying to say when it gives a verdict like the one at Chambery? Does it want to say that Hitler was right to eliminate the mentally disabled?"[37] Obviously, the association rejected this line of thinking, arguing that every disabled person has the right to life, but noted the need to have those rights codified and protected. It also noted that despite the efforts to educate their children and give them a pathway to work as adults, "our children are still not included in society."[38]

The need for inclusion and rights became a more important part of UNAPEI's mission, especially as a national organization created to advocate for all of the smaller associations, even as efforts to expand IMPs continued. While their approach had previously focused on developing resources for parents regarding the right to education for all French children, the story of Fausto Gourand set off a new period of advocacy in which the need for recognition of the basic rights of disabled children became the center of the association's mission. The French state was still the target of the group's efforts, but UNAPEI was more focused on ideological engagement with the meaning of the French ideals of *liberté, égalité, fraternité* and less on developing new IMPs. Still, the need for increased budgets for services and social support for families remained a significant part of the experience of these families, including the Gourand family. In a 1967 editorial, UNAPEI led with the statement, "The value of a civilization is measured by its capacity to care for its handicapped and deficient community which was once abandoned."[39] This phrase, a quote from the Minister of Social Affairs in 1966, illustrated the disconnect between the rhetoric of equality and the willingness to allow disabled people to experience tragedy and death, and the association used it as a rallying cry to assert a new role for itself. As context for the quote, UNAPEI provided statistics about the failure of the French state to provide the minimum support for disabled people, especially children, with only 16 percent of the needed placements in IMPs and other facilities being provided in 1966 and most families having few or no options for care.[40] The number of IMPs dedicated to developmentally disabled children did not match the estimated population, despite efforts to establish more effective evaluations to determine placement for these children; UNAPEI estimated a shortfall of over half a million placements by 1970.[41] In this sense, the association showed some sympathy for situations such as that of the Gourand family, but put the need for action on the French government to expand funding for more facilities beyond residential institutions, which were still a common solution to treating developmental disability, rather than solely blaming the mother for her actions.

By the end of 1967, UNAPEI noted that associations had been waiting for a solution to the failure to acknowledge the rights of disabled minors for nearly a decade and that change needed to happen quickly to stave off a looming crisis. The Fifth Plan, the most recent national five-year plan for economic growth, went into effect in 1966 but lacked enough funding to support the rapidly growing population of disabled persons in France. The association argued that the "presence of a disabled person in the household is an issue that concerns each among us" and called it a national scandal.[42] However, the attitudes that informed the Gourand verdict suggested that advocacy was needed to reframe the approach to reaching the larger French audience, given the speed by which that jury made their decision. The association looked to external sources for support while pressing the French government to recognize its responsibility to support all French families, and 1968 marked another important turning point for the association.

The International League of Societies for the Mentally Handicapped (ILSMH) was founded in 1964 to connect parents' associations throughout the world with the aim to help parents advocate for their children and obtain increased public services to help their children more successfully integrate into society. The organization grew out of the European League of Societies for the Mentally Handicapped and expanded to include members from Great Britain, France, Australia, Sweden, and the United States, among other countries. The ILSMH Third International was held in Paris in 1966, with UNAPEI contributing to the program. The conference included presentations from experts in juvenile law, medicine, and social work, as well as tours of facilities in Paris, including those that provided special education.[43] UNAPEI continued to send representatives to these meetings, notably the 1967 meeting in Sweden that introduced the Scandinavian concept of normalization of disability. Normalization was the social acceptance of disability combined with social services to help disabled people integrate into society, which became part of the mission of many French parents' associations by the end of the 1960s.[44] At the 1967 meeting, delegates argued that the legislative nature of "mental retardation" needed to be addressed directly and collaboratively despite the different national contexts of their representatives. ILSMH observed that while each country needed to assess how to respond to the failure to support disabled people and their families, there was not a single country with an adequate plan of action and there was a tendency to exploit this population with the promise of cures.[45] The organization also emphasized the need for more day clinics embedded within communities to help address prejudices against disabled people, as well as the importance of financial aid to families to ensure equity. For ILSMH, parents' associations were critical actors to engage in dialogue with government bodies and thus should make these goals central to their activities.

UNAPEI took direct inspiration from ILSMH by the middle of the 1960s as an obvious ally in its struggle to shape French public opinion and transform state policy. Following the Fourth International Congress in Jerusalem in 1968, UNAPEI reprinted the Declaration des droits du deficient mental developed during that meeting. This statement introduced a shift away from advocacy of a charity-based model toward one rooted in the concept of human rights.[46] These rights, as enumerated by ILSMH and UNAPEI, included "a right to proper medical care and physical restoration and to such education, training, habilitation and guidance as will enable him to develop his ability and potential to the fullest possible extent, no matter how severe his degree of disability. No mentally handicapped person should be deprived of such services by reason of the costs involved."[47] This statement became a guiding principle for UNAPEI and had been one of the rationales behind the creation of more IMPs and the attempts to establish expanded special education in France. ILSMH's Fourth Congress, where these rights were further enumerated, stressed that the failure of nations to provide adequate facilities was rooted in the lack of equal justice for disabled children.[48] This conclusion echoed UNIPEI's reaction to the Gourand decision and the social acceptance of filicide for disabled children. The declaration contained seven rights and asserted that they should be instantly recognized in the context of the proclaimed United Nations Declaration on the Rights of the Child from 1959, but UNAPEI observed that the French state failed to extend those protections to disabled children.[49]

The rights of intellectually disabled people have been a subject of political debate in the Western world for centuries, especially in the modern period with the emergence of mass politics. In Great Britain, France, and the United States, intellectual disability served as a method of exclusion for the extension of rights to a profound degree, especially given the commonality of institutionalization and the power of medical authority in the modern period.[50] During the 1960s and 1970s, there was a growing effort for the recognition of the rights of disabled persons (including disabled children) in France inspired by the civil rights movement in the United States, and parents' associations were important loci of this activity.[51] UNAPEI, in conjunction with ILSMH, emphasized the need for the French republic not only to recognize the rights of disabled children (and, by extension, perhaps adults) but also to defend those rights publicly through new legislation and budget prioritization. The approach to this advocacy was to highlight that the homeland for human rights was not living up to those ideals in its practices toward disabled children.

In an editorial from early 1970, UNAPEI noted that while parents had accepted that "their children would never be like other children" and that society "should accept their disability," the editorial board noted the double-edged sword of such an approach from the association.[52] The rejection of the curative model of psychoanalysis is evident in the editorial, and the association instead sought social acceptance for developmentally disabled children, including equal rights and inclusion in all activities. This turn marked a growing recognition by UNAPEI of what has been termed the social construction of disability and a distancing from the medical model, the latter of which informed psychoanalytic treatment of autism to some degree. The social model of disability points to how the conception of disability is rooted in the response to disabled individuals in terms of rights, treatment, and opportunities, rather than the medical experience of each individual as an explanation for their exclusion. Instead of focusing on individual deficit as the defining aspect of disability, advocates asserted that prejudice and inequality against the disabled (not their physical or mental impairment) led to their exclusion, which meant that the situation could be altered through action and legal reform.[53] In the case of associations, they hoped to find ways to promote inclusion as a logical response to the recognition that disability should not be inherently limiting. Thus, the recognition of the social model of disability meant that a civil rights movement was necessary, although parents in this case saw themselves as leaders of this international movement. They lacked a national platform that could connect them with the broader French public to obtain their aid in promoting the welfare of disabled children, but an incident in 1968 provided an opportunity to reach more people outside their organizations.

THE FIRE AT FROISSY AND THE NATIONAL STAGE

On November 25, 1968, a fire in a private residential facility for developmentally disabled children in the village of Froissy captured national attention and brought the issues faced by parents of disabled children into focus. The facility's population included children with all types of developmental disabilities, including autism, cerebral palsy, epilepsy, and Down syndrome. The fire took the lives of fourteen children, in large part because of poor conditions in the facility and the practice of administrators locking children in their dormitories on the third floor. Once news of the fire reached first national and then international news outlets, observers editorialized about the treatment of disabled children and the disgrace of their situation as the responsibility of all French society, which echoed the sentiments of the parents' associations. Following the fire at Froissy, UNAPEI and other organizations took a more militant and direct approach to secure the rights and privileges of their children, arguing that it was a life-or-death struggle to protect them. Even as the media attention quickly ebbed, associations continued down the path of awareness and advocacy that maligned the French state for its failure to prevent the tragedy.

The Chateau de Froissy, also known as La source, had been founded in 1959 to provide services for children with developmental delays. The fire in 1968 began in the middle of the night on the third floor, where sixteen patents between the ages of twelve and fourteen had been locked in their dormitory, with some of the children chained to their beds to prevent them from roaming the facility. La source did not have a working fire escape or any operant fire extinguishers, and the firefighters did not have access to a floor plan to identify the location of the children.[54] Thirteen children perished in the fire, and an additional child died in the hospital shortly after being transported there. The incident became front-page news across France, with media reports on national radio and television broadcasts as well, and reporters weighed in on the situation that led to the fire in editorials assigning blame to the French government and society. The associations understood that the moment was one in which to amplify their message of equality and inclusion to a newly receptive public.

In the first issue of *Nos enfants inadaptés* published after the fire, UNAPEI leaders called on members to contextualize the incident within the framework of the lack of resources dedicated to developmentally disabled children, echoing earlier rhetoric of the association's mission. Moreover, the editorial staff was grateful that media coverage had been respectful of the families of the tragedy while questioning how such an incident could happen in modern France. The association noted that it was time to pressure the French government to expand funding for families of disabled children, while also recognizing the need to "keep in our hearts a recognition of the poor children of Froissy for having given their lives for their brethren."[55] In the weeks after the fire, the Ligue française de l'ensignement et de l'éducation permanente, an association dedicated to promoting all forms of public education, assembled a collection of news articles from the press response to the fire, revealing that the tragedy resonated across different media outlets and that journalists had now discovered the challenges facing disabled children and their families.[56] The collection was offered without any commentary; rather, it presented sixteen articles in their entirety to illustrate how the conditions of facilities that housed disabled children, often hidden from view, had caught the attention of the French public.

In this collection, media commentators reflected on the issue of responsibility and what the culpability of French society was in failing to protect these children. The coverage shared a tendency: the sentimental presentation of the children as innocent victims without blaming the parents for their role in placing the victims at the facility. This interpretation of the events factored into the outrage that the fire generated in the pages of *Le Monde*, *Le figaro*, *Combat*, and *L'express*, to name a few of the newspapers and magazines that covered the event, with each directing their focus on the responsibility of both the French government and society in general for the accident, echoing the sentiment of parents' organizations. On the political left, the incident revealed the inequalities operant in contemporary society, although they were often couched in economic terms rather than addressing the specific rights of the disabled. For example, Françoise Giraud, in the December 16, 1968, issue of the center-left magazine *L'express*, noted the failure of the French government to manage the situation of health care for disabled children and the inability of private institutions to offer effective care that was within the means of many families, creating an unfair system that inherently led to tragedies such as that at Froissy. She asserted that this tension within the mental health system led to "les enfants perdus" such as those at Froissy and that a society as wealthy as France should be able to care for its vulnerable populations.[57] Giraud placed the blame for the incident at Froissy on the ability of French citizens to ignore the plight of disabled children because of their embrace of industrial capitalism. Similarly, *Esprit* noted that the fire revealed deeper inequalities that the French state could not solve in its current iteration, calling for profound structural change, a conclusion that could be read in the context of the editorial team's awareness of the challenges facing developmentally disabled children and their families.[58] Coming from a different political perspective, the conservative *Le figaro* noted the significance of the French Minister of Social Affairs Marie-Madeline Dienesch laying fourteen bouquets of flowers in honor of the dead children, but also stated that beyond symbolic gestures, the French state must recognize its moral responsibility, again sounding similar to the exhortations of parents' associations advocating for their children's rights.[59] The centrist *L'aurore* noted that while it would be easy to blame the Rokowskis—the proprietors of La source—the couple was not alone in their responsibility for the outcome: it was squarely the responsibility of French society.[60] Evelyne Le Garrec noted that the growing number of disabled children in France was not matched by resources from the state and recognized the specific efforts of UNAPEI to bring greater attention to these social deficits. La source was just one example of the potential for fatal failures in the French system.[61] The incident even made the international newswire, appearing in newspapers in the United States such as the *Boston Globe*, *Detroit Free-Press*, and *Pittsburgh News-Gazette*. Despite the political differences of these publications, there was a consensus among French journalists regarding the need for the government to take action to prevent further tragedies and the responsibility of French society to provide care for disabled children.

According to the national news radio program "Inter actualités" that aired immediately after the fire, the incident raised questions about the role of local authorities in monitoring the safety of La source. Reports of failures concerning fire exits, faulty wiring, and overcrowding were noted about three months before the incident, with no follow-up investigation. Also, the facility's permit allowed for the care for forty-five children, but when the firefighters arrived there were at least sixty children housed within the facility. Much like the reaction elsewhere, the emphasis of the reporting was that this was a preventable tragedy that illustrated the need for greater attention to the treatment of disabled children rather than placing blame on the institution itself.[62] As UNAPEI noted in January 1969, the media coverage brought the plight affecting families to light in a manner that was dignified and could truly affect change by bringing awareness to the situation.[63] Moreover, the rhetoric of these different outlets pointed to how parents needed help and were as much victims of this system as the children were.

THE POLITICS OF FROISSY

This sympathy also briefly appeared in the National Assembly, as the issue of care and financial support for disabled children was brought to Minister of Social Affairs Maurice Schumann in early 1969 as part of an inquiry after the Froissy fire. During parliamentary debate in January, Deputy Pierre-Bernard Cousté of Rhône asked the minister to move toward reforming government measures based on recommendations contained in the Bloch-Lainé report from a few years prior.[64] The inquiry focused on the failure of various state apparatuses to recognize the necessity for changing procedures considering the growing number of disabled children. A report issued by the Red Cross also noted that while some improvements had been made to many institutions, there was a national need to dedicate more resources to these children in recognition of their equal place in society.[65] The topic of Froissy did not last long in the National Assembly debates, however. It generated some immediate interest in December 1968, but by February 1969, references to the accident had all but faded from parliamentary discussion. During its brief appearance, Froissy became associated with the issue of educational rather than medical reform, which aligned with the shifting discourse of the parents' associations and their efforts to recast developmental disability as a social issue.

Within the National Assembly, references to Froissy appeared in debates during the fire's immediate aftermath. For example, in the November 29, 1968, session, Irma Rapuzzi of Bouches-du-Rhône, a member of the finance committee, presented a report to Minister of Education Edgar Faure about the state of education in France and referenced the incident at Froissy as symbolic of the needs facing disabled children. Rapuzzi referenced the media outcry concerning the deaths at the facility to address the need for greater allocation for institutional support, suggesting that the French public was becoming aware of a problem that the Senate had recognized for some time.[66] Rapuzzi suggested the positive development of special education in France and the Senate's fiscal support of these efforts that were already in motion prior to the accident. More significantly, Rapuzzi's report to Faure revealed the awareness of the public response to the fire within the National Assembly and the demand to address some of the issues in the immediate aftermath, including an official inquiry.

With all the attention focused on the incident, the National Assembly had to respond and immediately launched an investigation that focused on the failures in the operation of La source and the negligence of the institution's administrators and local officials. Drafted by Dr. Fonroget in association with the Inspection generale des affaires sociales, the report submitted on December 6, 1968, revealed a series of violations at La source, including overcrowding of facilities, failure to report the current population to local health authorities, the mixing of populations of boys and girls, and the lack of sufficient personnel to manage services properly. Existing guidelines required a ratio of one staff member to every five patients, but La source was operating at a ratio of one to thirteen. Fonroget's report pointed to the actions of the proprietors, the Rokowskis, in violation of rules as a primary cause for the outcome of the fire, although he also placed blame on local authorities because the facility had not been inspected properly since 1965.[67]

In Fonroget's assessment, the negligence of the Rokowskis was coupled with an equal level of negligence from the inspecteur de la santé and the departmental director of L'action sanitaire et sociale. This was a local failure and not the responsibility of the National Assembly. Yet, Fonroget consulted two local doctors familiar with the operation of La source and included their observations in his report on the incident to perhaps direct blame at broader government agencies. A pediatrician, Dr. Designolle, stated that in his opinion the children at La source were well treated and fed and had a happy nature. The children admitted to the facility showed remarkable improvement, even in cases where they had been previously housed in other facilities. Designolle noted that although La source was not a "model of the modern education of the profoundly retarded [*sic*]," this was not the fault of the staff, whose interventions showed a positive impact on the students.[68] The second expert, Dr. Grimberg, offered similar evidence of the sincere efforts of the Rokowskis and their staff to treat the children at La source, noting that the staff was pivotal in the education of the children to "adapt to a life as normal as possible." However, Grimberg also remarked that she was unaware of the violations on the facility's second floor.[69] Each of these observations emphasized the lack of malice on the part of the facility, suggesting that more funding could potentially prevent similar future accidents.

Ultimately, Fonroget pointed to the irregularities in the operation of La source and assigned final responsibility to its director, Madame Rokowski, suggesting that had she followed the regulations, no one would have died in the fire. Fonroget recognized that her actions merited sanction despite Rokowski's assertions that the limitations of the system and the needs of the families for facilities led to the decision to violate regulations and admit so many children at La source. At the same time, he suggested the need for greater oversight of private institutions.[70] After the fire, the children of La source had been placed either in other facilities or in the care of their families, but the inquiry report emphasized the shortcomings of the system itself and that the needs of disabled children and their families were not given enough attention (or funding) by the National Assembly. The closing of La source did little to address this line of reasoning or the obligations of French society, which had all but ignored this segment of the populace. While taking a less vitriolic tone than the media reports on the fire at Froissy, the inquiry nevertheless echoed their conclusions about where action was needed and galvanized parents' associations to accelerate their efforts.

The Froissy tragedy continued to appear briefly in the official records of the National Assembly as political advocates sought to use the attention it garnered to motivate action. The question of Froissy arose again on February 1, 1969, in the aftermath of the official inquiry. Cousté raised the issue of responsibility, suggesting that while the inquiry had laid out clear sanctions in terms of the accident, it was nevertheless imperative for the National Assembly to act on the recommendations of the Bloch-Lainé report. Minister of Social Affairs Schumann responded to Cousté with the recognition of implementing reform, but then suggested the limits of action due to fiscal shortfalls.[71] In a session on March 28, 1969, the issues that continued after Froissy, namely, the efforts of associations to address the lack of facilities and the lack of oversight of these facilities, were part of the broader debate about the role of the government in developing a response to these issues.[72] Despite the ongoing issue concerning the treatment of disabled children and the debate concerning the role of the National Assembly that appeared in the official record, references to Froissy faded by April 1969.

The brief energy that the accident at Froissy engendered for reform crested as a result of concerns about funding and disagreements about the nature of government intervention. Part of this disagreement hinged on the definition of disability and the understandings of the rights of disabled children. While some within the National Assembly saw the need for the government to provide greater assistance to families with disabled children, there was disagreement about which ministry should bear the responsibility, illuminating the differences in understanding disability as a medical or social issue.[73] These debates continued into the 1970s, but the National Assembly approached the issue of reform cautiously and slowly, which did little to change the institutional situation that led to the accident in the first place. This lack of action spurred activists to advocate for change, challenging the existing structure of institutions and pushing for even greater parental oversight concerning treatment and care.

The residential nature of La source highlighted a missing resource that parents seeking treatment for their children hoped to acquire—outpatient care. While the psychoanalytic sessions detailed in Chapter 1 suggested that disabled children were able to receive care while living with their parents, the more common approach was treatment within an IMP, which allowed for numerous services to be delivered from an array of professionals in a residential setting. After the Froissy fire, parents hoped to develop and secure more resources to keep their children embedded in their households so they might monitor and participate in their children's care. ASTIP had the Santos Dumont, but similar facilities were needed outside Paris to help families across France, and parents' associations continued to press for state support for expanding day hospitals. While they were trying to advocate for services, there was a recognition that perhaps a new approach would be needed to bring the family more directly into the care of their disabled children, in concert with professionals. In this sense, parents were increasingly seeking pathways outside the existing structure to improve the lives of their children while accepting that their condition was permanent. However, the public nature of the Froissy fire brought more voices into the discussion about the treatment of developmentally disabled children, and the public increasingly became a participant in the discussion about disability and childhood thereafter.

The growth of parental intervention in the 1960s marked a turning point for the position of parents within the discussion of autism, but much of the activity fell under the larger umbrella of advocacy for all disabled children. Yet there was not agreement about the connection between autism and disability because autism was still medically considered a form of psychosis, and thus it was curable. While groups such as ASTIP did focus specifically on autism, it was not as developed or visible at UNAPEI, which had become a more pronounced political force after the Froissy fire. Still, at this stage these associations were seeking to engage with the state to ameliorate limitations through funding and legislation to recognize the rights of disabled children. Given the French public's ability to discount the value of disabled life, associations also continued their awareness efforts to promote their children as belonging to French society. But several controversies in the coming decade would serve to refocus the efforts of associations to address concerns with the medical profession in a challenge over expertise concerning childhood disability. Even with all these efforts, however, the voices of the disabled themselves remained marginalized and the notion of autism as a disorder of childhood was reinforced.

NOTES

1. "20 Ans d'action," *Nos enfants inadaptés* 29, no. 1 (Spring 1969): 22–23.
2. Philip Roos, "Parents of Mentally Retarded People," *International Journal of Mental Health* 6, no. 1 (Spring 1977): 96.
3. Paul Longmore, "'Heaven's Special Child': The Making of Poster Children," in *The Disability Studies Reader*, ed. Lennard J. Davis (New York: Routledge, 2013): 34–41.
4. Allison C. Carey, Pamela Block, and Richard K. Scotch, *Allies and Obstacles: Disability Activism and Parents of Children with Disabilities* (Philadelphia: Temple University Press, 2020).
5. Chloe Silverman, *Understanding Autism: Parents, Doctors, and the History of a Disorder* (Princeton, NJ: Princeton University Press, 2012).
6. Amanda Apgar, *The Disabled Child: Memoirs of a Normal Future* (Ann Arbor: University of Michigan Press, 2023), 5–6.

7. Sarah Fishman, *From Vichy to the Sexual Revolution: Gender and Family Life in Postwar France* (New York: Oxford University Press, 2017), 37.
8. Ingo Bode, "A New Agenda for European Charity: Catholic Welfare and Organizational Change in France and Germany," *Voluntas: International Journal of Voluntary and Nonprofit Organizations* 14, no. 2 (June 2003): 209. While organizing charitable support for disabled children, the French Catholic Church had a complex relationship with disability and eugenics in general, noting the rejection of some elements of eugenic practices in France while recognizing its alleged medical authority. See Sharon M. Leon, *An Image of God: The Catholic Struggle with Eugenics* (Chicago: University of Chicago Press, 2013), 190n30.
9. Richard Bates, *Psychoanalysis and the Family in Twentieth-Century France: Françoise Dolto and Her Legacy* (Manchester, UK: Manchester University Press, 2022), 101.
10. Philippe Denis, "Le couple et la famille au prisme d'une revue: Histoire des *Feuilles familiales* (1938–1975)," *Revue d'histoire ecclésiastique* 84, no. 2 (1989): 396.
11. Gaston Falisse and Marie-Françoise Falisse, *Nos enfants handicapés* (Paris: Editions universitaires, 1962), 28.
12. Ibid., 36–37.
13. Ibid., 64–65.
14. Ibid., 101–2.
15. Brigitte Chamak, "Autism and Social Movements: French Parents' Associations and International Autistic Individuals' Organisations," *Sociology of Health & Illness* 30, no. 1 (2008): 76–96.
16. Natalie Bélanger and Nicolas Garant, "Educational Opportunities and Polysemic Notions of Equality in France," in *Disability, Human Rights and Education*, ed. Felicity Armstrong and Len Barton (Philadelphia: Open University Press, 1999), 139.
17. See Thérèse-Adèle Husson, Catherine J. Kudlick, and Zina Weygand, *Reflections: The Life and Writings of a Young Blind Woman In Post-Revolutionary France* (New York: New York University Press, 2001); and Margaret A. Winzer, *The History of Special Education: From Isolation to Integration* (Washington, DC: Gallaudet University Press, 1993), 65–68, for discussions on the development of education for disabled people in France during the eighteenth and nineteenth centuries.
18. G. Vattier, "Experimental Pedagogy in France," *Journal of Educational Psychology* 1, no. 7 (1910): 389–403.
19. Camille Robcis, *Disalienation: Politics, Philosophy, and Radical Psychiatry in Postwar France* (Chicago: University of Chicago Press, 2021).
20. Dominique Lerch, "Séparer, intégrer, inclure: Enfants handicapés à l'école," *Ethnology française* 39, no. 3 (2009): 445.
21. Pierre Doussinet, "La recuperation professionnelle et sociale des déficients sensoriels et des inadaptés psychiques," *Ligue française pour la santé mentale: L'hygiène mentale* no. 2 (1950): 40.
22. For example, see the exchange on September 26, 1966, concerning a shortfall in the budget for the care and education of disabled children and the need to address this issue; *Journal officiel de la République française: Débats parlementaires*, October 4, 1966, 3071.
23. See Magali Coldefy and Sarah E. Curtis, "The Geography of Institutional Psychiatric Care in France 1800–2000: Historical Analysis of the Spatial Diffusion of Specialised

Facilities for Institutional Care of Mental Illness," *Social Science & Medicine* 71 (2010): 2117–29.

24. Nicholas Henckes, "French Deinstitutionalization or the Irony of Success: Psychiatrists, the State and the Transformation of the French Psychiatric System, 1945–2010," in *Deinstitutionalisation and After: Post-war Psychiatry in the Western World*, ed. Despo Kritsotaki, Victoria Long, and Matthew Smith (London: Palgrave Macmillan, 2016), 119.
25. "Qui sommes-nous?" accessed January 30, 2023, https://www.papillonsblancs29.fr/histoire/.
26. Guy Corlay, "Le mot du president," *Papillons blancs ADAPEI* 20 (April–May 1970): 1.
27. "Formation chretienne de nos enfants inadaptés," *Papillons blancs des Côtes du Nord 1* (1964): 7.
28. "Address of Paul VI to the Members of the Executive Council of the International League of Societies for the Mentally Handicapped [February 5, 1971]," https://www.vatican.va/content/paul-vi/en/speeches/1971/february/documents/hf_p-vi_spe_19710205_mentally-handicapped.html.
29. "Activités medico-sociales," *Vie et bonté: Nouvelles de la Croix-Rouge française* 156 (May 1965): 6.
30. See the special issue "L'enfance inadaptée" of *Vie et bonté: Nouvelles de la Croix-Rouge française* 158 (August–September 1965).
31. Adam Feinstein, *A History of Autism: Conversations with the Pioneers* (Malden, MA: Wiley–Blackwell, 2010), 103.
32. Moïse Assouline, "Autisme: Adolescence, sexualité et vie sociale," *L'information psychiatrique* 89, no. 7 (2013): 568.
33. Paul Vernon, "Le role des associations de parents," *Esprit* 343, no. 11 (1965): 831.
34. Jean-Pierre Quélin, "La cour d'assises acquitte Mireille Gourand meurtrière de son fils malade et incurable," *Le Monde* (November 30, 1966).
35. "Mirelle Gourand a été acquittée," *Sud-Ouest* (November 30, 1966): 1–2.
36. Anne McGuire, *War on Autism: On the Cultural Logic of Normative Violence* (Ann Arbor: University of Michigan Press, 2016), chap. 5. McGuire discusses the phenomenon of filicide and the Western tendency to disregard disabled life, noting the unfortunate turn to violence as a not uncommon aspect.
37. "Renforçons notre action!" *Nos enfants inadaptés* 21 (Spring 1967): 1.
38. Ibid., 2.
39. "Editorial," *Nos enfants inadaptés* 22 (Summer 1967): 1.
40. Ibid.
41. "Les données de notre problème . . .," *Nos enfants inadaptés* 24 (Winter 1967): 3; and UNESCO, *International Yearbook of Education*, Vol. 28 (Geneva: International Bureau of Education and UNESCO, 1967), 133.
42. "Nous ne pouvons plus attendre!" *Nos enfants inadaptés* 24 (Winter 1967): 1.
43. M. Lemarchand, "International League of Societies for the Mentally Handicapped, 3rd International Congress," *Occupational Therapy* 29, no. 9 (September 1966): 22.
44. Burt Perrin, "The Original 'Scandinavian' Normalization Principle and Its Continuing Relevance for the 1990s," in *A Quarter-Century of Normalization and Social Role Valorization: Evolution and Impact*, ed. Robert J. Flynn and Raymond A. Lemay (Ottawa, ON: University of Ottawa Press, 1999), 181–96.

45. International League of Societies for the Mentally Handicapped, "Symposium: Legislative Aspects of Mental Retardation," June 11–17, 1967, 5–6, https://mn.gov/mnddc/parallels2/pdf/60s/67/67-ILS-ILS.pdf.
46. L. L. Gitter, "From Charity to Rights," *Academic Therapy* 4, no. 3 (1969): 189–90.
47. "En conclusion du Congrès de Jérusalem," *Nos enfants inadaptés* 29 (Spring 1969): 1.
48. Yizchak Genigar, "Fourth Congress of the League of International Societies for the Mentally Handicapped," *Journal of Learning Disabilities* 3, no. 3 (1970): 181.
49. "En conclusion du Congrès," 2.
50. Allison C. Carey, *On the Margins of Citizenship: Intellectual Disability and Civil Rights in Twentieth-Century America* (Philadelphia: Temple University Press, 2009), 2–3. For examples in Great Britain, see Simon Jarrett, "'Belief,' 'Opinion,' and 'Knowledge': The Idiot in Law in the Long Eighteenth Century," in *Intellectual Disability: A Conceptual History, 1200–1900*, ed. Patrick McDonagh, C. F. Goodley, and Tim Stainton (Manchester, UK: Manchester University Press, 2018), 162–89. For the broader French context, see Myriam Winance, Isabelle Ville, and Jean-François Ravaud, "Disability Policies in France: Changes and Tensions between the Category-Based, Universalist, and Personalized Approaches," *Scandinavian Journal of Disability Research* 9, no. 3–4 (2007): 160–81.
51. Jonathyne Briggs, "Les enfants perdus: Asylum Reform, Parents' Groups, and Disability Rights in France, 1968–1975." *French Politics, Culture and Society* 39, no. 3 (December 2021): 26–45.
52. "Notre vocabulaire et notre combat," *Nos enfants inadaptés* 33 (Spring 1970): 1.
53. Tom Shakespeare, "The Social Model of Disability," in *The Disability Studies Reader*, ed. Lennard J. Davis (New York: Routledge, 2017), 195–203.
54. "Tragique incendie dans un pensionnat de l'Oise," *L'impartial*, November 26, 1968, 1.
55. "Le drame de Froissy," *Nos enfants inadaptés* 29 (Spring 1969): 3.
56. Ligue française de l'enseignement et de l'éducation permanente, *Le drame de Froissy: La presse découvre l'enfance inadaptée* (Paris: Ligue française de l'enseignement et de l'éducation permanente, 1969).
57. Françoise Giraud, "Les enfants perdus," *L'express* 910 (December 16, 1968).
58. Jean-Pierre Lacouture, "L'incendie de Froissy," *Esprit* 337 (January 1969): 102–3.
59. Quoted in Ligue française de l'enseignement et de l'éducation permanente, *La drame de Froissy*, 3.
60. Ibid.
61. Evelyne Le Garrec, "Meme s'ils ne reunissent pas toutes les conditions de securite," in Ligue française de l'enseignement et de l'éducation permanente, *Le drame de Froissy*, 13–14.
62. «Inter actualités de 20H00 du 25 novembre 1968», http://www.ina.fr/audio/PHF06020491.
63. Ligue française de l'enseignement et de l'éducation permanente, *La drame de Froissy*, 4.
64. *Journal officiel de la République française: Débats parlementaires*, January 11, 1968, 93.
65. Croix-Rouge française, "Activités médico-sociales," *Vie et bonté* 3 (1969): 41.
66. *Journal officiel de la République française: Débats parlementaires*, November 30, 1968, 1455.

67. "Enquète sur l'etablisseiment 'la Source' Chateau de Froissy," Archives nationales (hereafter AN) 19 840 763/1.
68. "Note d'information," AN 19 840 763/1, 14.
69. Ibid., 13.
70. Ibid., 15.
71. *Journal officiel de la République française: Débats parlementaires*, February 2, 1969, 249.
72. *Journal officiel de la République française: Débats parlementaires*, April 2, 1969, 820.
73. *Journal officiel de la République française: Débats parlementaires*, May 24, 1969, 1436.

3

The Psychoanalytic State

In 1969, the French publishing house Gallimard released a translation of Bruno Bettelheim's acclaimed book *The Empty Fortress* as part of its Connaissance de l'inconscient series. The series explored different aspects of psychoanalysis, often highlighting more marginal figures in the field to bring attention to their interpretations of Freudian thought. Bettelheim had by this point secured a reputation in the United States as an authority on autism based on his work at the Orthogenic School at the University of Chicago, where he was the director (and oversaw Sammy Y.'s treatment when he arrived after his experience in Paris, as detailed in Chapter 1). *The Empty Fortress* presented three case studies from Bettelheim's work to illustrate his techniques in treating autism in the residential setting of the school. Based on his observations during his time in a concentration camp in 1938, Bettelheim's conclusions about autism were that these children had become emotionally disturbed as a result of destructive domestic environments in their home life, which led children to retreat to the "empty fortress" of autism. This book made a significant impact in the United States, where Bettelheim had a level of celebrity not unlike that of Françoise Dolto in France, and the French translation remains in print to this day. Bettelheim's book crystalized many of the strands of psychoanalytic thought concerning autism that developed during the 1950s and 1960s, but by the beginning of the 1970s, his ideas were being challenged by new research developments in the United States. Nevertheless, these ideas found fertile ground in France to thrive. Despite the efforts of parents to transform the dialogue concerning autism during the 1960s, by the end of the decade the interpretation of its origins as an expression of deliberate retreat from the negative emotional attitudes of parents had been reinforced thanks to the ongoing medical and social interest in psychoanalysis.

Psychoanalysis continued to grow in influence during the 1960s among psychology professionals and found an audience with the larger French public following the events of 1968. The intersection of psychoanalysis, philosophy, and sociology after 1968 was coupled with the increased presence of analysts in the media, which allowed for the spread of concepts to a broader constituency as part of a larger questioning of institutions following the protests.[1] Psychoanalysis

Perpetual Children. Jonathyne Briggs, Oxford University Press. © Oxford University Press (2025).
DOI: 10.1093/9780197683002.003.0004

was associated with a type of revolutionary rhetoric that questioned expertise as a way of challenging cultural power in the wake of 1968.[2] Intellectuals such as Felix Guattari, Gilles Deleuze, and Michel Foucault produced works informed by the interpretation of psychoanalysis as a method of social inquiry.[3] While Dolto, Mannoni, and others had developed their practice and interventions within the clinical context of the 1950s, the 1970s saw them reach a new level of influence on the French public concerning the framing of autism and its treatment thanks to their visibility in the French media. Within the profession, Freudian psychoanalysis consolidated its hold on clinical psychology even as it became more of a mass phenomenon in France.[4] While it had influenced government policy starting in the immediate postwar period, psychoanalysis profoundly entered into French popular culture and consciousness after 1968.[5] Even while the major psychoanalytic societies found discord concerning the training and credentialing of analysts, psychoanalysis occupied a privileged place within France at a time when it was under greater scrutiny in other countries, especially in the context of autism treatment.

The strength of psychoanalysis tethered discussions concerning autism to childhood, despite the growing number of autistic persons who were reaching adulthood since their diagnoses in the 1950s. As the French public became increasingly aware of the challenges facing autistic children, the image of autism remained one of childhood psychosis, which framed the issue as one facing children and their families, rather than more fully exploring how autism operated as a lifelong condition that impacted adults attempting to navigate society. Moreover, the narrative presented in professional literature, news stories, and documentaries about autism emphasized the effectiveness of psychoanalysis in curing the disorder and allowing children to reintegrate into society. This position thwarted the efforts of families to have a greater say in the treatment of the disorder and did not allow for input from autistic persons themselves.

Nevertheless, the advocacy of parents' associations for more equitable treatment for developmentally disabled children contributed to some important legal victories during the 1970s. The Law of 30 June 1975, recognized and codified the rights of disabled children to the same education and opportunities afforded abled French children, something the Union nationale des associations de parents et amis de personnes handicapées mentales (UNAPEI) and the Association au service des inadaptés ayant des troubles de la personalité (ASITP) had pushed for since the late 1960s as a possible solution to the limitations of medical facilities. This new law transformed the experiences of many families with disabled children, allowing them access to more resources to help integrate their children into society while fostering the continued alliance between parents and medical authorities. However, the law did not provide for autistic children, who were still understood to be experiencing childhood psychosis, which was not considered a disability and therefore was not affected by the law. This attitude was reinforced by several significant media events in the decade, but most notably by the broadcast of an extended documentary on Bettelheim and his work at the Orthogenic School. The popularity of this broadcast fueled a vigorous public debate about autism, forcing parents' associations into a defensive position and ultimately undermining the increasingly fragile alliance between parents and professionals by the end of the 1970s. As psychoanalysis became more and more entrenched in French psychology and medicine, parents sought new alliances outside France to understand how parents elsewhere found new forms of understanding what autism was and how it could be treated in different ways.

The increased public attention given to autism also reinforced that parenting was still understood as the primary responsibility of mothers in the 1970s. Despite the evident changes in women's experiences and attitudes during the 1960s, the continuity of mothering as the emotional core of the family remained a profound assumption within French psychoanalysis, particularly in its understanding of the origins of autism. Although some thinkers were not willing to directly blame mothers for the psychological retreat of their children, they often indirectly did so within the language of their published work and in their practice. Such conclusions questioned the viability of the role of parents in the education and treatment of their children without submitting to analysis themselves. Yet, by the end of the decade, more mothers were expressing their frustrations with the existing system by telling their own and their children's stories through narratives that pushed back against these assumptions. The conflict over expertise during the 1970s hinged on who understood the minds of autistic children better, analysts or parents, both of whom still marginalized the voices of autistic children as potential self-advocates.

ASSOCIATIONS AND THE FRENCH STATE

Parents' associations had gained traction in their efforts to lobby the French state by the end of the 1960s, but the lack of progress concerning any legislation or dramatic changes in the Sixth Plan—the central government's economic plan to allocate resources from 1971 to 1975—for funding to support disabled children kept these groups on the offensive in the early 1970s. The president of UNAPEI, Robert Morin, presented an open letter to Prime Minister Jacques Chaban-Delmas in the spring 1972 issue of *Nos enfants inadaptés* questioning the decision within the plan to have services that were provided through UNAPEI's centers paid for using charitable donations and to reduce budgetary spending for disabled children that year.[6] The efforts of UNAPEI to provide and expand services for developmentally disabled children had been successful through the creation of nearly 1,700 facilities by 1970, far more than the state provided in the same decade. Morin noted the different treatment of this population in comparison to that of other children and the contradictions of the situation in the context of the French constitution and the articulated right to education. The exclusion of developmentally disabled children was, in his estimation, normalized within French society based on the ideals of natalism and social norms concerning childhood.[7] The actions of French social services rested on the notion of shared responsibility between the state and parents, but Morin asserted that, in practice, only abled children were included in that equation.[8] In response, Morin and UNAPEI reasserted the vital role that associations played in the development of specialized services as a result of the failure of the state to provide for its citizens.

Later that same year, UNAPEI initiated a national petition seeking to redress the concerns of the association and bring greater attention to the situation facing its families. In it, the association called for French people to say "no to systemic ghettos, no to the nightmare of asylums as dumping grounds, no to the general indifference toward handicapped infants, profoundly or multiply handicapped youth, [and] the isolated handicapped in the countryside and new suburbs."[9] UNAPEI members lamented the continued segregation of developmentally disabled children from neurotypical children and the ramifications of their social treatment. These children were not considered children in the normative sense, and the tendency to encourage institutionalization and social removal remained powerful among professionals, at least from the perspective of the association. The failure of the French government to live up to its promises of reform only amplified those conclusions, and Morin expressed his frustration at the lack of action from the state concerning disabled youth.[10] The increase in family allowance with the Law of 13 July 1971, although it was recognized as helpful, did not allow for disabled children's use of multiple services such as *instituts medico-pédagogiques* (IMPs) or special education schools and put the onus on the family to provide for their children mostly within the household.[11]

The associations' efforts for legislative intervention did not result in equitable outcomes and only reinforced the perception of developmentally disabled children as somehow separate from other children. Authorities' treatment of these children and their parents revealed the root of parents' frustrations and suspicions of the state and the pervasive negative attitudes toward disability in French society. As an example, UNAPEI reprinted a column from *Le Monde* written by Swiss reporter Paule Giron to illustrate the larger impact of negative attitudes toward disabled children and their parents. Giron's eldest son, who was disabled, needed an identity card to enter France, which required a medical examination. When the doctor asked about his son, Giron responded that he was physically healthy but developmentally disabled as the result of a childhood accident. The doctor responded that Giron was the one saying his son was disabled, which Giron interpreted as accusatory and as doubting his son's condition.[12] Giron noted the hostility in the interaction and also that his son was witness to the exchange, and he wondered how immigrant families who did not speak French could possibly navigate such a system, given the challenges he faced even with his privilege. This anecdote was symbolic of the tension within the system that was supposed to support families and illustrated that the state and medical professionals could lack empathy for the conditions facing these households.

The inertia at the national level in the early 1970s concerning the issue of childhood developmental disability led UNAPEI to stress to its members the need to return to local advocacy and action through department-level associations. The Association départementale de parents et d'amis des personnes handicapées mentales (ADAPEI) consisted of local branches of UNAPEI focused on providing services and support to families within specific regions of France, and several branches formed across France. For many ADAPEI members, the primary service was the creation of a local IMP or vocational school to educate and prepare their children for adult life. However, even with this energy, there were concerns about sustaining efforts and the strength of these associations to deal with the complex work of creating these clinics. ADAPEI branches required the energy of parents, which perhaps was flagging in the face of the reality of the limitations of what could be accomplished within the Sixth Plan. In response, Jean-Anny Trescases, deputy president of ADAPEI–Pyrénées-Orientales, countered that the work of ADAPEI was valuable because it addressed concrete problems in a dignified and humane manner.[13] While UNAPEI continued its efforts to address national concerns, ADAPEI focused on building local resources to provide care for disabled children who were in need of direct and immediate services.

In its second decade of operations, UNAPEI had increasingly emphasized the importance of influencing national policy concerning the treatment of disabled children despite the lack of progress in terms of funding or legislation. The association changed presidents at the end of 1974, with Jacques Henry succeeding Morin. Henry noted the importance of Morin's efforts to engage with the state and society through various campaigns but recognized that a new generation of parents, siblings, and allies had emerged to seek new solutions to the issues facing disabled children. These "jeunes loups" would renew the association's commitment to secure the future of their children despite the lack of support from outside the group.[14] The emergence of a new generation of parents underscores how the understanding of autism remained focused on young children with less attention given to adults, even within associations. While the French state was considering passing a new law that would recognize and protect the rights of disabled children, UNAPEI and other associations took a more militant tack that would in turn challenge assumptions concerning autism from the medical community as part of their efforts. However, professionals continued to develop new practices and ideas based on the principles of psychoanalysis to treat autistic youth, whose numbers continued to climb in the 1970s.

EXPERIMENTAL SCHOOLS AND PSYCHOANALYSIS

Psychoanalyst Maud Mannoni continued her private practice with disabled children during the 1960s, growing in stature within the community of child psychologists as a result of her celebrated work with autistic children. She published two critical works—*L'enfant arrière et sa mère* [The Backward Child and His Mother] (1962) and *Le psychiatre, son "fou," et le psychanalyse* [The Child, His Illness and the Others] (1970)—detailing her experiences in analysis with autistic children and their families, but equally significant was her decision in 1969 to open a specialized clinic in Bonneuil-sur-Marne. There, she focused on residential treatment of this population by creating a type of living space that put her ideas into practice in a more social setting, rather than in individual therapy. Mannoni had embraced elements of the antipsychiatry movement that emerged in the 1960s as a critique of the psychological community, especially aspects directed toward asylum reform and improving treatment of developmentally disabled persons.[15] At Bonneuil, she sought to establish a new type of care guided by the principles of psychoanalysis and antipsychiatry to develop an alternative to existing clinics and

IMPs. She believed in the importance of children developing in a healthy and safe environment outside their home, often with the use of play therapy, which could not be guaranteed within the family home.

Mannoni had seen value in the therapeutic notion of play as a creative activity that permitted children to express imagination and establish relationships within the family, especially with their mothers. Thus, elements of play were incorporated into the daily activities of the clinic, although they were voluntary and children had input into the kinds of leisure that were available at Bonneuil. At the outset of the clinic, the population was twenty children, not dissimilar to the size of the populations at the clinics developed by parents' associations. The therapeutic architecture of Bonneuil was completely informed by the concepts of psychoanalysis and Mannoni's theories concerning the linguistic deficiencies of autistic children. She intended to create a space where the power of parental authority, as expressed through unconscious desire, was blunted by the freedom afforded these children in the unstructured space of the clinic. She believed that the recognition of autistic children as individuals was the first step in treating their psychosis: "The autistic child rarely received from his mother [any] recognition as a sexual or autonomous being."[16] At Bonneuil, she wanted to provide these children the opportunity to make a clean break from the expectations of their parents, which had led them to retreat into their inner world and undermined their development into autonomous individuals.

Mannoni also saw Bonneuil as a new type of clinic that recognized and rejected the inherent nature of psychology as a method of adapting patients to the needs of capitalist society, very much in line with the political valence of antipsychiatry in the 1970s. Her philosophy here served as a critique of the growing number of technical schools that parents' associations had advocated for as part of their efforts to help their children gain acceptance in French society; nevertheless, there were children at Bonneuil who did participate in apprenticeships and work with the blessing of the school.[17] There was a leftist critique of these types of facilities that emphasized their alliance with capitalism and their exploitative nature, with which Mannoni appeared to agree.[18] Mannoni's open campus approach was not unique; Fernand Deligny had developed his practices in special education for autistic children based on similar principles in Cévennes in the south of France.[19] Mannoni did not explicitly practice analysis at Bonneuil, but it informed much of her efforts with these children (as well as her overall focus on children) and she continued to publish her thoughts on her "treatment" there as a way to criticize the practices used in hospitals, asylums, and IMPs.[20]

Mannoni's team at the clinic included a key figure in the antipsychiatry movement in France: Roger Gentis. Gentis was another critic of the existing psychological establishment; he argued that the expansion of IMPs included facilities that operated for profit and forced care on patients.[21] He asserted that the expansion of these types of services was the result of the dehumanization of developmentally disabled patients and that the profession was invested in maintaining the system. Like Mannoni, Gentis believed this to be a logical extension of the concepts of capitalism.[22] The value of places such as Bonneuil was that they operated outside those parameters and instead allowed autistic children to "find a little peace . . . to treat them like other [children] . . . [and] do not stop them from speaking even with nothing to say."[23] Gentis's approach rejected the more structured nature of special education and the programs developing in the United States at the time, such as Treatment and Education of Autistic and Related Communication Handicapped Children, which sought to help autistic children establish methods of communication through a series of visual cues and other forms of nonverbal communication. Gentis understood the disorganized speech patterns of the children at Bonneuil as inherently valuable as a genuine expression of their inner desires and was suspect of any methods that could undermine them. As a psychoanalyst, he was also skeptical of how parents interacted with their children, hoping that putting some distance between them might help autistic children discover their individuality.

Bonneuil operated outside the French system of IMPs and day hospitals for its first six years of existence as a private institution and was eventually recognized as a facility approved for state funding in 1975. It drew a great deal of attention because of Mannoni's stature within the field of child psychology and the broader fascination with psychoanalysis. In 1974, Guy Seligmann filmed a documentary on the clinic, *Vivre à Bonneuil*, which aired on TF1 the following year and introduced Mannoni's clinic to a broader audience, coinciding with a general discussion that would be launched by the documentary on Bettelheim that introduced the interior of such facilities to the French public. Seligmann's conversations with Mannoni about her rationale behind creating the school revealed how she developed the practices there, and the documentary also offered glimpses into the lives of the children in her care.[24] While parents were involved in some of the scenes, the focus was primarily on the children and the need for them to separate from their parents so that they could grow beyond their limitations.

Parents' associations were interested in the work being done at Bonneuil because many parents were searching for any approach to treatment that would allow their children to be integrated into French society. Following the broadcast of *Vivre à Bonneuil*, Patrick Boccard interviewed Mannoni to introduce her approach at the clinic to the readership of *Epanouir* (the successor to *Nos enfants inadaptés*). Mannoni reaffirmed her conclusion that parental rejection created the foundation for autism, while noting that some parents were so exhausted that they could no longer speak with their children.[25] She did not limit her conclusions to the challenges within the household because she saw the alienation of autism as developing from a complex web of social relations, but she viewed relations with the people in the child's home as paramount.[26] Her approach integrated autistic children with other developmentally disabled populations at Bonneuil, as well as some neurotypical children, to model sociability for autistic patients through a form of institutional analysis. She also spoke about how the village played a role in the treatment, since Bonneuil was an open institution that encouraged students to interact with the residents around the clinic, again mirroring Deligny's approach at Cévennes.[27] Additionally, Mannoni discussed a mothers' support group at Bonneuil that met every Monday to share their experiences of being "abnormal mothers," revealing her awareness of how cultural norms shaped these parents' responses to their children.[28] Mannoni was sympathetic to the experiences of families, noting their struggle and the role that French society played in judging them, which amplified the emotional anxiety directed at their disabled children. At the same time, she recognized that she was not entirely in agreement with the ideas of parents' associations because she felt that many of their efforts at treatment and rehabilitation only created "good robots" for exploitation.[29]

UNAPEI had long been aware of Mannoni's work, dating from its review of her *L'enfant arrière et sa mère* from 1964, and approached it seeking understanding. In the review, Pierre Echavidre summarized the essence of her argument of maternal alienation as the engine driving autistic behavior and the infantilization of developmentally disabled children. With her sympathy to the prejudices that these children faced, Mannoni appeared as an ally. One of the logics of her work that Echavidre noted in his review was that there was the implication of true disabilities and false disabilities, although he expressed some skepticism because of the lack of data and the tendency for generalization. Moreover, the idea of false disability might reinforce some of the prejudices Mannoni was criticizing.[30] Parents approached Mannoni and her work with some trepidation, but did engage with her ideas. Despite the continued skepticism of some, the rising stature of psychoanalysis and Mannoni's continued influence in child psychology fostered ongoing interest in her efforts into the 1970s.

For example, in September 1970, a full five years before the documentary aired, ASITP conducted an interview with Mannoni about Bonneuil in its publication *Sésame*. The interviewer questioned her about her conclusions concerning madness (*fou*), that autistic children should not be considered mentally ill, and that they have the right to live with their "madness" as a path to therapy.[31] She quibbled with the interviewer about that interpretation and suggested that *Sésame* readers should explore other articles in different publications to gain a more nuanced understanding of her approach and her critique of psychiatry and its diagnostic apparatuses. She then offered details about the daily lives of patients at Bonneuil, noting the presence of special educators, psychoanalysts, and medical doctors on staff, as well as her collaboration with Françoise Dolto in its operation. The population consisted of boys and girls aged four to fifteen, who always worked with three staff members as well as several interns. Guided by the principles of radical psychiatry, Mannoni allowed the children to dictate the schedule at Bonneuil, although she did suggest coursework on cooking, budgeting, communication with others, and the arts.[32] Radical psychiatry was an intellectual movement that questioned the role of institutions in replicating forms of madness. It led therapists to engage in an inclusive therapy that considered the perspective of patients in their treatment and questioned the organization of clinics.[33] Mannoni put these ideas into practice for the benefit of autistic children, so they could find their own path to expressing themselves outside the influence of their parents and society.

While a central assumption in Mannoni's practice was the culpability of parents in the development of autism, there were elements of her work that interested associations seeking new methods of treatment to implement in IMPs and other clinics. The reproducibility of Bonneuil was not clear, but Mannoni's significance made her an obvious inspiration for associations that desired more effective treatments and outcomes for autistic children. Despite her assumptions about parents, her advocacy for autistic children made her an important ally to associations. Even as Mannoni's ideas were reaching a broader public, her colleague Françoise Dolto found greater celebrity with her work with autistic children and her parenting advice in general during the 1970s, leading parents to engage with her ideas and their continued influence on parenting norms.

PARENTING BY RADIO AND THE RETURN OF THE EXPERT

In 1968, Françoise Dolto appeared on the airwaves with Europe 1's short-lived "SOS Psychanalyste!," a call-in show in which she dispensed her advice to listeners who phoned in with their problems. She fielded questions primarily from children and adolescents (and sometimes from parents who were concerned about their children), often dispensing advice in the context of an emergency, as suggested by the show's title. Although she used a pseudonym (Docteur X), listeners quickly recognized Dolto, and the show attracted the attention of other psychology experts and, eventually, organizations that found her approach to therapy lacking and felt it undermined the intellectual sophistication of psychoanalysis.[34] The show ended its run in 1969, but it was not Dolto's last attempt to bring psychoanalysis to a mass audience. Dolto had already engaged with the public through her affiliation with L'école des parents (see Chapter 1), but her move into mass media during the 1970s solidified her expertise as the leading expert in child psychology in France outside any distinct institution. Although she was not associated with the more intellectual elements of the new wave of psychoanalytically informed thought that emerged after 1968, Dolto was well positioned to build on her expertise because of her long association with psychoanalysis and her ability to introduce psychoanalytic concepts to a larger audience.

While she was expanding her celebrity, she continued to engage in her specific work with autistic persons, evidenced in her 1971 *Le cas Dominique*. A collection of her clinical notes regarding her treatment of a fourteen-year-old boy with schizophrenia, *Le cas Dominique* follows a similar narrative trajectory as the earlier *Le cas Samy* from the 1950s.[35] Dolto approaches Dominique's case with deep attention to the relationship between him and his parents, particularly his frustrations at his inability to develop autonomous longing for his mother and the absence of his father. According to Dolto, this lack of a father figure, combined with the arrival of a sister, disrupted Dominque's healthy resolution of the Oedipal complex and led to his emotional withdrawal, as well as other behaviors such as bedwetting and shying away from touch.[36] As Richard Bates details in his rich history of Dolto's importance in postwar French culture, she continued to center the family in the origins of psychosis, albeit not in a biogenetic sense, but rather in ascertaining the behaviors within the family that led to the psychotic response in autistic children.[37] Her approach reinforced the position of psychoanalysis as the key to understanding and treating childhood schizophrenia, even as other conclusions were being developed outside France during this period that pointed to biological origins. Dolto's position as a preeminent and trusted authority on childhood and autism in France provided a bulwark for psychoanalysis to counter the influence of these developments among French child psychologists and medical professionals.

In her treatment of Dominique, Dolto relied on her combination of play therapy and psychoanalysis to address the behavioral struggles he exhibited in the home and at school. He had not responded to medication and his mother was now seeking psychoanalytic treatment. In her initial consultation, Dolto noted his tendency to play with toys but not in a normative manner: "He plays a little with toy cars but not in practical manner."[38] Over the course of twelve weeks, Dolto engaged Dominique in various forms of play in their sessions, including having him mold modeling clay and draw pictures as a method of communication for explaining his home life. Dominique was verbal, and Dolto encouraged him to narrate stories using his clay figures. While he at times replicated his favorite tales from the popular comic *Tintin*, he also told stories that Dolto believed indicated his repressed sexual longing and unfulfilled desire, as expressed through the shapes of his figures.[39] She interpreted his play as evidence of the corrosive structure of the family, which led her to redirect Dominique's transference so that he might recognize his own desire and become autonomous from his mother. While Dolto did not claim he was cured, Dominique had greater control over his behaviors and emotions when their sessions ended, giving the narrative a redemptive arc.

Much like Mannoni, Dolto emphasizes how children like Dominique are products of not only corrosive parenting but also a society that deprives them of "the chance to freely and humanly assume the responsibility of their own desires."[40] While his transference was recognized and redirected by Dolto, Dominique still needed to work to accept his own desire as part of his ongoing therapy, although without the antisocial behaviors that she extinguished through her treatment. In her conclusion, Dolto was critical of efforts to develop interventions that only addressed superficial aspects of autism without recognizing the larger context of frustrated desire. This interpretation did two things: one, it recognized the continued need to treat parents as part of therapeutic intervention, albeit with less blame assigned to them; and two, it questioned the expansion of clinics and special schools advocated by parents' associations as a method of assisting developmentally disabled children. The latter element continued to interest Dolto, who followed Mannoni's path and established centers for socializing these children in the 1980s. Upon its release, *Dominique* was feted by the French press as a significant contribution to the literature of child psychology, as well as an affirmation of Dolto's genius. Bates observes her tendencies to write in a style like detective fiction, which helped audiences understand the complexities of autism in a rather straightforward and simplistic manner that resonated with French readers.[41]

By the end of the decade, a few years after publishing *Dominique*, Dolto returned to the airwaves with a more successful radio program: *Lorsque l'enfant paraît* [When the child appears]. This fifteen-minute show was aimed at mothers, with Dolto offering advice, insights, and opinions on childrearing, education, and even homemaking. Airing at three o'clock in the afternoon, it attracted a national audience on France Inter and further bolstered Dolto's position as a national authority on children. On a typical episode, she would respond to a letter submitted to the show, as selected by her daughter, who worked as part of the production team. This approach allowed her a more measured response and the opportunity to steer the conversation in a more direct manner because the segments were produced before they aired. In these broadcasts, Dolto remained committed to her conservative values concerning the structure of the normative family as patriarchal, but she combined them with more practical advice in response to her listeners' requests.[42] Although the show ended in 1978, its ongoing popularity led to the publication of collections of letters sent to the show and compilations of broadcasts released on compact disc.[43] The success of Dolto's shows and subsequent publications was a manifestation of the "Doltomania" that swept through France in the 1980s, but built on her successes in the 1970s.[44] Although she did not solely address questions about developmentally disabled children, the show articulated her beliefs about normative family structures and the potential of harm in deviating from them.

The strength of these personalities in the media and the general interest in psychoanalysis meant that ideas about the origins of autism and its treatment remained firmly defined by professionals, especially for the French public. Mannoni and Dolto, while very different in their approach, both contributed to the continued linkage of autism and schizophrenia, even as research developments from Great Britain and the United States increasingly distinguished between the two diagnoses, which eventually led to their decoupling abroad.[45] Both certainly saw a role for parents to play in the treatment of their children, but in each case it was secondary to the position of the analyst, who could advocate for disabled children in a manner that recognized the potential harm caused by parenting and educators in replicating the existing system. Despite this negative image, parents continued their efforts through associations by establishing more facilities to treat their children and lobbying for their legal protections, bringing them into potential conflict with the psychoanalytic regime in French medicine that often questioned their motivation.

PARENTS AS PARTICIPANTS AND THE LIMITS OF LAW

The operation of Centre Santos Dumont in Paris by ASITP illustrated how the actions of parents' associations could disrupt the alliance between medical professionals and parents, given the day clinic's specialization in the treatment of autistic children and the position of parents in its operation. The role of these centers in the context of Bonneuil and the public work of Dolto came into question from professionals because parents had their own agenda concerning how their children should receive treatment and how they would participate in it. Additionally, UNAPEI increased its efforts to direct the National Assembly to implement laws recognizing and protecting the rights of disabled youth, which culminated in the passage of the Law of June 30, 1975. Although that law was a watershed in terms of the rights of disabled persons in France, its protections did not extend to all disabled children because of the way autism was framed in that country. Hence, despite the gains in establishing IMPs and other treatment facilities and greater recognition of the issue of autism among the French public, parents remained on the defensive during the latter half of the decade.

At the UNAPEI colloquium on infantile psychosis in 1971, the question of treatment at Santos Dumont was the subject of a report given by Dr. Bianca Lechevalier, a neuropsychiatrist and psychoanalyst who was asked to join the clinic's team. Lechevalier offered her assessment of the purpose of ASITP and its role at the clinic. She reiterated the concept at the heart of the associations' mission—namely, that disability impacts all of French society and not just the families in the association—while noting the level of commitment and care each family provides for their children. She then gave her assessment of autism: a pathological, early-onset disorganization of personality in children.[46] Lechevalier asserted that the best approach to treatment was working with a single population rather than mixing autistic children with other disabled populations. She also championed the ASITP in creating ideal facilities to work with autistic children in day hospitals, which allowed for greater adaptability and different methods.[47] For her, the institutions pioneered by parents' associations served as the benchmark for how new facilities should be constructed and underscored the important role parents should play in the consideration of treatment.

Parents were increasingly versed in the literature concerning autism and were looking to bring new ideas and perspectives into the conversation about treatment, while also looking to ideas outside psychology. *Sésame*, the publication of the ASITP, was already introducing readers to scholarship from Great Britain and the United States in translation, but in 1975, D. D. Rouqués offered a survey of the landscape of the literature on autism, including differences in the causes and treatment. Rouqués identified a schism among experts concerning organic versus psychogenic origins of autism, with the French medical community primarily leaning toward the latter.[48] Although there were some outliers, most notably Pierre Debray-Ritzen, who was a vocal critic of psychoanalysis, the understanding of autism as indicative of a psychological reaction to trauma found either in society or in the family made psychoanalysis the consensus solution. Rouqués's summation also included recently translated biographies from parents in the United States who were challenging the use of psychoanalysis there. In France, however, the strength of the consensus concerning psychoanalysis meant that the question of autism as a form of disability had little acceptance in the medical community in the mid-1970s.

In this context, the passage of the Law of June 30, 1975, failed to provide parents' associations with the victory they had been hoping for since the 1960s. The efforts of UNAPEI in pressuring legislative action on the issue of disability rights were not unique to France; activists throughout the Western world had developed momentum for recognition of the equality of disabled persons in a similar fashion.[49] After some debate, the National Assembly passed a series of laws that recognized the rights of the disabled population in France and echoed many of the sentiments advocated by parents' groups after the fire at Froissy: Law 75-734 and Law 75-735 of June 30, 1975. These laws enshrined the rights of the disabled to work, to a minimum level of support, and (the most pertinent to the Froissy incident) to integration in schools and society, which would help to supplement and potentially replace the reliance on IMPs as the only method of educating developmentally disabled children. Law 75-534 explicitly guaranteed access for disabled children in all facilities open to children while recognizing the role parents continued to serve in their education and treatment.[50] More importantly, these laws stated clearly the role that the French state needed to play in ensuring that disabled children had equal access to all the benefits of society, the very thing that parents' associations had been arguing for since the mid-1960s.[51] As Pierre Verdier argues, the laws transformed the meaning of private clinics and created the possibility of choice for parents of disabled children.[52] The right of integration brought greater resources to the families of disabled children, which afforded them more of a voice in their children's treatment and education.

The classification and diagnosis of developmentally disabled children became more significant because many of the children receiving treatment at IMPs were primarily considered noneducable and hence faced challenges integrating into the existing educational system. Nicholas Henckes observes that the classification of "handicap psychique" was not wholly included in the wording of the law because there was not a consensus about the relationship between these handicaps and other forms of disability; this ambiguity led to critiques of the law from psychologists and medical professionals.[53] This law was not the first—previous laws were passed in the late 1960s recognizing the rights of disabled adults—but it was the first to recognize the particular situation facing disabled children, who certainly did not have equity of opportunity or protection in comparison to other French children. Again, the issue was that *l'enfance handicapé* (childhood disability) was not explicitly a diagnostic category but rather a socio-medical one, and there was little agreement on whether autism was a handicap or an illness that could be treated through psychoanalysis and medication. This divide led professionals to question their lack of participation in the drafting of the law, which appeared to favor the ideas of parents' associations.[54] However, even as the legal protections emphasized the role that parents played in the amelioration of autistic behaviors, the position of psychology professionals was nevertheless reinforced by its ongoing classification of autism as an expression of infantile schizophrenia, which dictated psychoanalysis as the appropriate response. This belief would be reinforced by a media event that brought this conclusion to the French public through the introduction of an American thinker who was already known within the world of French psychoanalysis.

UN AUTRE REGARD SUR LA FOLIE

In October 1974, TF1, France's primary television network, aired a four-part documentary on Bruno Bettelheim and his work at the Orthogenic School at the University of Chicago. Directed by Daniel Karlin, *Un autre regard de la folie* (Another look at madness) showed the American educator and analyst working closely with parents and children in the salon of the school as part of his treatment of autistic children. *Un regard* combined footage of his students' lives at the residential school with an extended interview between Bettelheim and Karlin detailing how the former developed his methods to treat autism. Over the course of three more episodes, the documentary provided an extended view of the daily routine at the school and the students' therapeutic regimen. Because of labor issues in French broadcasting, these documentaries were the primary programming available on television that month, airing on all three national networks to an audience of over three million viewers. Given the efforts of parents' associations to engage the public in understanding the challenges facing autistic children, the Bettelheim documentary found a curious audience, and responses to it after the airing revealed the growing contention between psychology professionals and parents that was playing out in the French media.

Karlin's decision to film the documentary rested on his desire to introduce Bettelheim's work to a larger French audience to offer hope for the treatment of autism. *La forteresse vide* had not made the same impact in France that it had in the United States, where it was hailed as a definitive statement on the origins and treatment of autism.[55] In his introduction to the French edition, translator Roland Humery emphasized Bettelheim's credentials from his experiences in Austria before the Second World War, which strengthened his claims of psychoanalytic expertise, and his internment as a political prisoner at Dachau and Buchenwald, which provided the framework for his analysis of autistic persons. In Humery's summation of the work, he explained that autistic persons operated from the same position as the "musulmans" did in Bettelheim's observations of his time in the concentration camps; both were muted, withdrawn, and listless, with this reaction in autistic persons stemming from rejection by their families.[56] Humery also emphasized the importance of individual psychotherapy sessions with the children at the Orthogenic School as the most compelling part of the treatment to draw them out of their emotional isolation.

In his practice, Bettelheim used a form of milieu therapy that established a frame of emotional reference for emotionally disturbed children, which he understood autistic children to be. At the Orthogenic School, this included the creation of a well-defined hierarchy that would allow children to develop in a normative manner.[57] At the same time, students were encouraged to explore their individual interests without explicit direction, similar to the approach Mannoni practiced at Bonneuil. They were separated from their parents as a requirement of this treatment, reinforcing notions of parental blame. The guiding principle for this approach was Bettelheim's belief that segregation led to healing to remedy "ego deficits."[58]

Although French readers were slow to engage, the critical response was overwhelmingly positive, as critics found merit in *La forteresse vide* and saw it within the context of the recent interest in psychoanalysis. In an extensive review in *Esprit*, Gennie Luccioni observed that the validity of the psychoanalytic model had been shown as "extraordinary fruitful" in France but that Bettelheim provided three powerful cases to reinforce that conclusion.[59] Jean-Michel Palmer of *Le Monde* praised Bettelheim as a historical figure in the history of psychoanalysis, emphasizing the importance of his most famous case, Joey the Machine-Boy, which had already appeared as an excerpt in *Le nouvel observateur* in early 1970.[60]

In these reviews, Bettelheim's magnum opus on autism was placed in conversation with the theoretical works of child psychoanalysis, although critics emphasized that *La forteresse vide* lacked the sophistication of Jacques Lacan, D. W. Winnicott, or Melanie Klein.

While his work had not had the broad interest of other psychoanalytically informed publications in the early 1970s, it did attract the attention of some French child care specialists who wanted to understand his ideas more precisely in order to introduce his methods to French parents. One notable example was Geneviève Jurgensen, a speech therapist who worked at the Orthogenic School between 1970 and 1972. While working at an IMP in Paris, she read *La forteresse vide* and decided to travel to Chicago and study at the University of Chicago under the supervision of Bettelheim. Her memoir of her experiences in Chicago, *La folie des autres*, detailed her reaction to Bettelheim's ideas and to psychoanalysis in general, which was not something she had used as a speech therapist working with children.[61] Jurgensen offered insights into the operations at the school, detailing her responsibilities in working with five young women assigned to her care, each of whom exhibited various levels of behavioral challenges. Early on, she failed to understand how Bettelheim's methods worked, and at first, she expressed disappointment and frustration with her role because she felt more like a babysitter than a therapist. Her time was spent monitoring children and ensuring that they completed day-to-day tasks.[62]

Bettelheim's milieu therapy encouraged the children at the school to explore through play to develop a healthy fantasy life, which he believed they lacked as a result of overbearing parenting. This improvisational approach was based on his belief that children needed to feel safe and secure to be able to emerge from their autistic prisons. Jurgensen chronicled her struggle to continue working in this environment, but noted that she saw the students become more social and joyful, demonstrating Bettelheim's ability to help them develop in a healthy manner.[63] Upon graduation, Jurgensen decided to return to France, and Bettelheim encouraged her to contact Serge Lebovici and continue her career there. She advocated for Bettelheim's approach as a highly effective form of treatment that could bring relief to French families.

ASITP reached out to Jurgensen on her return and asked her to write about her experiences for the association's bulletin to inform their members about Bettelheim's successes. She reflected on the work done at the Orthogenic School and the methods there: "It is useful for the [autistic] child to not be endlessly confronted with the reality of his parents because autistic children report that this leads to the distancing between themselves and reality."[64] She encouraged parents to read *La forteresse vide* for themselves as a way of clarifying Bettelheim's conclusions about their culpability in their children's disorder, while also noting the important connections between his work and that of Dolto. Readers sent questions ahead of Jurgensen's article, and she offered answers to affirm his conclusions about mothers' desires that their autistic children not exist.[65] However, many of the readers were seeking more practical advice about how to handle the behavior of autistic children and were not as interested in its origins. ASITP provided summaries of Bettelheim's work for its readers and his concept of the "extreme situation" to place him within the context of work on autism.[66] All of this served to validate the psychoanalytic nature of autism, even as it suggested that the condition was curable if children were removed from their homes.

Parents' associations had long been engaged with the scholarship concerning autism, but Karlin's documentary was an effort to bring Bettelheim to the attention of the French public who were less aware of the details of his practice. Karlin had come to Bettelheim through his interest in the French education system, especially once he learned of the treatment of disabled children in the system. A neurologist friend recommended Bettelheim's book to Karlin, who became engrossed immediately. Karlin was especially interested in the applicability of Bettelheim's concepts and approaches, in contrast to the more esoteric nature of French psychoanalysis.[67] After contacting the school, he gained permission to film there after a visit in April 1974. By that point, Bettelheim had retired as director and had time to work with Karlin on the project. Karlin hoped that with a documentary, he could highlight Bettelheim's successes and bring reform to the practices of special education and the application of psychoanalysis in France.

The film cut between long interviews between Bettelheim and Karlin and footage of the daily activities of educators and students inside the school. Bettelheim opened the documentary with an extended critique of institutionalization, countering that patients who had been deemed incurable and abandoned in the American psychiatric system had achieved positive results at the Orthogenic School.[68] Karlin, however, was presenting Bettelheim to a French audience, so he included interviews with students from the school addressing the situation in France: "The people of France realize, realize that here [the United States] or in France, those who are mentally challenged are not also nutcases."[69] Karlin expressed concern that Bettelheim's conclusions were misunderstood in France, leading him to recount examples of French people who did not explain his ideas correctly. He believed these encounters spoke of negative entrenched public attitudes concerning developmentally disabled persons, something that had concerned parents' associations for over a decade.[70]

L'AFFAIRE BETTELHEIM

Following the broadcast of the documentary, TF1 aired a panel discussion of psychologists, analysts, and educators (although there was no representation from parents' associations) to discuss the film. The panel did not establish a consensus on the merits of Bettelheim's work or his position as "a great philosopher and child analyst."[71] This debate over the documentary became an intellectual flashpoint concerning the appropriate treatment of autism, which was increasingly under question from parents and some medical professionals. Bettelheim, for his part, inserted himself into the debate by coming to France several times afterward to participate in conferences and defend his work.[72] The documentary elicited a series of responses from parents' associations, whose skepticism was rooted in the broadcasting of yet another example of mother blaming that required a response.

The Bettelheim documentary drew immediate attention in the pages of *Épanouir*, especially for its role in bringing awareness of autism to the French public, even if it did not present the entire experience. While laying out some of the reactions of medical and psychiatry experts in general, UNAPEI offered a detailed response from Dr. Robert Lecuyer, the association's resident medical expert, who found the general tenor and presentation of the documentary favorable and optimistic but lacking some clarity of method and treatment. Lecuyer objected to Bettelheim's conclusion that autism was caused by poor parenting and expressed regret that this idea had been broadcast to such a large audience.[73] *Épanouir* also included a statement from the ASITP, which emphasized how parents had been ostracized publicly as a result of the documentary's oversimplifications of the causes of autism. In addition, the statement questioned whether some of the children presented were actually autistic, a criticism of Bettelheim's work that arose in the United States as well. These parents engaged with his ideas, and some were willing to accept that psychoanalysis was a possible method of treatment, despite the limited success they had experienced so far. However, most parents rejected the psychogenic thesis as not useful in helping autistic children, which they were already aware of through their readings of *La forteresse vide* and their discussions with Jurgensen. Although the parents affiliated with the ASITP recognized Bettelheim's passion for helping developmentally disabled children, they feared his conclusions and their potential effects on French viewers' understanding of how autism should be treated.[74]

Given the continued influence of the documentary in 1975 through rebroadcasts, ASITP offered its own extended response in the pages of its bulletin that summarized reactions from working groups within the association that met to discuss Bettelheim throughout that year. These groups discussed the impact of the documentary on the existing organization and practice within IMPs and day hospitals in the Paris region that specialized in the treatment of autism. In its survey of these facilities, ASITP asserted that many of them practiced several elements purported to be used at the Orthogenic School, namely, the flexibility of treatment, the recognition of the individual desire of each child, the integration of learning and curriculum, and the use of psychoanalysis; the list included Mannoni's school in Bonneuil. The institutions surveyed also noted that there were different levels of treatment based on the severity of symptoms, allowing for a variety of approaches to operate at each institution, combining psychoanalysis, special education, and medical interventions to address the potential biological aspects of autism.[75] The combination of residential and day hospitals reveals efforts from ASITP to promote the place of parents in the care of their children, in stark contrast to Bettelheim's conclusions about the need for separation.

In their reflections from the conference, the professionals who participated noted that "the 'parents of psychotics' would no longer be isolated, culpable in a role that constantly signifies this uniqueness," and that these parents must be treated as all other parents to avoid compounding difficulties and alienation, stressing the importance of parental support and solidarity. They recognized the "extraordinary intervention" of the parents of ASITP.[76] In addition to the conference, ASITP founder and president Denise Ribadeau-Dumas organized a debate in 1975 among the Faculté de medicine de Paris about other therapeutic approaches outside psychoanalysis and institutionalization, which included luminaries from the world of child psychology such as Serge Lebovici and Roger Misès. The attendees also viewed documentaries on the work of Alfred and Françoise Brauner, two educators with an interest in autistic children who were also staunch allies of parents. The collective debated questions of genetics as an origin of autism, which might also have biochemical aspects that inform autistic behaviors.[77] Much of the debate served as an anodyne to the framework established in Bettelheim's documentary and pointed to research done in the United States on biological aspects. Even participants with a psychoanalytic orientation such as Lebovici and Misès offered a counter to Bettelheim's conclusions that focused solely on the parents. ASITP remained engaged with professionals but found that the influence of the documentary was shaping public opinion about autism in a manner that excluded the viewpoint of parents.

In the French media, voices emerged to counter the impact of Karlin's film and in some cases launched an attack on the dominance of psychoanalysis as a method of treatment, noting that it had been eclipsed by other interventions elsewhere in the world that showed greater efficacy. One of Bettelheim's most vocal French critics, a pediatrician and the director of the Necker enfants-malades de Paris hospital, Pierre Debray-Ritzen, completely rejected psychoanalysis as a form of treatment for autistic persons. In an interview with the journal *Elements* shortly after *Un regard* aired, Debray-Ritzer panned French television for dedicating over four hours to the work of Bettelheim without offering any other viewpoint concerning the current state of child psychiatry in France. He repeated similar criticism in *Le figaro*, calling Bettelheim fraudulent in his diagnoses of his students and questioning his outsized influence.[78] When asked to explain his position, Debray-Ritzer launched into a deeper condemnation of psychoanalysis, noting that it exhibited "an extraordinary naiveté . . . envisioning itself as having definitely established its position and refusing to debate [it] with other schools of thought. Because it is necessary to remember that Bettelheim is neither a doctor nor a psychiatrist: he is a psychoanalyst. His lack of scientific rigor is quite apparent in his book."[79]

Debray-Ritzen was a conservative who was skeptical of much of the new philosophy that emerged in the 1960s and 1970s, and he questioned the link of psychoanalysis to philosophy in France.[80] He believed in the importance of scientism, although he combined this viewpoint with a belief in the moral nature of science.[81] As an outspoken critic of the antipsychiatry movement and what he perceived as its negative effect on the treatment of developmentally disabled children, Debray-Ritzen asserted that the antiscientific nature of psychoanalysis fostered an atmosphere in France that allowed for the easy digestion of charlatan ideas offering simple explanations such as Bettelheim's. "It is a very complete childhood illness that completely cuts the child off from the world. Psychiatry has acknowledged its relative ignorance [concerning autism]. Bettelheim claims that this illness is the product of psycho-affective factors as do all psychoanalysts."[82] His position was rooted in his emphasis on experimental rigor, which he believed to be an inherent element of the natural sciences, as a pathway to help children, and he found that the public fascination with psychoanalysis after 1968 was accompanied by its own "superstitions" of Freudianism, including Bettelheim's work.[83]

Other French experts were divided, often finding merit in the documentary and seeing its value as part of the discussion in France. Both Mannoni and Misès were hesitant in their support of the film's conclusions and offered faint praise.[84] Others, such as *Le nouvel observateur* medical columnist Norbert Besaid, followed Debray-Ritzen's criticisms to some degree, although he questioned the conclusion of autism as a biological condition and thus incurable. Besaid also noted that the documentary could provide false hope for some parents, especially those who did not have the means to send their children to facilities like the Orthogenic School.[85] Other important voices in the conversation were those of the Brauners, who had worked with ASITP to promote various forms of special education as an intervention to improve the lives of autistic children. Their clinic, the Externat médico-pédagogique de Saint-Mandé, was part of the constellation of facilities in Paris that aligned with parents' associations. The Brauners recognized the impact of the documentary in crystalizing the connection between psychoanalysis and autism for the French public, especially given the presentation of efficacy of Bettelheim's approach in the documentary.[86] They later reflected on its continued influence in a more negative way as they themselves distanced their approach from psychoanalysis in the 1980s.[87]

More documentaries appeared in France, revealing a growing interest in what had been marginalized as a rare phenomenon during the 1970s. Films on Mannoni's clinic at Bonneuil as well as Fernand Deligny's retreat in Cévennes presented pathways for autistic children to exit their "psychosis" with treatment reliant on philosophy as much as psychology. Bettelheim's acceptance was symptomatic of the entrenchment of psychoanalysis as a viable intervention and the public's continued fascination with it in France. During the 1970s, parents' associations continued to work with professionals despite the continued assumption of their role in the onset of symptoms and the conclusion that autistic children should be removed from their families in order for treatment to be effective. *Un regard* did not introduce anything novel to the French conversation about autism; rather, it merely expanded its audience while sidelining the voices of parents and autistic persons. Associations' work with professionals and their place in expanding facilities were confounded by the inherent blaming in psychoanalysis and the lack of engagement with other methods among professionals. The increased mediation of stories of autism during the 1970s—through broadcasts and Dolto's radio program—brought it to the attention of more people. However, unlike with the Froissy incident, parent blaming was an inherent part of the discourse that made a sympathetic public less likely.

The legal change that the Law of June 30, 1975, promised never materialized, and the remainder of the decade saw parents increasingly on the defensive about their part in their children's condition. The membership of these associations increased because of rising numbers of developmentally disabled children, but the question of diagnosis remained contentious in France because professionals predominantly considered autism an expression of childhood psychosis. Existing associations began to question this linkage, especially considering changes outside France at the end of the 1970s, but new associations appeared that rejected it outright and instead sought medical and legal reform to discredit psychoanalysis. Since this was more of a public issue, parents also began to tell their stories to that same public through memoirs that showed their emotional commitment to their children and the ways the existing system had failed them. This new approach reasserted the importance of parents as the arbiters of care for autistic children, in many ways reaffirming more traditional concepts of family, in contrast to the pervasive culture of psychoanalysis and the questioning of tradition after 1968. It also heralded the arrival of a more combative approach from parents that reconnected them with allies from outside France to provide new areas of conflict over the treatment of autism.

NOTES

1. Sherry Turkel, *Psychoanalytic Politics: Jacques Lacan and Freud's French Revolution* (New York: Basic Books, 1978), chap. 3.
2. D. V. M. Bishop and Joel Swendsen, "Psychoanalysis in the Treatment of Autism: Why Is France a Cultural Outlier?" *BJPsych Bulletin* 45, no. 2 (2021): 91.
3. Dagmar Herzog, *Cold War Freud, Psychoanalysis in an Age of Catastrophes* (New York: Cambridge University Press, 2017).
4. Élisabeth Roudinesco, "Psychoanalysis," in *The Columbia History of Twentieth-Century French Thought*, ed. Lawrence D. Kritzman (New York: Columbia University Press, 2006), 100.
5. Richard Bates, "Democratic Babies? Françoise Dolto, Benjamin Spock, and the Ideology of Post-war Parenting Advice," in *Ideologies in Action: Morphological Adaption and Political Ideas*, ed. David Laycock, Maiken Umbach, and Mathew Humphrey (New York: Routledge, 2020), 203.
6. The emphasis on charity in the postwar period concerning disability was coupled with a mediated image of disability as a burden that could undermine families and therefore needed the support of affluent individuals in society; see Paul K. Longmore, *Telethons: Spectacle, Disability, and the Business of Charity* (New York: Oxford University Press, 2016), chap. 12.
7. Robert Morin, "Lettre ouverte," *Nos enfants inadaptés* 41 (Spring 1972): 1–2.
8. Arie Rimmerman, *Family Policy and Disability* (New York: Cambridge University Press, 2015), 28.
9. "Pétition nationale," *Épanouir* 45 (September 1972): 5.
10. Robert Morin, "L'heure de verité," *Épanouir* 52 (June 1973): 2.
11. "Quelques precisions sur la Loi du 13 Juillet 1971," *Épanouir* 52 (June 1973): 30.
12. Paule Giron, "Ici, nous n'aimons pas beaucoup les étrangers tares," *Épanouir* 62 (June 1974): 22.
13. Jean-Anny Trescases, "Rôle d'une ADAPEI," *Épanouir* 65 (October 1974): 9.
14. Jacques Henry, "Les jeunes loups," *Épanouir* 67 (December 1974–January 1975): 2.
15. Jonathyne Briggs, "Les enfants perdus: Asylum Reform, Parents' Groups, and Disability Rights in France in the 1970s," *French Politics, Culture, and Society* 39, no. 3 (December 2021), 38–39.
16. Maud Mannoni, *Education impossible* (Paris: Seuil, 1973), 79.

17. Catherine Vanier and Kareen Malone, "The Experimental School in Bonneuil-sur-Marne . . . with Commentary from a North American Context," *Frontiers in Psychology* 8 (October 2017): 2.
18. For example, see Antoine Lazarus, "Handicapés hors-la-loi," *L'idiot international* 3 (February 1970): 20.
19. Jonathyne Briggs, "Reinventing Play: Autistic Children and the Normativity of Play in Postwar France," *Historical Reflections/Réflexions historiques* 45, no. 2 (Summer 2019): 58–60.
20. Roland Jaccard, "Un lieu de vie: Bonneuil-sur-Marne," *Le Monde*, December 20, 1973, https://www.lemonde.fr/archives/article/1973/12/20/un-lieu-de-vie-bonneuil-sur-marne_2560081_1819218.html.
21. Maud Mannoni, *Un lieu pour vivre: Les enfants de Bonneuil, leurs parents et l'équipe des "soignants"* (Paris: Seuil, 1976), 47.
22. Roger Gentis, *Les murs de l'asile* (Paris: François Maspero, 1970), 5.
23. Roger Gentis, *N'être* (Paris: Flammarion, 1977), 59.
24. Guy Seligmann, dir., *Vivre à Bonneuil* (Paris: Office de radiodiffusion-télévision française, 1975).
25. Patrick Boccard, "À l'écoute de Maud Mannoni," *Épanouir* 75 (September 1975): 20.
26. Sophie Wustefeld and Timothy Scott Johnson, "Maud Mannoni and Piera Aulagnier on Mental Illness and Disability: Parents at the Boundary between Society and Childhood (France 1960–1980)," *Psychoanalysis and History* 21, no. 2 (2019): 193–94. Wustefeld and Johnson reject the simplistic interpretation of parental blame in Mannoni's work.
27. Briggs, "Reimagining Play," 58.
28. Boccard, "À l'écoute," 22.
29. Ibid., 25.
30. Pierre Echavidre, "L'enfant arriéré et sa mère," *Nos enfants inadaptés* No. 12 (Winter 1964): 17.
31. "Un entretien avec Maud Mannoni," *Sésame: Bulletin de l'ASITP* 17 (September 1970): 16.
32. Ibid., 22.
33. Camille Robcis, *Disalienation: Politics, Philosophy, and Radical Psychiatry in Postwar France* (Chicago: University of Chicago Press, 2021), 3–7.
34. Richard Bates, "Mediating Trauma and Anxiety: Letters to Françoise Dolto, 1976–1978," *Journal of Medical Humanities* 42, no. 2 (2021): 269.
35. Françoise Dolto, *Le cas Dominique* (Paris: Seuil, 1971); an English translation by Ivan Kats was published as *Dominique: Analysis of an Adolescent* (London: Souvenir Books, 1973).
36. Sian Morgan, "Childhood Psychosis," in *Theory and Practice in Child Psychoanalysis: An Introduction to the Work of Françoise Dolto*, ed. Guy Hall, Françoise Hivernel, and Sian Morgan (New York: Routledge, 2009), 52–53.
37. Richard Bates, *Psychoanalysis and the Family in Twentieth-Century France: Françoise Dolto and Her Legacy* (Manchester, UK: Manchester University Press, 2022), 160.
38. Dolto, *Dominique*, 12.
39. Ibid., 38.
40. Ibid., 252.
41. Bates, *Psychoanalysis and the Family*, 160–61.
42. Ibid., 203.

43. See Françoise Dolto, *Lorsque l'enfant paraît, Tome 1* (Paris: Seuil, 1977); Dolto, *Lorsque l'enfant paraît, Tome 2* (Paris: Seuil, 1978); Dolto, *Lorsque l'enfant paraît, Tome 3* (Paris: Seuil, 1979); Françoise Dolto, *Lorsque l'enfant paraît—integrale*, France Inter FA5222 (2008), CD-ROM, nine compact discs. Since 2019, Radiofrance has streamed archived episodes via podcast, showing continued interest in Dolto's show.
44. Camille Robcis, *The Law of Kinship: Anthropology, Psychoanalysis, and the Family in France* (Ithaca, NY: Cornell University Press, 2013), 131.
45. For example, see I. Kolvin et al., "Studies in the Childhood Psychoses. II. The Phenomenology of Childhood Psychoses," *The British Journal of Psychiatry: The Journal of Mental Science* 118 (April 1971): 385–95; and Ivar Lovaas et al., "Some Generalization and Follow-Up Measures on Autistic Children in Behavior Therapy," *Journal of Applied Behavior Analysis* 6, no. 1 (1973): 131–65.
46. Bianca Lechevalier, "Pourquoi des associations de parents," *Sésame: Bulletin de l'A.S.I.T.P.* 21 (October 1971): 7.
47. Ibid., 9.
48. D. D. Rouqués, "Tour d'horizon à propos de la psychopedagogie des enfants psychotiques," *Sésame: Bulletin de l'A.S.I.T.P.* 35 (April 1975): 15.
49. For example, see Fred Pelka, *What We Have Done: An Oral History of the Disability Rights Movement* (Amherst: University of Massachusetts Press, 2012); Jameel Hampton, *Disability and the Welfare State in Britain: Changes in Perception and Policy, 1948–79* (Bristol, UK: Policy Press, 2016); and Sharon Barnartt and Richard Scotch, *Disability Protests: Contentious Politics, 1970–1999* (Washington, DC: Gallaudet University Press, 2001).
50. Loi n° 75-534 du 30 juin 1975 d'orientation en faveur des personnes handicapées, https://www.legifrance.gouv.fr/loda/id/JORFTEXT000000333976.
51. Robert Morin, "L'heure de vérité," *Épanouir* 52 (June 1973): 3.
52. Pierre Verdier, "Les décrets d'application de la loi rénovant l'action sociale et medico-sociale," *Journal du droit des jeunes* 6, no. 226 (2003): 23–24.
53. Nicolas Henckes, "Entre maladie et handicap: Repenser la critique psychiatrique de la loi du 30 Juin 1975 d'orientation faveur des personnes handicapées," *ALTER, European Journal of Disability Research* 6 (2012): 242–54.
54. Ibid., 247.
55. Edward Dolnick, *Madness on the Couch: Blaming the Victim in the Heyday of Psychoanalysis* (New York: Simon & Shuster, 1998), 169–73.
56. Bruno Bettelheim, *La forteresse vide: L'autisme infantile et la naissance du soi* (Paris: Gallimard, 1969), 7–8.
57. Bruno Bettelheim and Emmy Sylvester, "A Therapeutic Milieu," *American Journal of Orthopsychiatry* 18, no. 2 (1948): 191–206.
58. Literature on the Orthogenic School, n.d., Orthogenic School Archives, University of Chicago Special Collections.
59. Gennie Luccioni, "Libarie du mois: Bruno Bettelheim: La forteresse vide," *Esprit* 390 (March 1970): 630.
60. Jean-Michel Palmier, "La forteresse vide de Bruno Bettelheim," *Le Monde*, March 21, 1970.
61. Geneviève Jurgensen, *La folie des autres: L'expérience d'une jeune éducatrice française à l'École orthogénique de Bruno Bettelheim* (Paris: Robert Laffont, 1973), 27 and 29.
62. Ibid., 101.

63. Ibid., 132–33.
64. Geneviève Jurgensen, "Souvenirs et impressions d'une educatrice française sur l'école de Mr. Bettelheim," *Sésame: Bulletin de A.S.I.T.P.* 35 (April 1974): 28.
65. Ibid., 34.
66. Rouqués, "Tour d'horizon," 12.
67. Bruno Bettelheim and Daniel Karlin, *Un autre regard sur la folie* (Paris: Club français du livre, 1975), 10.
68. Ibid., 56.
69. Ibid., 91.
70. Daniel Karlin and Tony Lainé, *La raison de plus fou* (Paris: Editions sociales, 1977), 18.
71. Jacqueline Baudrier, "La concurrence des chaînes 'Pouic Pouic' et Jean Rostand," *Le Monde*, August 1, 1974, https://www.lemonde.fr/archives/article/1974/08/01/la-concurrence-des-chaines-pouic-pouic-et-jean-rostand_3090653_1819218.html?xtmc=&xtcr=3.
72. Jacques Hochmann, *Histoire de l'autisme: De l'enfant sauvage aux troubles envahissants du développement* (Paris: Odile, 2009), 369.
73. Robert Lecuyer, "Quelques réflexions 'simple' à propos des émissions sur Bruno Bettelheim," *Épanouir* 67 (December 1974–January 1975): 5–7.
74. Denise Ribadeau-Dumas, "La voix des parents de A.S.I.T.P.," *Épanouir* 67 (December 1974–January 1975): 7–9.
75. "Dans le sillage retombées de l'emission de television de l'automne 74 sur l'école orthogenique," *Sésame: Bulletin de l'A.S.I.T.P.* 38 (December 1975): 7–12.
76. Ibid., 11–12.
77. Denise Ribadeau-Dumas, "Un debate à la faulte de medecine de Paris sur l'approche scientifique et therapeutique des psychoses infantile (29 avril 1975)," *Sésame: Bulletin de l'A.S.I.T.P.* 36 (December 1975): 25–26.
78. Jonathyne Briggs, "The Enduring Fortress: The Influence of Bruno Bettelheim in the Politics of Autism in France," *Modern Intellectual History* 17, no. 4 (2020): 1163–91.
79. "Bruno Bettelheim est-il un charlatan?" *Élements* 8–9 (1974): 1.
80. Pierre Debray-Ritzen, *La scholastique freudienne* (Paris: Fayard, 1972).
81. Élisabeth Roudinesco, *Why Psychoanalysis?*, trans. Rachel Bowlby (New York: Columbia University Press, 2001), 88.
82. "Bruno Bettleheim est-il un charlatan," 1.
83. Pierre Debray-Ritzen, *L'usure de l'ame* (Paris: Albin Michel, 1980), 13 and 445.
84. "Autour de Bruno Bettelheim," *Le Monde*, October 19, 1974.
85. Norbert Besaid, "Le foie, vous dis-je," *Le nouvel observateur* 9961 (October 21, 1974): 51.
86. Alfred Brauner and Françoise Brauner, *Vivre avec un enfant autistique* (Paris: Presses universitaires de France, 1978), 11.
87. Alfred Brauner and Françoise Brauner, *L'enfant déréel: Histoire des autismes depuis les contes de fées fictions littéraires et réalités clinques* (Toulouse, France: Privat, 1986), 198–202.

4

Parental Expertise as Resistance

On March 21 and 22, 1981, the Union nationale des associations de parents et amis de personnes handicapées mentales (UNAPEI) organized a conference in Vichy to examine the purported equivalence between psychosis and autism, bringing together psychologists, medical doctors, analysts, and parents, including some participants from outside France. The two-day event introduced some new concepts into the discussion concerning the disorder and again reminded participants that the children who had inspired the creation of UNAPEI in 1960 were now adults. The discussions were summarized in a pamphlet published by the association for its members after the conference, with topics ranging from the state of research in a global context to advice on the role parents needed to play as part of the treatment team. The importance of proper diagnosis appeared in many of the experts' contributions, signaling a place where France was diverging from the medical norms of other nations. Many of the examples provided pointed to the limitations of the existing research in France due to the conflation of psychosis and autism and the need to develop new lines of inquiry to understand the relationship between autism and other developmental disorders. Perhaps most significant was that, following the conference, UNAPEI pushed for an educational rather than medical or psychoanalytic solution and affirmed its support for "interventions that work within the family structure for the wellbeing of all our children."[1] One of the major participants was Edward Ritvo, an American psychiatrist from the School of Medicine at the University of California, Los Angeles, who postulated a genetic origin for autism and questioned the appropriateness of psychoanalysis as an intervention for the disorder.

At the conference, more voices from outside the French system were introduced to participants to reframe the discussion of therapy for autistic children, although there were also examples of the types of assistance needed for autistic adults. Growing interest in special educational and behavioral techniques such as Treatment and Education of Autistic and Related Communication Handicapped Children (TEACCH) and applied behavior analysis led to the formation of new parents' associations in the 1980s that wanted to establish these approaches at *instituts medico-pédagogiques* (IMPs) and other facilities to achieve improved

Perpetual Children. Jonathyne Briggs, Oxford University Press. © Oxford University Press (2025).
DOI: 10.1093/9780197683002.003.0005

outcomes for their children in the hopes of mainstreaming them in French society. The conference at Vichy was but one of many similar events held by UNAPEI that signaled another shift in policy for the association. While politicking and lobbying remained important, the introduction of more scholarship from the United States and Great Britain became a central part of the association's mission after 1981, as an increasing number of translated articles from foreign academics appeared in the pages of the bulletin. UNAPEI hoped for a more open dialog about these approaches and their potential use in France to broaden the conversation beyond analysis, as had happened elsewhere. However, the shift in approach that occurred in anglophone countries was met by a retrenchment in France of psychoanalysis, particularly apparent in conflicts over changes in diagnoses that appeared in the *Diagnostic and Statistical Manual of Mental Disorders* (*DSM*)-*III* in 1980, which disconnected autism from schizophrenia based on clinical research published in the 1970s.[2] The revisions in the *DSM*, which had informed global understandings of psychological disorders, led to the creation of a French psychological diagnostic manual, the *Classification française des troubles mentaux de l'enfant et de l'adolescent* (*CFTMEA*), in 1983. The *CFTMEA* clearly embedded autism in childhood because it approached diagnosis from a psychoanalytic perspective and contributed to the French divergence concerning autism.

Undoubtedly in reaction, new associations took a more aggressive stance in challenging psychoanalysis for autistic children, while others sought a cure through various biological interventions and pseudoscientific approaches. One association, Pro Aid Autisme, took direct aim at the work of Bruno Bettelheim, who remained influential as a result of continued public awareness of the 1974 documentary, while also partnering with parents in Belgium whose children had a wider range of treatments available to them. Another organization, Association pour la recherche sur l'autisme et la Prévention des Inadaptions (ARAPI), was founded by parents to press for changes in how French medical professionals approached autism research that was more international in scope and rooted in scientific principles and new lines of inquiry. The combative tone of these organizations set the stage for conflicts between professionals and parents who attempted to pressure French medicine to move away from psychoanalysis completely, disrupting the alliance between the two groups that had developed since the 1950s.

The positions of associations were also strengthened by the emergence of parental memoirs, which offered a picture of autistic children within their family life that differed from the one portrayed in the theory and rhetoric of psychoanalysis. Inspired by a growing number of translations from American authors, French parents adopted a form of storytelling that emphasized their empathy with their children's struggles and the struggle to deal with the sense of blaming and shaming they read into and experienced with psychoanalysis. This new form of autism literature centered on the parents' experience and reified the place of autism in childhood, even as parents recognized that it was a lifelong disorder. The publication of these memoirs brought the stories of these families into the public in a new way that elicited more sympathy for their situation and challenged parent blaming, revealing a new way for parents to engage with the French public. Psychoanalysts, for their part, remained dominant in intervention, even with the pushback from parents, controlling important aspects of diagnosis and medical organizations. Despite the increased public conflict, the voices of autistic children remained marginalized in the discussions of the 1980s, even as the number of autistic adults climbed, as the voices of parents dominated the discourse and framed the debates about treatment.

UNAPEI AND PARENT EXPERTS

One of the shifts in orientation for parents' associations in the 1980s was the move toward identifying methods of prevention for various developmental disabilities. UNAPEI dedicated itself to introducing scientific research from around the global to its members and the French public through numerous conferences and public campaigns. The meeting at Vichy in 1981 was the first of these types of events organized by the association, but others followed, including a symposium in 1982 on the "Prevention of Physical and Mental Congenital Anomalies." UNAPEI remained the most visible national parents' association, and its ability to introduce foreign research and connect with scholars from beyond France made it a vital resource for its members. ASITP continued its work in alliance with UNAPEI but also found common cause with other autism-focused organizations developing in the Western world, such as Autisme Europe. The new engagement with international organizations brought into sharp contrast the French divergence in comparison with the rest of the Western world and energized a new generation of parent advocates. By the 1980s, outside France, psychoanalysis had fallen out of favor as an intervention for autism, and techniques based in behavioral psychology, primarily applied behavior analysis, had attracted more resources and research.[3] However, the continued understanding of autism as a form of childhood psychosis created resistance to the introduction and acceptance of these techniques in France, and parents were often at a loss for how to change this situation.

UNAPEI leaders were interested in exploring these ideas and their potential use in France, hoping to inform parents and their allies of the research conducted abroad. The lack of the inclusion of autism among the disabilities protected by the Law of June 30, 1975, made this struggle even more profound. To help parents learn about the possibilities available to them, UNAPEI organized several conferences that brought together foreign experts, interested French professionals, and parents, which would establish how UNAPEI attempted to align French practices with those elsewhere starting in the early 1980s. As UNAPEI president Jacques Henry noted at the time, the meeting held in Caen in 1980 marked a change in the orientation of parents' associations and the treatment of autism, thanks in large part to their discovery of therapeutic breakthroughs outside France.[4] Several important engagements occurred between the association and American psychology researchers, including Eric Schopler at the University of North Carolina (UNC) and Ritvo at the University of California, Los Angeles, whose work moved beyond the emphasis of origins that had been at the heart of psychoanalytic thinking on autism. Instead, these researchers developed interventions that helped with communication and physical symptoms, which theoretically prevented autistic children from participating in an integrated education, and provided evidence of the need for their inclusion. The hopes of this outcome energized associations to revisit the issue of the equal rights of autistic children during the 1980s and create a schism between the associations and medical professionals, who continued to advocate for psychoanalysis.

Ritvo was a crucial voice; he understood how the tunnel vision of linking autism and psychosis had not only closed off other critical avenues of research in France but also proliferated parent blaming as a defining aspect implicitly. Like Pierre Debray-Ritzen, he was a vocal critic of Bettelheim and his influence on definitions of autism among the broader public. He recognized that Bettelheim's remaining defenders, including Daniel Karlin and British analyst Melanie Klein, needed to be challenged to allow for his infamous thesis to finally be discarded. Klein's influence in French psychoanalysis was evident in the work of most child psychologists since the 1950s, and her theories provided a foundation for many French analysts' conclusions about the mother–child bond and its relationship to autistic behaviors. Ritvo also lamented the continued impact of Karlin's documentary in establishing the framework of the autism debate in France, especially given how Bettelheim's work had been supplanted by new theories in the United States.[5] Ritvo's research on twins had not explicitly revealed what the causes of autism were, but for him it definitively ruled out it being an expression of childhood schizophrenia and pointed instead to a genetic cause.

UNAPEI positioned Ritvo as keynote speaker at the Vichy conference in 1982, allowing him to address the entirety of the attendees and introduce his own ideas about the organic and neurological nature of autism. The shift to understanding autism as biological in nature would align it with other disabilities and decouple it from its connection with childhood, giving parents a way of reformulating their efforts about needed interventions and providing an alternative to parent blaming. Ritvo noted that, in his experience, many parents had autistic behaviors and these traits had become more pronounced in their children. His presentation at Vichy highlighted his own research, offering his evidence of effective pharmaceutical interventions to ameliorate more profound delays among autistic children while outlining the history of global autism research. Ritvo observed that two major interpretations concerning the origins of autism developed in the 1960s—one biological and one psychosomatic—with the latter receiving the lion's share of attention. He argued that some elements of autism, including repetitive motor movements and impaired verbal communications, were rooted in the neurological impact of disorder and were not deliberate or subconscious responses, as psychoanalysts had interpreted them.[6] For Ritvo, autism was a syndrome that had nothing to do with the social class of parents or their frigidity toward their children; rather, it was a genetic disorder.

In his presentation at the conference, pediatrician and child psychologist Didier-Jacques Duché laid out his argument about the best place for autistic children to receive treatment, engaging directly with the question regarding the family having a role in treatment. Duché worked with disabled children at the Hôpital

Necker and had expertise on the situation in France in a way that Ritvo did not. He spoke of the challenges facing families with disabled children and indicated that there was a tendency for families to be overprotective, which could undermine efforts at treatment. Nevertheless, Duché praised the work of UNAPEI and the efforts of parents in creating important facilities that allowed children to remain in their home while receiving excellent care.[7] While he recognized some validity to psychoanalytic observations about the symbiotic nature between disabled children and their mothers, he did not pathologize it in this instance and instead recognized it as a response to the situation these children faced.

The success of the conference in introducing new ideas to parents led to more meetings from UNAPEI, as its reorientation to a research focus engaged parents in a new way. While associations had previously used their bulletins to inform parents of research, the shift in the 1980s brought parents into direct contact with foreign experts who offered an alternative view of autism that could not be reconciled within the existing framework of psychoanalysis. These conferences led some associations to advocate for specific interventions while arguing for the importance of parents becoming experts. This trend echoes what Chloe Silverman observed in the case of the United States, where parent-experts were a driving force in the shift away from psychoanalysis there in the 1970s.[8] The emergence of parent-experts necessitated a shift in treatment that permitted greater parental involvement without blame. While many French parents sought to challenge the strength of psychoanalysis in France through approaches similar to those of their American counterparts, they did not have the same success in achieving that goal during the 1980s.

Another important moment at Vichy was the growing recognition that autism was a lifelong disorder that impacted adults. The assertion of autism's genetic origins decoupled the disorder from childhood and pointed out that the population of autistic adults would continue to grow, meaning that more resources were needed for them to receive therapy and assistance. The focus on children in the discussion of treatment, rights, and advocacy had obscured the needs of adults, even as many autistic children had reached the age of majority in terms of treatment at IMPs and other associational facilities. A panelist from Aix-en-Provence asserted the need for associations to engage more with autistic adults, who had not received the same attention as children despite the difficulties they shared. In Aix, a centre d'aide par le travail had been built in 1977, just five years after the establishment there of IMP La Bourgette to help autistic children, but advocate Marie-Jo Schmitt argued that it was important for UNAPEI and other associations to recognize that autistic adults needed "a place by our side" for these efforts to be effective and inclusive.[9] Schmitt's plea suggested that autistic adults should have equal participation in advocacy and help shape policy, but associations did not prioritize this approach at the time, again suggesting the frozen relationship between autism and childhood and the primacy of parental views within associations. It is not clear how autistic adults were to participate in these conferences, nor is there much to suggest that they had been given any role at this point in shaping policy for associations.

UNAPEI continued to hold conferences during the 1980s, bringing more foreign experts to its proceedings. At the same time, a new element appeared in its advocacy that built on the organic turn it embraced for understanding autism: prevention. UNAPEI hoped to inform all current and future parents about autism to encourage screenings and prevention, which would require more research, greater publicity, and new awareness campaigns. With the recognition of the role of genetics, parents' associations pressed for more funding for biological research into autism, even as medical professionals continued to cede authority for treatment to psychoanalysts. At the 1982 UNAPEI meeting, the theme was prevention, and parents were increasingly curious about a cure, since the assumption was that autism was a physical syndrome.

Outside the conferences, many association members communicated directly with foreign researchers to understand how their techniques might be adapted for use in France. Eric Schopler, who fell on the organic side of the autism debate, had developed the TEACCH method at UNC by the early 1970s based on his awareness of communication difficulties for many autists. Through a series of pictures that were designed to provide templates for nonverbal communication, autistic children could convey their feelings and desires, albeit in a simplistic manner, and create narratives through interactions with storyboards. Because it used a visually oriented vocabulary, TEACCH was easily translated into other languages and remains a common intervention throughout the world. French parents reached out to Schopler and his collaborator, Gary Mesibov, in the late 1970s to develop a French version of TEACCH that could be used in IMPs with the participation of parents. TEACCH also operated outside the boundaries of facilities and could be implemented within the home. The method was embraced by parents who had not found success with psychoanalysis and who wanted to participate in their children's therapy. Parents in the early 1980s invited Schopler and Mesibov to come to France to teach them their method, so they could subsequently teach others, and whole associations formed around its advocacy, most notably Pro Aid Autisme, which was founded in 1985. Schopler and Mesibov had already developed a training technique as a result of their work at Maudsley Hospital in Great Britain, allowing them to create a European network of interested parents and professionals that included people from France.[10]

TEACCH was based on principles of behavioral psychology, and because it relied on visual communication, it did not align with the French emphasis on spoken language as the pathway to treatment. Within the sphere of French psychology, behavioral psychology had been a subject of criticism since its development in the early twentieth century, and the resistance to its theories remained entrenched within the "psy" field into the twenty-first century.[11] Behaviorism was a counterpoint to psychoanalysis, with the latter being deemed less appropriate for French patients, and the techniques developed from it attracted little interest from French psychologists in the 1980s. Rémy Amouroux characterized French psychology within the postwar intellectual milieu as resistant to the totalitarian nature of behaviorism and its disinterest in philosophical questions and observed an element of anti-Americanism inherent in that position.[12] As some parents discovered in their efforts to engage with TEACCH, the resistance from the medical establishment thwarted early efforts to introduce the method as an approved intervention (and thus eligible for financial support) in IMPs.

One such parent, Neil Offen, shared his experience of the growing divergence between France and the United States with respect to autism treatment. His son Paul had been born in Paris in 1980, and the family soon after relocated to Provence, where services were less available to track Paul's development. After Paul's pediatrician had characterized him as nervous, Offen sought more services for his son and found them lacking. Professionals also recommended Paul for special education because of speech delays and his lack of social engagement with other children. Eventually, Offen determined that his son might have autism, leading him to a psychologist who wanted to determine the emotional trauma in the family before making an assessment. When Paul reached the age of four, Offen took him to the United States to receive a diagnosis of autism and then connected with the TEACCH center at UNC. On his return to France shortly after, Offen attended the annual conference held by UNAPEI, during which he was told that for Paul's sake he should return to the United States, which he did.[13] Gloria Laxer, a French special educator and UNAPEI ally, gave Offen this advice, noting the failures of the French state to develop an appropriate response to the growing challenges facing autistic children and their families.

Unlike the earlier case of Samy, in which French and American child psychologists could collaborate on the same case thanks to shared approaches, the waning of psychoanalysis elsewhere fostered a French exceptionalism that made the field of psychology resistant to similar collaboration by the 1980s. The main influence from America, Bruno Bettelheim, had his theories increasingly questioned by psychologists, leading professionals in the United States to disregard his conclusions about autism; in France, they remained part of the discussion.[14] Associations were limited by the lack of support from French authorities for new methods and their growing distance from other parent groups in Europe and North America, which had been important early allies in the 1960s. The attempt to gain expertise and have more participation in deciding on interventions led some associations into direct conflict with the medical establishment, as authority over autism led to parental hostility and resistance.

CONFRONTING THE SYSTEM

The failure to obtain recognition for new treatments developed in the United States energized the formation of new parents' associations that were deliberate in their attempt to undermine the monopoly of psychoanalysis as an intervention in France. These associations rejected the French deviation, especially given the proximity of groups in Britain, Belgium, and West Germany, which were practicing many of the techniques already, and instead positioned themselves as fighting for the medical rights of their children. These new associations consisted of members who were active in other associations—UNAPEI and ASITP, for example—but wanted to focus on undermining the position of psychoanalysis within French medicine as a method of promoting other potential methods that parents had discovered in their research. Their approach, however, did not account for how entrenched psychoanalytic theory had become in French culture during the 1970s and how its language had long framed public thinking about autism. Association members were trying to fight two battles: first, the recognition of autism as a disability and not an illness, which would change the trajectory of services available to autistic people; and second, the need to use a variety of educational and behavioral approaches to help autistic persons participate more fully in society. They saw psychoanalysis as the barrier to achieving success and thus concentrated on discrediting it during the 1980s.

Nicole and Pierre Toureille, parents of an autistic child, were among the first to develop an interest in the TEACCH program, hoping to introduce it within IMPs as a legitimate and accepted approach in France. The Toureilles had sent their child's tutor to the United States to learn TEACCH, but they wanted all French families to have the same opportunity to use the method, so they developed a version of the program for French clinics.[15] Nicole Toureille became an ambassador of sorts for TEACCH, connecting with a group in Belgium led by Théo Peeters, a neurolinguist who pioneered special education interventions and was an outspoken critic of psychoanalysis. He was an advocate for parents, believing they played a vital role in the education of autistic children, and at the same time he argued for the recognition of a "culture of autism" that emphasized the humanity and experience of autistic persons from an empathetic perspective.[16] Peeters developed a number of international collaborations during his career and was a major inspiration for Toureille's association Pro Aid Autisme, launched in 1985 to promote the use of TEACCH, defend the rights of disabled children to be full participants in French society, and question the efficacy of psychoanalysis in the context of emerging research on autism.

Pro Aid Autisme published the first issue of its bulletin in 1988, outlining the work the association had completed so far in its first three years, including the opening of a special educational center in Issy-les-Moulineaux and supporting the travels of educators to study in Belgium and the United States to then train parents and professionals in the use of TEACCH. Promoting TEACCH was the primary function of the association. Its secondary function was advocacy, not unlike many other associations that had formed since 1960, but in this case, its aim was to convince the French public to change its outlook on autism as an illness. This change was necessary to elevate the position of autistic persons and promote their full inclusion in society, since disabled people had recognized rights thanks to the 1975 law.[17] In order to press this change, however, psychoanalysis needed to be abandoned, because analysts only understood autism as a form of psychosis and appeared unwilling to change their position. As Toureille observed, "a strong current of French psychiatry does not see autism as a specific disorder of organic origin," meaning that psychoanalysis exerted a hold on French thought that prevented innovation in developing new treatments.[18]

This critique would be a primary aspect of the activities of the association, especially against the continued influence of Bruno Bettelheim, whose work also attracted the condemnation of Peeters. The president of Pro Aid Autisme, Emmanuel Hirsch, echoed the rhetoric of earlier arguments made by UNAPEI about the human rights of autistic children, including the right of education, which was limited by psychoanalysis and the ossification of the treatment of autism through methods that had been abandoned elsewhere. Hirsch believed that it was time to return to those arguments because autistic children and their families had waited long enough for change and needed their rights to be protected.[19] The demonization of parents and the dominance of psychoanalysis stood in the way of that change, at least according to the leadership of Pro Aid Autisme. Bettelheim's death in 1990 gave Toureille the opportunity to revisit the influence of Karlin's documentary and the fact that Bettelheim was presented as a success story with little questioning, which continued to impact autistic persons and their loved ones. She noted that the cultural strength of analysts allowed them to ignore changes outside France, such as the reclassification of autism in the *DSM-III*.[20] Longtime critic Debray-Ritzen also contributed another condemnation of Bettelheim that emphasized his lack of credentials as a physician, psychologist, or even analyst.[21]

The parents of Pro Aid Autisme shared in letters to Toureille their stories and experiences of struggles with diagnoses and navigating the medical system while trying to find the best care available for their children. Mme D. of Somme related her inability to get her son Frédéric diagnosed and how experts talked only of psychosis and institutionalization. Mme C. of Eure spoke of her nonverbal son who had not responded to the therapies provided for the past few years and her own alienation from the professionals treating him. She also expressed her frustration at what she saw as incompetence from specialists who focused on the idea of psychosis. Mme G. of Essonne detailed her sense of hope after reading Peeters's *Autisme, la forteresse éclatée*, a response to Bettelheim's famed work that had inspired Toureille to organize the association and publish the work in France.[22] Mme G. lamented the lack of options in France that used Peeters's methods and noted that autistic children were destined to become vegetative adults because of the conditions of their treatment. Another Mme D., this one from Seine-et-Marne, refused to have her daughter undergo psychoanalysis, but had few options otherwise. These letters revealed the challenges in seeking treatment outside the accepted pathways for many parents and the isolation that they experienced within the system. That these letters were all from mothers underscored both the continued position of women as the primary caregivers in families, despite other changes in society at this point, and how resistant they were to the implication that they were responsible for their children's condition.

The parents of Pro Aid Autisme were looking for answers that they felt psychoanalysis failed to provide, and the experience of navigating the French system made many of them reluctant experts who wished to share their knowledge with other parents. They often shared the paradoxical experience of being blamed for their children's condition while at the same time being encouraged to abandon their children to the system, especially as they approached adulthood. For example, Mme D. of Doubs chronicled her experience getting treatment for her son Luc at an ADAPEI facility. Despite the efforts of the staff, Luc struggled with gaining competencies and following an educational plan. As a result of his inability to reach goals, Luc represented the type of case where parents were encouraged to "forget the child," which Mme D. saw as defeatist.[23] Another mother, Mme D. from Loiret, wrote to the bulletin to get information to connect with previous letter writers because she felt that she shared their experiences of professional interaction while getting treatment for her epileptic son. This networking of parents gave them a method of comparing expertise and sharing emotional responses to the psychology community's reactions to their children.

Like other associations, Pro Aid Autisme promoted the creation of facilities to treat autistic children but made sure to differentiate them from facilities for the "mentally ill." Toureille, in her survey of autistic care in 1990, noted the presence of autistic persons under the age of twenty in psychiatric hospitals despite the availability of other venues, illustrating the inertia within the medical field and the continued preference of isolating this population. Furthermore, the treatment of autistic persons along with other developmentally disabled populations had shown little evidence of success. Noting the high cost of care, Toureille also reminded readers of the data concerning the effectiveness of TEACCH and the ability to implement it within a day hospital at a much lower cost.[24] Toureille was advocating for increased funding toward IMPs and other facilities that could provide TEACCH, which was one of the guiding principles of the association. Pro Aid Autisme was not alone in this approach—another association, Association Ile-de-France pour le développement de l'éducation et la recherche sur l'autisme, also established facilities that used TEACCH—but the larger national associations did not favor a single method in facilities and allowed that decision to occur at the local level.

While Pro Aid Autisme took a hard stance against psychoanalysis and Bettelheim's continued influence, another new association took a very different approach in its charter and practice. Building on the momentum generated by the conferences organized by UNAPEI, a collection of experts and parents wanted to introduce and develop more scientific research on autism in France and created the Association pour la recherche sur l'autisme et la prévention des inadaptations (ARAPI) in 1983 with Gilbert Lelord. Its founding in Tours was important because Paris had remained a powerful base of psychoanalytic thought in the 1980s, and being outside the capital provided a different intellectual space for research.[25] ARAPI, like Pro Aid Autisme, consisted of members from other associations but had a more specific purpose to support and promote research on autism that operated outside psychoanalysis (primarily neurology), with parents helping to direct the lines of research inquiry. ARAPI developed out of collaborations with Institut national de la santé et de la recherche médicale (INSERM), the French public organization responsible for health research that operated within academic networks throughout France.[26] This connection gave ARAPI the important veneer of scientific respectability while simultaneously providing a pathway for research that lacked a laboratory setting in France, including behavioral psychology.[27] Furthermore, ARAPI can be understood in the larger context of French efforts to question notions of illness and health through organized research and internal inquiry within the profession.[28] The establishment of a scientific committee put researchers in contact with the international colleagues despite the French divergence, including Schopler at UNC. Despite the earlier frustrations, Schopler noted his continued belief that France could establish a broad program of education based on research done by Lelord and his associates to align the French with the same breakthroughs that had occurred in the United States, Great Britain, and Canada.[29]

Like other associations, ARAPI issued bulletins to its members, although their publication did not start until the late 1990s. The lag between the formation of the association and the publication of its first bulletin reveals how much had changed in the landscape of autism in France, as well as the continuity of norms. The expansion of university-supported research continued into the 1990s, but the persistence of psychoanalysis characterized the French response in pediatric practices. The association organized conferences to disseminate information about research developments in education and treatment, but called on its members to be public advocates to broaden the conversation. As Lelord reminded them, "autism is now better known to the public. Images of child and adult autists are sometimes presented in films and television. The medical and social problems facing these patients deservedly preoccupies state power [*pouvoirs publics*]. However, there is still much to be done in this field."[30] Diagnosis was one of the aspects that concerned ARAPI, especially given the divergence from the norms in anglophone countries following the reclassification of autism in the *DSM-III*. British researcher Lorna Wing, an important advocate for the work of Hans Asperger and for understanding autism as a spectrum of experiences, spoke before a colloquium in Tours in 1985, asserting that "the ethical problem of autism is not in the evaluation but the non-evaluation."[31] The question of what organization controlled diagnostics became an issue during the 1980s, as psychoanalysts rejected the *DSM-III* and the American Psychological Association's reassessment of autism as distinct from schizophrenia.

ARAPI was instrumental in reconnecting French associations with other advocacy groups in francophone Europe and in the establishment of international organizations such as Autism Europe in 1983, which combined regional and national associations originating in western Europe. The increased development of transnational bodies in Europe preceded the eventual creation of the European Union in 1993, and Autism Europe had established itself as a lobbying organization by then to promote its "Charter for Persons with Autism" as a goal for all European states, which was drafted in 1992.[32] Elements of the charter did not conform to French norms concerning autism, revealing that the divergence was increasingly in contrast to the norms of European agencies. Autism Europe was an important ally to ARAPI, providing specialists for conferences during the 1980s.[33] ASITP was also interested in the work of Autism Europe at the outset, particularly its publications that offered a different narrative about autism than the one in France.[34] The internationalization of autism research meant that French researchers needed support to keep up with breakthroughs abroad, which was difficult because of the continued favoritism toward psychoanalysis. As Pro Aid Autisme member Catherine Cohen asked, "Why in France are we so sealed off from these new methods [of intervention]? Notably, those that have shown their effectiveness elsewhere, in other countries . . . why are all these questions without an answer?"[35]

The collaboration between parents and scientific professionals provided further energy to the pushback against psychoanalysis, centering the experience of parents and championing research with reproducible results. Psychoanalytic culture in France was resistant to both of these concepts as a whole, as Lacanian influence on the practice of analysis had emphasized a rejection of professionalization and credentialing in favor of a more broad and open approach to training that was a personal journey to understanding psychoanalysis outside medical studies and university studies.[36] The culture of "psychoanalysis, especially as interpreted by Lacan, became for the French not a medical technique, as it did in the United States, but an extension of philosophy. They looked to it not for cure of specific symptoms but for an understanding of the human condition and general guidance in dealing with human relations. They sought it not so much a science as a path of wisdom."[37] The alliance between ARAPI and parents' associations rejected this conclusion and emphasized the need for applied research that could ameliorate conditions in a way that parents approved of, moving their experience of autism to the front of the discussion. Nevertheless, the question of diagnosis and treatment remained under the control of psychoanalysts, who sought to keep its place secure in the treatment of autism.

DIAGNOSTICS AND OLD WINE IN NEW BOTTLES

The publication of the first edition of the *CFTMEA* illustrated French psychology's resistance to the conclusions drawn by foreign research on autism. Under the direction of Roger Misès, the working group that established the *CFTMEA*'s definition of autism gave it a profoundly psychoanalytic character in reaction to the changes in the *DSM-III* in 1980. Misès, an influential psychoanalyst who had worked with Serge Lebovici in the 1950s, brought his experience to bear on developing the *CFTMEA* as a useful tool for identifying and treating childhood psychosis. The creation of the *CFTMEA* occurred in the context of ongoing French psychiatric criticisms of diagnostic tools as "Anglo-Saxon creations" that failed to engage with the larger meanings of developmental disabilities through the tendency to label disorders rather than explore their origins and implications to French society.[38] The *CFTMEA* was another significant factor in the French divergence because it remained an influential reference in the psychology field in France into the twenty-first century. However, the criteria in the *CFTMEA* would make it another target for parents' associations who were pushing French medicine to distance itself from psychoanalysis.

The architect of the *CFTMEA* was a proponent of Bettelheim's theories about the familial environment as a driving force for autism, although Misès did not believe that Bettelheim was working through psychoanalysis; "Bettelheim's thinking was not really psychoanalytical, but personal," which dovetailed with Misès's own concerns about the determinism of anglophone diagnostics.[39] While Misès rejected the removal of autistic children from their parents as an effective strategy, he nevertheless supported the conclusion of autism as a form of psychosis requiring analysis for proper treatment.[40] With the overwhelming acceptance of the *CFTMEA* within the medical field, parents' efforts to advocate for other approaches faced the renewed institutional alliance between medicine and the state because the *CFTMEA* strengthened the classification of autism as a form of mental illness and not a disability, reasserting the primacy of analysis as the method of intervention for autistic behaviors. This impasse impeded efforts to create a holistic approach based on the TEACCH method that required the participation of doctors, educators, and community leaders because the reliance on psychoanalysis thwarted discussion of a national policy.

Moreover, the changes in the *DSM-III* marked a rethinking of what autism was for psychologists in the United States. While Leo Kanner's early work still influenced the language of diagnosis, the change in the diagnostic criteria illustrated a recognition of different experiences of autism because autistic persons could exhibit some of the symptoms but not necessarily all of them. Clinical genetic work done in the United States was critical to unmooring autism from schizophrenia and pointing to a biological origin. The new category that was created in the *DSM* emphasized the developmental aspect of autism as well as its locus in childhood—*infantile autism* was the name given—thus, it still emphasized the association between autism and childhood despite the revision.[41] The *CFTMEA* defined autism as infantile psychosis, similar to how it had been defined in the *DSM-II*, but did not offer much in the way of symptoms to evaluate and diagnose, leaving that work to the individual therapist. The criteria offered in the *CFTMEA* provided a set of specific conditions that constituted autism, in contrast to the expanded range of symptoms listed in the *DSM-III*, likely leading to lower rates of diagnosis in France.[42]

Misès admitted that the *CFTMEA* was created in direct opposition to the *DSM-III* as well as organicist theories about autism, which increasingly informed the outlooks of associations.[43] Jacques Hochmann, in his history of autism, notes that Misès hoped to preserve the work done on autism in France as well as other psychoanalytically informed work against the deluge of clinical research that only accounted for symptoms and lacked the consensus that defined French medicine.[44] Moreover, therapists purported their successes in treating autistic children through a combination of methods that were informed by psychoanalysis, reifying the interpretation of autism as a retreat from the world that could be reconciled by proper analysis.[45] Through the intervention of an analyst, autistic children were able to develop representations that had become distorted and led to their psychological retreat.[46] Within the Lacanian literature, autism, as a form of psychosis, represented the failure to develop a sense of the other and therefore to develop within the social domain.[47] Lacan's formulation of the psychic subject as an expression of a system between the real, the imaginary, and the symbolic allowed analysts to understand autistic behaviors as disruptions in the symbolic that prevented subjects from marking coherence between the real and the imaginary, which could be developed through the proper work of analysis.[48] This explanation connected with the *CFTMEA* and its formulation of autism as an example of schizophrenia.

Even as parents' associations were pressing for different models of intervention, supporters of psychoanalysis were able to weather this challenge through their control of diagnostic criteria. The politics of diagnosis became part of the tension between associations and professionals because diagnosis numbers remained low for autism in comparison to other Western nations, especially given that the *International Classification of Diseases* (*ICD*), a diagnostic tool of the World Health Organization, aligned with the *DSM-III* beginning with its tenth edition in 1990. The *ICD-10* incorporated the concept of the spectrum to establish a broad range of disorders that could be understood as aspects of autism, including Asperger syndrome, Rett syndrome, and pervasive developmental disorder, which did not appear at all in the *CFTMEA* until later editions in the twenty-first century.

Parents learned about the differences between French and foreign diagnostics through their continued engagement with academics outside France, who provided them information about why the changes had developed elsewhere and the impact they had on treatment. These interactions showed parents an alternative to psychoanalysis that pointed to the importance of diagnosis in defining autism for the broader public. One such interaction was between ASITP and Donald J. Cohen, a child psychologist working at Yale University who was allied with several parents' organizations in the United States. Cohen came to France in 1985 to speak with parents and offer his expertise on the changing framework established by the *DSM-III* and its impact on treatment options. He provided a definition of autism that focused on it as a developmental disorder that impacted many functions, including motor movement, speech, and social relations. Although it was increasingly diagnosed in early childhood, autism was recognized as lifelong disorder that had many permutations. Cohen also explained that special education had been effective in the United States in limiting some of the developmental delays in speech and socialization, especially with early intervention, allowing autistic persons to participate more fully in society.[49] He also argued that psychoanalysis and medication should only play a small role in the treatment of autism, although they were the common responses from French medicine.

With the retrenchment of psychoanalysis in French medicine, thanks to the legitimacy of the *CFTMEA*, these conclusions were dismissed in France and the response continued to be analysis and medication as the norm. Psychoanalysts developed their own research cluster to counter the influence of foreign scholarship in the form of the Centre d'etudes et de recherche sur l'enfant dans le discours analytique (CEREDA) in 1983 to improve collaboration among analysts and hold colloquiums that emphasized the effectiveness of their interventions in treating infantile psychosis. CEREDA also released several collections to propagate their ideas beyond these conferences in support of Freudian thought. Through their alliance with French medicine, psychoanalysts were able to maintain their authority in the realm of autism despite the accelerated efforts of parents' associations in the 1980s. The influence of books by Bettelheim, Françoise Dolto, and Maud Mannoni led some parents to respond to their inability to shift the dialogue by sharing their experiences through more narrative means as a method of shaping public opinion through emotional discourse.

PARENTS IN THE PUBLIC SPHERE

During the 1980s, the issue of autism became one that attracted renewed attention, thanks to increased press coverage, the continued appearance of documentaries and television specials, and radio programs. Parents' associations were put on the defensive and their members suggested the need for these organizations to engage with the discussions that were happening without their input. As Henri Doucet, president of ASITP Île-de-France, summarized, "it was no longer prudent to abstain" from these discussions.[50] While many new associations had launched, their rhetoric was often limited because of the lesser reach of their publications and media emphasis on centering professionals and connecting with members. One place where parents attempted to push back against this was in the realm of autism literature—the narratives that shaped public understanding of autism. These narratives took all types of forms, including scientific literature, biographies, documentaries, films, and news coverage. Psychoanalysis, with its inherent reliance on storytelling, had been a dominant force within French autism literature, especially the conversion stories of Mannoni, Joyce McDougall, Dolto, and Bettelheim.[51] The publication of Clara Claiborne Park's memoir *The Siege* in 1967 offered a new narrative that moved beyond parent blaming and showed parents as engaged, involved, and emotionally available to their children, countering the assumptions of poor parenting.[52] Once the book was translated into French in 1972, it became an example of how parents could tell their own stories in a dramatic and emotional manner to connect with audiences who did not understand the daily challenges facing autistic persons.

Park's book chronicled her challenges in navigating the American medical establishment and her quest to find new treatments and therapies for her daughter Elinor, an experience shared by many parents during their activism in the 1980s. One of the things Park took aim at was the refrigerator mother thesis and the notion that her parenting was the cause of Elinor's autism. In counterpoint to assumptions about parents of autistic children, Park asserted her high level of emotional bonding and understanding of Elinor's needs that underscored her expertise in communicating with her daughter. Her experience with quotidian interactions made Park a cypher for Elinor's needs and desires, solidifying Park's role in the treatment and care of her daughter. Park's book attracted the interest of ASITP once it appeared in translation and it was included in a bibliography complied for parents for reference.[53] Park's approach to her biography signaled to French parents how they might better tell their stories to explain to the public that they did not conform to the tidy narratives of psychoanalysis and instead presented the parents in an empathetic light.[54]

One of the first examples of parent memoires in French was Marcelle Hénault's 1973 biography *Mon fils Emmanuel*.[55] In her recounting of the struggles in getting educational support for her disabled son, Hénault centered the family experience and emphasized the importance of parents working with educators while noting that the supportive attitude of the family often took professionals by surprise. The Hénault family lived in Normandy, far from the locus of professional activity and psychoanalytic debate in Paris, and was deeply religious, often turning to religious figures for support. Emmanuel was born in 1951 and was a bit underweight, but had no other obvious differences at first. However, he faced serious health issues as an infant, including a whooping cough scare at three months old, and from these physical challenges a developmental disability developed, initially and erroneously diagnosed as a form of Down syndrome by doctors at the time.[56] Often, the subsequent opinion offered was to find a residential placement for Emmanuel and forget about him. Yet the Hénault family emphasized their determination to keep him at home and obtain care and an education for him. The challenges they encountered are similar to ones other parents had spoken of, but *Mon fils* presented them in a narrative form that emphasized many of the same elements of Park's work, namely, the special understanding that parents had of their disabled children.

The impact of these books increased in the 1980s, thanks to the publication in 1979 of Francine Fredet's *Mais, Madame, vous êtes la mère*, which opens with Fredet recalling the titular exhortation at the time of her son Vincent's diagnosis as a type of accusation and expression of responsibility.[57] She detailed her confusion at the response to her efforts to get Vincent help through psychoanalysis, with the narrative of her story focused on the challenges posed by the medical establishment. As the immanent French historian of disability Henri-Jacques Stiker noted at the time, the combative nature of psychiatrists obfuscated the limits of their knowledge about autism and did little to help disabled children or their families, which he saw exemplified in Fredet's text and her frustrations with the system.[58] Fredet shared her experiences with her nonverbal son and navigating a variety of institutions—public schools, IMPs, and psychotherapy centers—to get Vincent what she hoped was the best care. Professionals thought they understood her role in Vincent's condition, but Fredet did not exhibit the symptoms of the anxious or frigid mother stereotype associated with autism.

Fredet's frustrations are evident—the idea of struggle was central to parents' autism narratives. She detailed the early years of Vincent's life and his first diagnosis at age two, noting that the family continued to provide a loving home and support for him in the face of his increasingly violent behavior.[59] Despite her efforts, Vincent's situation became untenable by the time he was fifteen, and he could no longer receive treatment within the home. He was institutionalized for three years, and the professionals who took over his care were adversarial to Fredet as a reminder of the durability of assumptions about the role of mothers in fostering autism. Eventually, Fredet's efforts to find care for her son created divisions within her marriage, as exhaustion and frustration began to affect her relationship with her husband and impact her daughter's behavior. *Mais, Madame* concluded when Vincent was twenty-two and left home, moving to a residential hospital. Fredet uses the language of struggle to frame her narrative, ending with her hope that her story serves as inspiration for other mothers to embrace the struggle.[60] Unlike the examples found in the psychoanalytic narratives that had captured the attention of the French public, Fredet as a mother was highly engaged, active and inquisitive about her son's condition, seeking to participate where she could and advocate where she could not, similar to many of the parents participating in parents' associations. Fredet's work reveals how resistance to that stereotype became part of the emerging counternarrative of parents seeking approaches outside psychoanalysis. Ultimately, the challenge for her was the dual conflict between Vincent's behavior and the continued accusations from many in the medical community despite all her attempts to work within it. As her book emphasized, the care and love of parents were more valuable than the efforts of psychological professionals, who questioned the sincerity of the former, making psychoanalysis a barrier to the proper treatment of autistic children, as associations had claimed it was. *Mais, Madame* dramatized this experience in a way that resonated beyond the population of associations.

Fredet's attempts to deal with her child's violent behavior were echoed in another important example of parent-centered autism literature: Françoise Lefèvre's 1990 autobiographical novel *Le petit prince cannibale*.[61] Lefèvre was an award-winning novelist who brought a literary style to the biographical approach of autism literature, giving her work a more dramatic flair. She borrowed heavily from Antoine de Saint-Exupéry's celebrated novella *Le petit prince*, using the story as a metaphor for autism. She imagined her son lived on a different but violent planet, and the former became a common analogy offered to explain the different experience of autism.[62] Lefèvre's narrative differs greatly from the more straightforward narratives of Park and Fredet because Lefèvre ventures into fantastical storytelling while at the same time moving the focus away from her child's impact on the family. And rather than framing the story in empathic and inspirational terms, Lefèvre employed a more hyperbolic and fantastical language to give readers the sense of the challenges of raising an autistic child and finding care for them. For example, she notes that her son Sylvestre (Hugo in real life) "behaved like a terrorist," while also noting that French "society brutalizes maternal sentiment."[63] Lefèvre rooted the drama of the novel in her own experiences with her son during the 1980s, including a scene in which Sylvestre asks his mother to call him by a new name, which Hugo discussed later in his own memoir.

Lefèvre fictionalizes herself as the character Blanche in the story, but in essence sets up a similar conflict experienced by other mothers within the narrative of psychoanalysis. However, the major difference is that Blanche recognizes that Sylvestre inhabits "a mysterious kingdom" and that Blanche must engage with him through his own special language. Unlike the emphasis on the insights of the analyst that dominated the literature on autism in the 1970s—such as books by Dolto and Mannoni (see Chapter 3)—*Le petit prince cannibale* focuses on the special connection between mothers and their autistic children, not as a target of treatment but rather one of understanding and acceptance that illuminates the interiority of these children. Even with the conflict that permeates Lefèvre's narrative, there was still a rejection of the psychoanalytic model as a method of explaining that conflict and her son's interior life. Instead, Sylvestre's resistance was couched within a narrative of the typical challenges of children's struggles in development and learning to interact with the world to remind readers that all children experience struggles in childhood. In this sense, Lefèvre was trying to highlight how all parents had to deal with problematic children as part of childrearing and that while autism presented some challenges, it did not make autistic children so radically different from other children.

Le petit prince cannibale earned the Prix Goncourt des lycéens in 1990, elevating its status considerably. Lefèvre's empathy with her son Hugo's struggles invited her readers to challenge their own preconceptions of childhood and normativity while reminding them of their own disappointments and frustrations in childrearing. Lefèvre's story combines her sense of modesty as a parent with a portrait of her son's resistance to her, with the author experiencing sadness and understanding.[64] She also asked, "Isn't it better to think that he [Hugo] is a little prince rather than a psychotic child, exhibiting behavioral issues and strong autistic tendencies?"[65] Reviewers noted the novel's presentation of the "near-impossible" maternity, especially in the context of Lefèvre's conflicts with the French medical community, and how the novel dramatized the conflict of communication through an honest presentation of this family's life.[66] Hugo Horiot, Lefèvre's son, wrote a response to his mother's work a few decades later and became an important contributor to the autism self-advocacy movement in France in his adulthood (see Chapter 6). The recognition of *Le petit prince cannibale* validated the biographical approach taken by mothers to tell their stories to challenge the practices of French medicine in a public setting, amplifying the methods taken by associations in the 1980s in general. More parent-centered examples followed, with mothers continuing to tell their stories about the joys and aggravations of raising autistic children from their perspective. However, even with greater public awareness, parents still had little effect on undermining the place of psychoanalysis in French medicine, with Lefèvre's novel at the end of the decade chronicling many of the same experiences as Fredet's, which began the decade.

LA GRANDE CAUSE NATIONALE 1990

Every year since 1977, the French prime minister selected a cause through a public process based on proposals from nonprofits and associations, awarding them the support of the French media to spread their message and organize campaigns to raise funding to help with their cause. In 1990, the French government selected UNAPEI as the beneficiary of *la grande cause nationale*, and UNAPEI president Bernadette Wahl wanted to use the opportunity to "leave the psychology ghetto" through a public campaign mobilizing families and allies (including entertainers) to create a Charter for the Dignity of the Mentally Handicapped and an expansion of facilities through increased government funding.[67] Wahl couched her plans in the combative rhetoric that had been developed in parents' associations during the 1980s, bringing these ideas from the pages of bulletins to mainstream newspapers to reframe the meaning of autism and other developmental disabilities and counter the common misconceptions of disability among the French public. It appeared that the more combative efforts of parents' associations paid off because the French government recognized the validity of their struggle through the selection of UNAPEI.

And yet, psychoanalysis persisted. Child psychologist and parent Catherine Milcent presented her assessment of the situation in 1991 with the publication of *L'autisme au quotidien* [Autism at present], which addressed the continued influence of psychoanalysis in defining autism in France. She recognized that there was some value in the empathic and intellectual elements of psychoanalysis but lamented how its adoption had invalidated other forms of treatment in France and its limitation in understanding the different experiences of autistic persons. Moreover, she also recognized the difficulty in challenging its authority, stating, "Psychoanalysis is irrefutable because its power of interpretation is infinite; it can assimilate all things."[68] Thus, the efforts to expand research and bring parents more into therapeutic interventions could be ignored, since these approaches did not address the issues that psychoanalysis engaged with, namely, the origins in disrupted family relations. Nevertheless, Milcent remained optimistic that France would adopt elements of foreign research on autism to help autistic persons adapt to social expectations as part of their integration into society.

The continued challenge of classification muted the impact of *la grande cause nationale* in 1990 because autism was still considered an illness rather than a disability, despite the protestations of parents' associations and the conclusions of foreign researchers. The associations maintained their aggressive stance against psychoanalysis, but by the 1990s had returned to their earlier efforts to lobby the French government for recognition of autism as a form of disability, thus covered by existing laws that protected the rights of the disabled. And parents had become more prominent in the discussion thanks to their support of research, the expansion of special educational techniques in IMPs during the 1980s, and their alliances with new international organizations. Their storytelling also contributed to their changing place in the discourse because they presented a complex yet sympathetic story of their families that did not conform to the assumptions of psychoanalysis. The growing conflict between parents and psychology professionals erupted into the public view in the coming years and led to legal conflict between the two groups, especially with parents asserting their own expertise over their children's condition. The centering of the parent experience during the 1980s still marginalized autistic voices, but the 1990s would signal a shift in advocacy with the formation of associations directed by autistic persons, which added an important voice to the discourse.

NOTES

1. Union national des associations des parents d'enfants inadaptés, *Rencontres de Vichy (2e): Autisme et psychose* (21–22 mars 1981): back cover.
2. Nicole E. Rosen, Catherine Lord, and Fred R. Volkmar, "The Diagnosis of Autism: From Kanner to *DSM-III* to *DSM-5* and Beyond," *Journal of Autism and Developmental Disorders* 51 (2021): 4254–55.
3. The emergence of applied behavior analysis in the United States began in the 1960s but became more visible with the growing strength of parents' advocacy in the 1970s and 1980s, especially given its appearance in parents' memoirs in that era.

The integration of parents into therapeutic practice was an important aspect of its eventual dominance of autism treatment in the United States and elsewhere. See Chloe Silverman, *Understanding Autism: Parents, Doctors, and the History of a Disorder* (Princeton, NJ: Princeton University Press, 2012), 95–100.

4. UNAPEI, *Rencontres de Vichy*, back cover.
5. Edward R. Ritvo and Gloria Laxer, *Autisme: La vérité refusée* (Paris: SIMEP, 1983), 18.
6. UNAPEI, *Rencontres de Vichy*, 6.
7. Ibid., 8.
8. Silverman, *Understanding Autism*, chap. 3.
9. UNAPEI, *Rencontres de Vichy*, 11.
10. Gary B. Mesibov, Victoria Shea, and Eric Schopler, *The TEACCH Approach to Autism Spectrum Disorders* (New York: Springer, 2004), 10.
11. Rémy Amouroux and Nicholas Zaslawski, "'The Damned Behaviorist' versus French Phenomenologists: Pierre Naville and the French Indigenization of Watson's Behaviorism," *History of Psychology* 23, no. 1 (2020): 2.
12. Rémy Amouroux, "Beyond Indifference and Aversion: The Critical Reception and Belated Acceptance of Behavior Theory in France," *History of Psychology* 20, no. 3 (2017): 314.
13. Eric Schopler and Gary B. Mesibov, "Parent Essays," in *High-Functioning Individuals with Autism*, ed. Eric Schopler and Gary B. Mesibov (New York: Plenum Press, 1992), 275–81.
14. Jonathyne Briggs, "The Enduring Fortress: The Influence of Bruno Bettelheim in the Politics of Autism in France," Modern Intellectual History 17, no. 4 (December 2020): 1163-1191.
15. Eric Schopler and Gary B. Mesibov, "Guest Editor's Introduction: Cross-Cultural Priorities in Developing Autism Services," *International Journal of Mental Health* 29, no. 1 (2000): 11–12.
16. Théo Peeters, *Autism: From Theoretical Understanding to Educational Intervention* (San Diego, CA: Singular Publishing Group, 1997).
17. "Pro Aid Autisme, une ambition morale et sociale," *Pro Aid Autisme: La forteresse éclatée* 1 (Spring 1988): 2.
18. Nicole Toureille, "Mais combien sont-ils et où pas sont-ils," *Pro Aid Autisme: La forteresse éclatée* 8 (November 1990): 2.
19. Emmanuel Hirsch, "Éditorial," *Pro Aid Autisme: La forteresse éclatée* 2–3 (Summer and Fall 1988): 1.
20. Nicole Toureille, "Éditorial," *Pro Aid Autisme: La forteresse éclatée* 6 (March 1990): 1.
21. "La mise au point du Pr. Debray-Ritzen," *Pro Aid Autisme: La forteresse éclatée* 6 (March 1990): 18.
22. Théo Peeters, *Autisme: La forteresse éclatée* (Paris: Pro Aid Autisme, 1988).
23. "Boite à lettres," *Pro Aid Autisme: La forteresse éclatée* 7 (July 1990): 24.
24. Nicole Toureille, "Mais combine sont-ils et où sont-ils?" *Pro Aid Autisme: La forteresse éclatée* 8 (November 1990): 2.
25. Adam Feinstein, *A History of Autism: Conversations with the Pioneers* (New York: Wiley–Blackwell, 2011), 104.
26. INSERM, *Autisme infantile: Colloque international INSERM–CNRS à l'initiative de l'ARAPI* (Paris: Editions INSERM, 1987).

27. Amouroux and Zaslawski, "Beyond Indifference," 11.
28. Janine Pierret, "The Social Meanings of Health: Paris, the Essonne, the Herault," in *Le sens du mal: Anthropologie, histoire, sociologie de la maladie*, ed. Marc Augé and Claudine Herzlich (Paris: Éditions des archives contemporaines, 1983), 218-256.
29. Quoted in "Editoral," *Pro Aid Autisme: La forteresse éclatée* 12 (September 1991): 12.
30. "Rapport moral," *La lettre de l'ARAPI* 2 (June 1998): 1.
31. "Les débuts du Conseil scientifique," *La lettre de l'ARAPI* 63 (2013): 6.
32. Autism Europe, "Charter for Persons with Autism," Accessed March 13, 2023, https://www.autismeurope.org/wp-content/uploads/2017/08/charter-for-persons-with-autism-1.pdf.
33. Jacques Masson, "La genèse de l'ARAPI," *La lettre de l'ARAPI* 63 (2013): 4.
34. "Editoral," *A.S.I.T.P. Île de France bulletin de liaison* 5 (May 1983): 1.
35. Catherine Cohen, "Association des parents et amis des handicapés du Ministère des finances," *Pro Aid Autisme: La forteresse éclatée* 11 (June 1991): 6.
36. Élisabeth Roudinesco, *Jacques Lacan & Co.: A History of Psychoanalysis in France, 1925–1985* (Chicago: University of Chicago Press, 1990), 225.
37. Eugene Webb, *The Self Between: From Freud to the New Social Psychology of France* (Seattle: University of Washington Press, 1993), 22.
38. Charles Durham, "Evolution of Services for People with Autism and Their Families in France: Influence of the TEACCH Program," *International Journal of Mental Health* 29, no. 1 (2000): 25–26.
39. Quoted in Feinstein, *History of Autism*, 74.
40. Roger Misès, Nicole Garret-Gloane, and Yvonne Coinçon, *L'enfant déficient mental: Approche dynamique* (Paris: PUF, 1975), 34.
41. Rosen, Lord, and Volkmar, "Diagnosis of Autism," 4255.
42. Roy Richard Grinker, *Unstrange Minds: Remapping the World of Autism* (New York: Basic Books, 2007), 97.
43. Roger Misès, Nicole Garret-Gloanec, and Yvonne Coinçon, "Classification de l'autisme et des psychoses précoces, plaidoyer pour des convergences," *L'information psychiatrique* 86, no. 3 (2010): 223–26.
44. Jacques Hochmann, H*istoire de l'autisme*: De l'enfant sauvage aux troubles envahissants du développement (Paris: Odile Jacob, 2009), 458.
45. For example, see Claire Synodinou, *Autisme infantile: Approche thérapeutique* (Paris: Aubier, 1985).
46. Didier Houzel, "The Psychoanalysis of Infantile Autism," *Journal of Child Psychology* 30, no. 2 (2004): 225–37.
47. Leon S. Brenner, "The Autistic Mirror in the Real: Autism in Lacan's Mirror State," *Theory & Psychology* 31, no. 6 (2021): 957.
48. Jacques Lacan, Écrits*: The First Complete Edition in English*, trans. Bruce Fink (New York: W. W. Norton, 2006), 38.
49. Claire Chastenet, "Rencontre avec le Professor Cohen," *A.S.I.T.P. Île de France bulletin de liaison* 12 (July 1985): 2.
50. Henri Doucet, "Le mot du president," *A.S.I.T.P. Île de France bulletin de liaison* 10/11 (March 1985): 1.
51. John Duffy and Rebecca Dormer, "'The Pathos of 'Mindblindness': Autism, Science, and Sadness in 'Theory of Mind' Narratives," *Journal of Literary and Cultural Disability Studies* 5, no. 2 (2011): 203–5.

52. Clara Claiborne Park, The Siege: The First Eight Years of an Autistic Child (New York: Harcourt, Brace, and World, 1967), published in French as Histoire d'Elly, le siège (Paris: Calmann–Levy, 1972).
53. M. Rossignol, "Bibliographie," *Sésame: Bulletin de l'A.S.I.T.P.* 42 (December 1976): 38.
54. Marga Vicedo, *Intelligent Love: The Story of Clara Park, Her Autistic Daughter, and the Myth of the Refrigerator Mother* (Boston: Beacon Press, 2020), 149.
55. Marcelle Hénault, Mon fils Emmanuel (Tours: Mame, 1973).
56. Hénault, *Mon fils Emmanuel*, 20.
57. Françine Fredet, *Mais, Madame, vous êtes la mère* (Paris: La Centurion, 1979).
58. Henri-Jacques Stiker, *A History of Disability* (Ann Arbor: University of Michigan Press, 2019), 2.
59. Fredet, *Mais, Madame*, 27.
60. Ibid., 192–93.
61. Françoise Lefèvre, Le petit prince cannibale (Paris: J'ai Lu, 1990).
62. Ian Hacking, "Humans, Aliens & Autism," *Daedalus* 138, no. 3 (2009): 44–59.
63. Lefèvre, *Le petit prince cannibale*, 28 and 16.
64. Jean François Gomez, *Le temps des rites: Handicaps et handicapés* (Quebec City: Presses de l'Université Laval, 2005), 47.
65. Quoted in Jacqueline Delville, Joseph Duchêne, and M. Mattys, eds., *Éthique et handicap mental* (Namur, Belgium: Presses universitaires de Namur, 1997), 260.
66. Michael Bishop, "Review of Le Petit Prince cannibale by Françoise Lefèvre," *World Literature Today* 65, no. 3 (1991): 457; and Paule Constant, "Review of *Sans histoire, plus de mots*, by Frédéric Bonhomme, Caroline Tiné, Françoise Lefèvre, and Anne Garréta," *Revue des deux mondes*, 1990, 168.
67. "Le handicap mental grande cause nationale 1990," *Le Monde* (February 10, 1990).
68. Catherine Milcent, *L'autisme au quotidien* (Paris: Odile Jacob, 1991), 27.

5

The Deepening Divergence

On March 25, 1989, Barry Levinson's drama *Rain Man* debuted at French cinemas. A critical and commercial success during its theatrical run, *Rain Man* was pivotal in presenting autism to a broader audience and holds a special place in the history of autism as an example of what Stuart Murray calls an *autism event*: a fiction that attains a sort of "status of social documents in the ways in which their presentations of the condition were received."[1] Dustin Hoffman's portrayal of Raymond Babbitt, an autistic adult who is reunited with his younger brother after his father's death, provided a powerful example of the challenges facing autistic persons in society. The box office success of the film in France and its nomination for a César in 1990 revealed the large audience it attracted as well as its critical acclaim, but *Rain Man* also cultivated an enduring social interest in autism among the French, serving as a touchstone for further discussions of the disorder.[2] The presentation of autism in the film reinforced a number of stereotypes, even as the understanding of autism expanded to include a variety of experiences during the 1990s, but it also drew greater attention to the population. For Gilbert Lelord and Théo Peeters of Pro Aid Autisme, the film also served as further indictment of the French medical profession because *Rain Man* revealed that the rest of the world had moved on from psychoanalysis and parental culpability; the continuation of this "very dark page in psychoanalytic and medical history in France was an enormous social injustice."[3]

The increased public awareness of autism in France through a greater number of media representations amplified existing tensions between parents' associations and psychology professionals during the 1990s and 2000s, leading to direct conflict between these groups. While Pro Aid Autisme had been a loud minority among parents' associations in the 1980s, newer groups adopted the same approach to challenging the status and assumptions of psychoanalysis after 1990, with the continued proliferation of associations dedicated to specific interventions and pressing for a biological cure. The need for increased support for diagnoses to better understand the extent of the autistic population was another driving force in advocacy during this period. Some of these associations embraced approaches that promised results but lacked research, while others looked to blame the medical

Perpetual Children. Jonathyne Briggs, Oxford University Press. © Oxford University Press (2025).
DOI: 10.1093/9780197683002.003.0006

industry in a different manner through the emergence of an antivaccination movement in the wake of the now-discredited work of British gastroenterologist Andrew Wakefield that linked autism to the measles, mumps, and rubella vaccination in 1998. Even with the challenge to psychoanalysis drawing the attention of many parents' association, a fragmentation of the broader movement developed at the end of the twentieth century as more and more information from outside France attracted the attention of parents while illuminating the limits of their expertise. European integration and the development of extragovernmental bodies shaped the debates in France as well, especially with the French divergence in treatment operating counter to accepted ideas in western Europe. The European Union and its attendant organizations provided opponents of psychoanalysis with a powerful new resource in their pushback against its position in French medicine following its establishment in 1992.

The legal recognition of autistic rights also occupied a significant amount of attention from associations, especially given the failure of the 1975 law to do so. With *la grande cause nationale* as mental disability in 1990, more French people became aware of the issue, but lawmakers remained slow to address it. Given the existent protections for disabled rights, it became imperative to have autism legally recognized as a disability and not a form of mental illness, but psychoanalysts maintained their authority over the issue and served as a barrier to this outcome. Nevertheless, the push for rights gained momentum in the 1990s through the work of advocates, leading to the passage of the Loi Creton in 1996 and expanding the parameters of debate at the beginning of the twenty-first century. The alliance between the French state and parents' associations became stronger during the 1990s, with associations persisting in their push for expansion of special education and integration for autistic persons through the direct lobbying of leaders. Yet, issues concerning the classification of autism remained unresolved because psychoanalysis continued to influence diagnoses and treatment as it maintained its value among French thinkers and doctors as the way to understand autism. Given the emergence of conflicting information about the origins and treatment of autism, psychoanalysis provided continuity for French medicine, in contrast to the continually shifting perspectives of parents, and gave its practitioners resolve to maintain their approach despite the growing strength of criticisms in the public sphere. By the 2000s, these criticisms, dubbed *la bataille de l'autisme*, led to legal battles about the portrayal of psychoanalysis in the French media.

Even with these changes and the cultural influence of *Rain Man*, the primary conceptualization of autism remained rooted childhood, wherein autistic persons were imprisoned by the disorder and trapped in an infantile state. Public campaigns in the 1990s relied on the notion of poster children to spread awareness, but this approach followed the earlier patterns of advocacy by emphasizing the relationship between autism and childhood. Psychoanalysts continued to focus on intervention in early childhood as the primary treatment for autism. Through the metaphors of lost childhood, advocates' and professionals' efforts reified the location of autism in childhood, but autistic self-advocates were developing their own strategies to improve treatment and understanding based on their experiences rather than those of their parents or doctors. Much like it was for the association movement, international solidarity was key in this development because allies were needed to help autistic persons chart their own path within the powerful influence of parents and professionals. The 1990s were significant in the genesis of an autistic self-advocacy movement in France due to support from abroad.

CARRYING ON LA CAUSE

The announcement of *la grande cause nationale* in 1990 brought together allies who had been spearheading local efforts to improve the treatment of disabled individuals to shift the conversation to a national level. The successes of parents' associations in building *instituts medico-pédagogiques* (IMPs) and other educational facilities had not kept pace with the number of individuals in need of services, much less with the recognition of what happens to disabled adults once they aged out of these facilities. While associations continued to build and operate private facilities focused primarily on children, the French government supported the expansion of a new type of facility that followed principles of psychoanalysis to educate parents about preventing childhood traumas that could lead to psychosis. The government responded to pressure from parents' associations to fund their facilities by instead funding facilities based in psychoanalytic theories, illustrating how little impact the associations had on changing the conversation within French medicine.

One of the central points of discussion in the 1990s was the treatment of developmentally disabled adults. An important ally who pressed the French government to address this concern was Michel Creton, a film and television actor who took up the cause of equality for disabled persons in France. Creton led a public campaign that affirmed the humanity of disabled individuals and asked for improved conditions in their treatment within the health system. Moreover, he drew attention to how the Law of 30 June, 1975, although it was important in the recognition of disabled rights, was limited in its effects because of its focus on children. His concern was what happened when these rights waned as children became adults. Creton also noted that because of the law, facilities were designed to handle children, and there was a lack of facilities for adults and their specific needs, a situation that had developed from the historic association between autism and childhood. In 1989, he pressed for the National Assembly to adopt an amendment to the law that would force health professionals and administrators to address this shortcoming. Named in his honor, the Creton Amendment passed unanimously in January 1989 as a modification of the 1975 law that affirmed the rights of disabled adults to remain in IMPs and other educational facilities past the age of twenty if they had not gained placement at an adult facility.[4]

Creton's advocacy meshed well with the larger trends in 1990 and the selection of Union nationale des associations de parents et amis de personnes handicapées mentales (UNAPEI) for the national cause of that year. The campaign UNAPEI designed—"Vivre ensemble c'est pas débile"—fit with Creton's embrace of the disabled rights cause. Creton had been engaged with the issue of disabled rights since the mid-1960s, when he learned of the challenges of the system.[5] Using his celebrity, Creton rallied support for the proposed changes to the 1975 law to prevent the lawful discharge of disabled adults from facilities: "We [French society] expel them from institutions where they [the disabled] have always lived in order to put them in asylums at the age of eighteen or twenty. It is legal and it is this legality that we should ask to be abolished."[6] Creton questioned the effectiveness of institutionalization as a form of treatment and argued that the work done with disabled children was undone by the neglect shown to adults within asylums.[7] Unfortunately, his interest in the situation for adults did not resonate with the priorities of UNAPEI and its focus on the improved treatment and social integration of disabled children in the years prior to 1990.[8]

However, Creton and the association did come together after 1990 to organize large events that emphasized the social importance of the dignity of developmentally disabled persons, with UNAPEI creating a national petition in 1992 recognizing disabled rights that attracted more than 120,000 signatories across France. The mass mobilization of members and allies of parents' associations led to a number of demonstrations in France in the 1990s to recognize the need to further reform the 1975 law to guarantee the equal treatment of autistic people and their integration into French society.[9] The broadening of the disability rights movement internationally helped associations gather allies, and the greater recognition of the needs of the developmentally disabled population kept the momentum going for French associations to continue to challenge the monopoly of psychoanalysis and press for more accessibility for disabled persons. UNAPEI found allies among other associations that focused on advocating for other disabled populations, especially concerning issues of budgeting, classification, and available facilities.

Associations continued to offer services outside the conventions of psychological intervention, such as Treatment and Education of Autistic and Related Communication Handicapped Children (TEACCH), and securing funding for such services remained a priority for members. While TEACCH had been introduced with the expectation that it would allow autistic persons greater integration in French society, this outcome still faced numerous obstacles in the 1990s despite the increased public awareness of autism. Pro Aid Autisme noted the dearth of diagnoses as a barrier preventing the French from recognizing its biological origins.[10] The Association au service des inadaptés ayant des troubles de la personalité (ASITP) emphasized the lack of acceptance of autistic people as an obstacle to their equality.[11] In its bulletin, Union des familles de malades mentaux et de leurs associations stressed the need for psychoanalysis to recognize the transformation in the family in order to understand how it failed to account for the social changes in the meaning of family at the end of the twentieth century.[12] One thing that connected these various associations was that autism in France remained defined as a form of psychosis thanks to the unwavering influence of psychoanalysis and its ability to counter criticism from parents' associations.

As the associations sought to establish more facilities to offer their educational approach in the 1990s, Françoise Dolto founded a network of centers based on the therapeutic ideas she developed in her practice. The first of these centers, *les maisons vertes*, was established in 1979; they were designed to create a space for very young children and their parents to interact. During the 1980s and 1990s, the number of these spaces increased across France, thanks in large part to Dolto's reputation as a preeminent expert on childrearing. She expressed concern about the need for parents to connect with their infants to ensure their proper development, but she wanted to create an alternative to the *école maternelle* and the *crèche*, state-run facilities that specialized in the care of infants and young children; she felt that these facilities did not support parents and fostered anxieties that could be detrimental to the family.[13] Unlike those services, the *maisons vertes* required parents to stay with their children to foster a healthy family environment, although this approach tended to assume that mothers would be the parent in question.[14] These facilities welcomed children from birth to age four. One of the theoretical elements of this approach was to manage the emotional impact of parental separation by working with parents to help them develop appropriate behaviors that would not negatively impact their child's development, which points to the persistence of psychogenic origins of autism as an undercurrent.[15]

First established in Paris, the *maisons vertes* consisted of a space in which parents could interact with their children and watch them interact with other children, and areas of each clinic were demarcated by a red line indicating the space in which parents were permitted. This red line became a signature for each of the clinics that followed, despite their uniqueness in layout.[16] The play spaces designated for the children were filled with toys for them to play with as a method of socializing them by allowing their parents to observe and comment on their play (or even, at times, engage in imaginative play). Proper play had long been a central goal of child psychology, and the *maisons vertes* reinforced this concept in their organization and purpose. However, despite the influence of psychoanalysis on Dolto's thinking about childhood and disability, the *maisons* did not direct activities or analyze the children or parents who used the facility; instead, they offered insights for parents that were improvised but psychanalytically oriented.[17] The principles behind its operations were nevertheless influenced by many of the primary elements of child psychology, especially the work of Anna Freud.[18] While the *maisons* were not designed explicitly for use by disabled children, Dolto hoped that families with children facing developmental difficulties would use the centers as a method of building confidence and social skills to allow them to integrate into the existing education system by subtly introducing parents to psychoanalytic ideas outside the context of the clinic or school.[19]

The *maisons vertes* were successful in attracting parents and received media attention thanks to Dolto's celebrity status, leading to the expansion of the program throughout France. The French government eventually recognized the value of these centers, dedicating a protected line of funding in the budget for them after 1996.[20] Dolto's support of the *maisons* as an effective way of promoting healthy French families underscored her continued emphasis on early intervention as a preventative for infantile psychosis, counter to the more varied understanding of autism developing outside psychoanalytic thinking. More attention had been given to adult concerns regarding autism and its treatment, but the popularity and expansion of the *maisons* reinforced concerns about shaping parental behavior to create proper development, echoing the ideas that structured parental outreach programs during the 1950s and suggesting that understandings of childhood and parenting had not changed much for Dolto in the intervening years. During the 1990s, the number of *maisons* grew because of their popularity and state support, and by the turn of the century there were over two hundred spaces established on Dolto's model in France, each operating independently, and a few in neighboring countries.[21]

The *maisons vertes* reveal that psychoanalysis maintained support from the French state, even in areas that had been contested by parents' associations since the 1980s. Although it was not overtly psychoanalytic, Dolto's concept framed the concerns of proper development in similar terms while providing a new type of service that would attract parents to use it, even parents with disabled children. The usage of the *maisons* illustrated how they filled a gap for many parents, but there was nothing specific implemented for disabled children, who were treated as other children were. Unlike the facilities established by associations, which followed specific pathways to promote language and communication, the *maisons* operated in the spirit of Dolto's more personal notion of psychoanalysis and emphasized sociability as the primary outcome through a regulated separation that allowed children to gain autonomy while assuring parents of their children's normative behavior. For Dolto, this sociability was verbal; thus, parents of children who did not conform might be identified as in need of intervention. Again, the significant difference between the various facilities was the target of intervention—for the facilities of parents' associations, it was the children, whereas at the *maisons* it was the parents—that underscored that the gulf between the two views had not narrowed much since Dolto's work in the 1950s. The strength of the *maisons* suggested the limits of the 1990 UNAPEI campaign to inform French society about the challenges facing developmentally disabled children as a result of the continued influence of psychoanalysis in child care norms and the popularity of Dolto's clinics.

AGAINST THE HEGEMONY

The state of French psychiatry and its deep relationship with psychoanalysis endured in the 1990s despite the efforts of parents' groups to broaden the conversation. French thinkers justified the divergence in France based on their perception of the American domination of global psychological thinking through the power of the *Diagnostic and Statistical Manual of Mental Disorders* (*DSM*), which emphasized a focus on treating symptoms and failed to address deeper questions about the mind and the human condition. The resistance to the *DSM* was contextualized within the French Cartesian tradition that aimed to treat both the mind and the body, something French professionals saw as lacking in the anglophone response to mental illness. Psychoanalysts saw the emphasis on classification and symptoms as evidence of a regression of psychological thinking that necessitated the continued exploration and use of psychoanalytic theory to properly treat mental illness and understand patients as individuals.[22] And while French analysts questioned the behaviorist aspects of much foreign scholarship, they were not completely isolated because they engaged with the works of British psychoanalytic thinkers such as Frances Tustin and Donald Meltzer. Tustin had developed a theory of autism based on her concept of infantile fantasy, wherein autistic behaviors were expressions of an internal emotional state that was organized through unconscious expressions of fantasy. She published her conclusions in her 1972 work, *Autism and Childhood Psychosis*, but her theories came into conflict with the epidemiological research being done at the time in Great Britain that postulated an organic origin for autism.[23] Tustin's work had arrived in France as part of the translation of foreign psychoanalysts in the 1970s, and these works attracted interest in the wave of post-Kleinian thinkers who fell out of favor in Britain.[24] Meltzer, another British psychoanalyst, shared the French concern with understanding and treating the autistic state of mind, and his works appeared in French translation in the 1980s. Meltzer's theory of infantile aesthetic conflict resonated among psychoanalytically oriented French thinkers, who saw him engaging with primordial concepts to understand the how the rejection of beauty could lead to autism in children.[25] The continued relationship between child psychology and psychoanalysis found support in the works of such thinkers while taking on an activist element to solidify its place in the shifting world of international psychology and to counter the growing dissonance within France.

An important figure to emerge in the 1990s was Bernard Golse, the director of child psychology at the Saint-Vincent-de-Paul Hospital in Paris and head doctor at a day hospital for autistic children. Golse worked with Serge Lebovici, linking back to the one of the originators of French child psychology, and was also engaged in theoretical work based on his experiences since the 1980s. As the attacks on psychoanalysis increased in the 1990s, Golse became a lightning rod in the debates as a public defender of its significant place in the treatment of autistic children. He published numerous texts to strengthen psychoanalysis's claim on understanding and treating autism effectively, couched in his own interpretation of attachment theory and the inner life of infants, while engaging in public debates against critics seeking to implement other forms of treatment.

Golse's clinical work in Paris influenced the structure of his theories about the autistic mind, and he was interested in the same questions that fascinated Bettelheim, namely, how the sense of self developed in conditions that were unconventional or challenging, such as those assumed in cases of infantile psychosis. For him, autism was tied to the foundation of being and personhood and their psychological origins.[26] He understood autism in the same terms as previous analysts, namely, that it was a reaction to psychological trauma, but he added that it was a refuge by the rejection of the self (*je*) with an affinity to narcissism.[27] For him, the logical location of this trauma was in the family, which provided a way of reformulating parent blaming into a new theoretical shape. He was also interested in exploring dual forms of treatment that provided therapies in tandem, with hopes of the child gaining autonomy to allow for individual therapy. Golse was part of a larger team of psychoanalysts working out of the Centre de guidance de l'Institut de puericulture de Paris, which had been founded in 1971 and published numerous tracts designed to help parents understand the challenges of childrearing. These publications were developed from annual meetings of researchers working on questions of parenting, the role of the extended family, and issues of discipline, recalling the earlier work of the École des parents in the 1950s. Working closely with another important figure, Michel Soulé, Golse contributed to consolidation of the position of psychoanalysis within French medicine through his practice and his public engagement with the debate over autism treatment as a parenting expert.

Moreover, the issue of classification became a significant part of psychoanalysts' response to challenges from nonexperts, especially given the transformation in the diagnosis of autism in the 1980s. The notion of the autism spectrum—a collection of developmental disorders rather than a single type of response—appeared in the work of British psychologist Lorna Wing based on her discovery of the work of Hans Asperger during the 1970s. Asperger's findings emphasized a type of high-functioning experience combined with social deficits as an expression of autism. Wing's "The Relationship between Asperger's Syndrome and Kanner's Autism" from 1991 popularized the concept of the spectrum to tie together the radically different experiences of autistic people and their struggle with communication while recognizing the variety of symptoms and behaviors that could constitute autism.[28] Seeing Asperger's syndrome as a variant of Kanner's initial formulation of autism led Wing to revolutionize thinking concerning autism in the 1990s; her reformulation was embraced by parents' associations because of her own history as the parent of an autistic child and her role in establishing the National Autistic Society in Great Britain. Wing's concept influenced further revisions to the *DSM*, but in France it had little impact on treatment because psychoanalysts favored a different approach to diagnosis that ignored much of the work that contributed to the spectrum concept.[29] There was a question about whether disorders with a biological aspect should be called autism, and a distinction between disorders was important to establish for psychologists to better understand the psychotic position of autistic persons.[30] Parents' associations and their allies had adopted the *DSM* definition for the most part, at least as a starting point to better understand how to improve the lives of autistic persons.[31]

Despite the call from parents' associations and the professionals working with them to recognize biological aspects of autism, analysts remained tied to psychogenic concepts and emphasized the need to remove autistic children from their troubled home situation as part of treatment. The reformulation of these tenets of psychoanalytical thought illustrated that the challenge of framing proper parenting remained at the heart of analytic interventions, even as the character of what parenting might entail or how families might be formed had changed dramatically since the 1950s. The dynamics of motherhood in France changed with the transformation of labor, as more women continued to work while parenting, and the state accepted a larger role in intervening in the lives of families as a matter of public policy. Despite the double commitment of working and mothering for women, the French state took a supportive approach starting in the 1970s to recognize the rights of women to work outside the home. And by the 1990s, the French government sought to establish a new family policy based on gender equity that sought to establish a more mutualist concept of child care that included fathers.[32]

Yet analysts and theorists emphasized the critical role played by mothers based on Freudian theories (and at times Lacanian reformulations of those theories), with experts often articulating conservative ideas of parenting and motherhood that had little connection to the reality that many mothers experienced in 1990s France. Many psychoanalysts' concerns remained fixated on maternal attachment (as the first object of desire), but recent work on patterns of breastfeeding and maternal militancy suggests that French culture has a different concept of breastfeeding than anglophone countries, which could be based in social concerns about overattached mothers (*mères fusionelles*).[33] During the so-called mommy wars of the early twenty-first century, French mothers were often celebrated as objects of emulation among anglophone mothers for raising obedient and well-behaved children while exhibiting social notions of womanhood and having a career.[34] Yet the stereotyped notions of obedient children also established social expectations that parents of disabled children sometimes struggled to achieve, even with the support of the state. The activism of mothers against psychoanalysis focused on how little help they felt the intervention provided, more than a judgment on how they were perceived within these theories.

Within the psychology field, analysts emphasized the value of their approach as more humane and empathetic to autistic persons and argued for its continued role despite the increased pressure to move to a special educational model in France. Jacques Hochmann, a child psychologist and author of *Histoire de l'autisme* (2009), asserted the worth of a "French model" that recognized elements of neurological and biological concepts concerning autism but nevertheless included psychoanalysis as part of a litany of interventions.[35] Hochmann recognized the influx of ideas into the discussion concerning autism from external experts but questioned the efficacy of those ideas and whether they had shown that psychoanalysis was not helpful in the treatment of autism. The continued rejection of foreign models reinforced the value of psychoanalysis as the most valuable tool in conceptualizing what autism was and how to alleviate its challenges for young patients, which ultimately justified the French divergence and kept parents' associations on the defensive.

RENEWED ACTIVISM

The passage of the Creton Amendment and the pressure on the National Assembly to address the question of autism as a disability led parents' associations to organize a series of conferences that structured how to advocate for changes in the laws concerning autism. Since French medical professionals were unwilling to reclassify autism as a developmental disability, associations turned to the French government to change the legal status of autistic persons to have their rights recognized and protected. Law 96-1076 of 11 December 1996, also known as Loi Chossy, did just that, although not without issues that would cause friction with the medical establishment. The new law exposed the limits of inclusion as an attainable goal for associations, with stereotypes concerning autism still having a powerful influence on its social meaning. Also, this new law constituted an expansion of the 1975 law that prevented discrimination against the disabled population by recognizing autistic persons as part of that population. The legal shift of autism from mental illness to disability exacerbated further the tensions between parents and professionals, although the parents in this case had the state supporting their position.

The issue of diagnosis was a key part of the formation of the association Autisme France in 1989. Autisme France splintered off from ASITP, with a second association also forming from this split, Sésame Autisme.[36] Florence Vallade has argued that this split was the product of the ascent of the behaviorist-educational model of intervention and the outright rejection of psychoanalysis, which had developed from the work of ARAPI in the 1980s; this schism was predicated on a moral understanding of autism that led to a crusade for biogenic and educational interventions.[37] The limited effort on diagnosis by the medical community led Autisme France to press the government to mandate diagnoses to understand better the size of the autism population in France and the different challenges it faced. One of the main criticisms launched by Autisme France was that the dominance of psychoanalysis undermined other areas of potential intervention such as special education, leaving families with limited resources outside the medical sector. In 1994, Autisme France published a white paper on the issues facing autistic children and their families in France, which was derived from phone calls the association received at their national hotline established that February. In the document, parents offered details of their children's activities, interests, and struggles, but they also noted their own methods of connecting with their children and how that connection was ignored when they brought them for treatment. For example, one parent detailed their interaction concerning their ten-year-old child who was nonverbal and lacked autonomy; the recommendation was institutionalization and medication, which the parent called a "chemical straightjacket" that ignored the child's ability to communicate through alternate means.[38] After thirty-six pages of similar testimony from parents, Autisme France argued that the voluminous usage of its hotline in 1994 suggested a deeper issue in France than the official numbers outlined and urged its members to write to Simone Veil, then Minister for Social Affairs, Health and Urban Issues, to force her to intervene in this health crisis.[39] These letters focused on five themes: the absence of adequate structures, the rejection of psychiatric hospitals, the lack of diagnosis, and the lack of both therapeutic and educational support.

The 1994 white paper followed this data presentation with a litany of the association's aims, which included ending the social isolation of the autistic community. This echoed the earlier sentiments of ASITP from the 1970s, showing both continuity and the inability to achieve that goal in the interim. Autisme France hoped that the recognition of autism as a form of disability might be the crucial first step to achieving their goal because it would provide the autistic community with the legal protections it lacked. To attain this step, diagnosis was critical. Diagnosis would have the practical effect of challenging the connection between autism and childhood psychosis, which the association asserted was subjective and lacked a precise definition, as well as the variety of experiences on the autism spectrum adopted by international medical authorities.[40] Another institution that Autisme France hoped would intervene was the Comité consultatif national d'ethique, an independent French advisory organization composed of medical professionals that formed in 1983 to provide guidance and opinions on issues in health and medicine. While this organization did not offer its opinion in the 1990s, it weighed in on the issue of autism in 2007, showing that the advocacy efforts of associations were slow in reaching their targets. Last, the 1994 white paper demanded that the French state create a different class of professionals who could explicitly work with autistic populations based on the guideposts of the Law of June 30, 1975, while at the same time looking to European programs such as Educautisme to help train special educators, who were sorely needed in France.[41]

Following the passage of the Creton Amendment, Autisme Île-de-France continued to participate in working groups organized by the Secrétariat d'état chargé des handicapés et accidentés de la vie in 1991. While the questions posed at the working groups focused on the situation concerning autistic persons receiving treatment in existing facilities, the association saw it as an opportunity to reformulate the concept of autism in France.[42] One of the successes from *la grande cause nationale* in the previous year was the alliance between parents' associations and France Télécom, whose corporate patronage brought greater attention and resources to the issue of autism beginning in 1991 by partnering with Autisme France.[43] As France's primary communications company, France Télécom established the organization Volontaires pour les personnes avec autisme in 1991, allowing employees to volunteer to work with autistic children and adults where needed. The support of France Télécom provided capital to associations to formulate more ambitious political plans in the 1990s, and the company (now Orange) continues to support the cause to the present day.[44]

However, even with increased funding for advocacy, associations faced challenges in directing policy concerning the types of interventions approved for the treatment of autism, even after showing evidence of effectiveness. Having tried and failed to challenge psychoanalytic practices in the public arena, associations returned to government lobbying as a method of implementing their ideas despite the strength of the psychology field. These efforts were met with openness from legislators who were sympathetic to the cause of autism since the previous law had unintentionally excluded them from the same rights afforded to other disabled French people. This exclusion led parents' associations to return to a question that had guided them in the 1960s, namely, how to secure state support for programs that they felt improved the lives of their children more than the orthodox treatments. And much like in the aftermath of the Froissy fire, associations hoped the Inspection générale des affaires sociales (IGAS) would be an important ally in pressuring the National Assembly for action.

On November 21, 1994, IGAS submitted a report to Veil concerning the low level of support provided for young autistic persons and their families. The IGAS report noted a dysfunctional system that lacked coordination between health and social sectors and was incapable of serving the existing population of autistic children because it identified only 2,000 places in psychiatric institutions and 2,200 places in day hospitals and IMPs. According to the authors of the report, one of the reasons behind the systemic failure of state intervention was the doctrinal debates concerning autism between its organic and psychological origins. To put an end to this conflict, IGAS proposed that Veil establish a unity of the two elements within the research on child psychology. In addition, the IGAS condemned the terminology used to characterize autism that stemmed from the lack of diagnoses in France and recommended the creation of national centers specializing in the diagnosis of autism to address the shortfall.[45] The IGAS did not blame any specific sectors within its report; rather, it felt that Veil could take this opportunity to develop a coherent strategy that recognized the specific challenges that autistic persons and their families continued to face. From the psychoanalytic perspective, however, the IGAS report was primarily a political act and lacked clear guidance on how to deal with important questions in the health sector.[46]

Nevertheless, Veil did take up the reform of the state response as one of her strategies to change the national intervention strategy. Her ministry issued the Circulaire n° 95-12 du 27 avril 1995, which identified the problems that led to the IGAS report, established goals and a timeline for achieving recommendations in that report, and named the important parties that needed to be included these efforts. The circular noted the divergent definitions of autism between the *DSM-IV* (which had recently appeared in 1994) and the *Classification française des troubles mentaux de l'enfant et de l'adolescent*, while recognizing the lifetime experience of autism as the population aged into adulthood. The ministry noted that other definitions existed and that the clinical data were incomplete, leading to later diagnoses and interventions for autistic persons. To address this situation, a national plan was required that coordinated with regional authorities, and Veil welcomed the input of associations such as Autisme France and UNAPEI. The circular also asked that a regional coordinator be appointed to help with the creation of Comité technique regional sur l'autisme composed of "decision makers, financiers, activists, and families."[47] While associations welcomed these proposals, they were concerned that they should just be the beginning of reform because they failed to address the long-term issues that developed concerning autism and the indifference of French society.[48]

With the increased attention of the state, the issue of autism had reached a more overt political phase in its history in France. However, the articulation of the political issues remained focused on issues of childhood and development, but in this case the culprit had become the failing system of treatment and education that did not provide the resources for these children to become functioning adults. The French government remained committed to interventions in child care and reforming the benefits system to help support French families, especially with the higher percentages of women in the workforce following the 1970s. The accessibility of services for children was a priority supported by socialist and conservative regimes in the 1980s and 1990s, but these services were primarily aimed at abled children through *crèches* and *écoles maternelles*.[49] The IGAS report illustrated how the French state had previously ceded its authority concerning autistic children over to medical professionals, while revealing how the government tacitly accepted that autistic children were treated differently than other French children. Veil's decision to treat autism in the same manner as other forms of disability changed the entrenched policy of the French state that had been in place in some form since the 1950s.

As Veil was reshaping the policy of her institutions, Jean-François Chossy, a deputy from the Loire, formed a working group within the National Assembly that initiated a series of legal drafts, culminating in Law 96-1076 of December 11, 1996, also known as the Loi Chossy. The Loi Chossy revised the 1975 law to include autistic persons explicitly in the rights extended to disabled French people, a direct political challenge to the medical classification of autism. Autism hereafter in France was legally considered a form of disability, aligning France with other Western states and potentially bridging the French divergence. Moreover, the Loi Chossy mandated the extension of social and medical-social services to autistic populations regardless of age, recognizing the need to support adult populations as well. As Article 2 stated, "Any person with a disability resulting from autistic syndrome and related disorders, whatever their age, benefits from multidisciplinary care that takes into account their specific needs and difficulties. Adapted to the condition and age of the person and taking into account the means available, this care can be educational, pedagogical, therapeutic and social."[50] This language accounted for the types of private care provided by associations as well as special education services, which were explicitly referenced in the 1996 revision, while signaling the awareness of autism as a lifelong disability.

However, the implementation of these initiatives was uneven, and by the late 1990s, associations had become critical of the situation. Max Artuso, president of Autisme France, argued that the existing services in France were in danger of being dismantled as a result of reduced financial support because Veil's promised expansion had not appeared. For Artuso, the situation echoed the previous struggles of the parents' associations and illustrated for him how miserable the situation was in France compared to the rest of Europe.[51] In the view of Autisme France, France was trapped in a repeating cycle because of the ability of the psychoanalytic lobby to frame the conversation while maintaining the privileged position of psychoanalysis within that framework. To break this cycle, the association recommended the right to educational support as opposed to psychoanalysis, which would modify the initial contact of the psychological sector in cases and nullify the influence of analysts on treatment and approaches.[52] Autisme France wanted to talk about education to emphasize the need for nonmedical interventions to circumvent the medical field's authority on the situation.

One of the founders of Autisme France, Pierre Fouquet, questioned why educators were required by law to report mistreatment but at the same time were silenced in their attempts to report on medical professionals. He believed that these professionals were protected by the existing system, which they had contributed to building, and given the existent dogmatism within the psychology sector, it was necessary to shake the past. The need to work within education, however, did not mean that associations were abandoning all treatment. Addressing the association's members, Fouquet recognized that some professionals had embraced the educational approach and that the turn to new approaches was not akin to "replacing Freud with a pony."[53] While special education had a long history in France, it was dismissed by professionals concerning autism despite the increased convergence of concepts and classifications within special education during the twentieth century.[54] Yet this convergence took place within local and national contexts that could disrupt categorization and, in the case of France, diagnoses that led to classification, thwarting the convergence to a degree. Associations recognized what was happening outside France and thought that the 1996 reforms would bring France into alignment with other countries. The open hostility between Autisme France and analytic professionals marked the nature of conflict after the failure of the Loi Chossy to transform the experience of parents in a radical fashion, leading to more barbed criticism directed from associations invested in the educational model.

THE EUROPEAN DIMENSION

The most profound impact of Loi Chossy was providing a legal definition of autism as a disability, which made available more state funding for autistic children and promised more attention to the situation of autistic adults. While it appeared to bring the French situation into alignment with the conception of autism in Europe, associations continued to look to foreign resources to transform the situation in France, creating important alliances that pressured the French government as a result of its position within the developing European Union. Such alliances had been part of associational strategies since the 1960s, but with the passage of the Loi Chossy, associations now had legal leverage to introduce techniques that had been thus far marginalized in France. The slow change in implementing policy and the continued strength of psychoanalysis did not allow for a revolutionary moment in 1996, however, and parents were faced with similar choices at first and made some difficult decisions about how to intervene despite the legal protections. The continued influence of the illness discourse led some parents to leave France to seek treatment elsewhere, even after the Loi Chossy mandated the provision of more services.

For example, the connection between groups in the Low Countries and French associations grew stronger with the work of Pro Aid Autisme and the role played by Théo Peeters in the association. The connection led to increased awareness of practices in Belgium, which offered TEACCH and applied behavioral analysis as common interventions by the 1990s, although the French psychoanalytic approach had shaped earlier practices in some regions.[55] By the turn of the century, the failures of implementing structural change after the Loi Chossy necessitated a form of therapeutic tourism for some French families (at least those with means) to travel to Belgium for treatment. Autisme France identified this issue in 1999, noting the "exile" of 3,000 adult autists because of the inability to find space within France.[56] One destination was the Centre d'acceuil Séquoia in Namur, where Daniel Flawinne welcomed autistic children and adults for care, with many of his patients coming from France. Other Belgian institutions near the French border claimed many residents originated from France. In 2007, an official count of these French medical refugees was determined to be 3,500 of the total 13,000 places in the Wallonia region, with nearly a quarter occupied by French patients.[57] The proximity of Belgium, Great Britain, Spain, and Italy, all of which had turned to a large degree from the psychoanalytic model by the 1990s, made France's divergence starker and afforded some families a real alternative form of care nearby.

This proximity also brought French norms into conflict with supranational organizations that advocated for autistic rights worldwide, as well as the organizations within the nascent European Union. Autism-Europe had formed in 1983 as an international organization to link the efforts of national and regional organizations to advocate for the rights of autistic individuals as disabled people. It drafted an important charter, which was adopted and ratified by the European Parliament in the European Social Charter of 1996, that detailed the rights of autistic people, although again much of the language was focused on children.[58] This decision, coupled with the passage of the Loi Chossy, challenged the psychoanalytic establishment within the health sector in France on the issue of autism and led to a legal challenge against the French state in July 2002. Autism-Europe lodged a complaint with the Council of Europe alleging multiple violations of nondiscrimination provisions of the Social Charter by France in the treatment of autistic individuals, which was the first collective complaint issued to the European Committee of Social Rights (ECSR) based on Article 15 of the charter.[59] This passage noted the obligation of member states to "take necessary measure to provide persons with disabilities with guidance, education and vocational training," and the complaint of Autism-Europe was that the French state had failed in fulfilling its obligation to educate autistic persons, noting that the IGAS report of 1994 had already identified a problem that had not yet been rectified.[60]

Autisme France was a driver of this complaint, and its work after the passage of the Loi Chossy was in large part an attempt to bring French norms in line with how international organizations were operating at the turn of the century. However, the French state had done little to expand services and options for autistic persons, leading to the Belgian solution for some and the increased use of sedation to treat individuals in institutions. Neither the integration of autistic children into the existing educational system nor the expansion of special education had been achieved more than five years after their right to education had been ratified. Some issues within the French educational system had not helped, especially with its continued reliance on technical language and its paradoxical resistance of labeling, making integration a difficult task.[61] The alliance between Autisme France and Autism-Europe provided a new pressure point that associations could apply against the French state that forced a response in ways that earlier efforts did not. The complaint outlined data from Autisme France about the failure of the French plan born out of the Veil circular to provide the needed places to educate autistic persons, asserting that the state had only provided or planned a total of 7,853 places against a total need of 75,000 places; the French state countered that only it would only be short 39,514 places by 2003.[62] The discrepancy between the association's figures and the official state data pointed to the ongoing issue concerning diagnosis, but in either case the state failed to address the growing gap in services.

The ECSR gave its ruling on November 4, 2003, finding France in violation of Article 15 of the charter with respect to the education of autistic people. Despite the advocacy for legal change to help autistic persons and secure their rights to inclusion and education, the ECSR ruled that France had failed to enforce these laws and demanded that the French state immediately begin work to rectify its failure to accommodate the rights of autistic individuals. Chossy drafted an important report on the situation in France in 2003, but the ECSR still believed that it was imperative that the government develop a national, long-term plan on addressing the service gap, while stressing the need for greater use of diagnostic screening, research in autism, changing the quality of existing support, and providing greater support for families.[63] Many of the outcomes that parents' associations had hoped for were listed in the reforms that the ECSR saw as necessary in France, but again their position was rooted in their understanding of what their children needed and less engaged with what the position of autistic persons themselves had hoped for. Nevertheless, the decision broadened the scope of the conflict over the meaning of autism, bringing supranational bodies directly into the debate and adding new forces to counter the French divergence to align French treatment with that in Europe.

PSYCHOANALYTIC RESISTANCE

Despite the mounting pressure to change the place of psychoanalysis in the treatment of autism, French professionals remained committed to maintaining its presence as a guide for understanding the deeper meaning of the disorder. While Golse remained active in promoting his observations on treating autism, new voices emerged that sought to push back against behaviorist approaches they deemed unfit and ineffective in explaining autism in a profound or durable manner. These voices asserted their position of being true advocates for their patients and countered that the efforts of associations were not helpful for effectively mitigating autistic behaviors. Thinkers such as Laurent Danon-Boileau asserted that psychoanalysis provided unique tools to think about the communication issues that autistic children expressed and a solid framework that provided observers a clear logic to explain the mutism or echolalia associated with the disorder. Danon-Boileau's book detailing his clinical experiences, *L'enfant qui ne disait rien* [*The Silent Child*], appeared in 1995, as the French government and parents' associations continued to grapple over the issues of diagnosis and education.[64] Much like earlier analysts, Danon-Boileau took the position that psychoanalysis provided a method of structuring the lack of communication through specific narratives of psychodynamic origin. Given the nature of political debate, *The Silent Child* appeared to be having a different conversation about autism, but the reception of the book shows how durable this approach was, even with the political changes of the Loi Chossy. Moreover, the success of the book in France illustrates how receptive French audiences remained to the concepts of psychoanalysis and perhaps that they valued a different conversation about autism.

An analyst affiliated with the Sociéte psychanalytique de Paris and a professor of linguistics at the University of Paris–Descartes, Danon-Boileau had developed a clinical practice specializing in cases of mutism and other communication disorders. Like earlier child analysts such as Sophie Morgenstern and Serge Lebovici who worked on mutism and autism, Danon-Boileau framed his conclusions through his psychoanalytic training, but he also wanted to find a connection to the scientific aspects of his field, perhaps as an example of the "French way" for which Hochmann advocated. *The Silent Child* outlined his clinical practice with six clients who exhibited issues in speech communication and Danon-Boileau's interventions in these cases that achieved results. Reminiscent of Dolto's work in *Dominique*, Danon-Boileau's method was one that was highly personal and differentiated for each client without a specific plan, although his emphasis on the symbolic meaning of their speech linked the various cases through his reliance on a psychoanalytic interpretation of linguistic theory and Lacanian concepts to react to the behaviors of his patients.[65]

In his recounting of his sessions with Kim, a young girl with some speech difficulties, Danon-Boileau observed her free play during therapy, noting her activity with sorting various plastic animals and interpreting meaning in her choices. He was particularly interested in her interactions with a toy crocodile and her staging of scenes involving violence between the animals.[66] The association of the crocodile and the mother was a common connection made by French analysts, and Lacan postulated the image of the "crocodile mother" as a symbol of the mother's unconscious desire to subsume the child within her desire against the wishes of the father.[67] While he intervened in the play to try to understand Kim's intentions more clearly, he made a note of her choices in playing with the crocodile and what it suggested about Kim's inner world. Danon-Boileau did not claim to work only with autistic clients; however, given the connections between mutism and autism in French child psychology coupled with the reluctance of diagnoses from professionals, the specific conditions of clients remained obfuscated.

In some cases, Danon-Boileau recognized traits tied to autistic persons—low communication, repetitive behaviors, and lack of understanding social cues—in his patients. Sessions with Rachid, a likely autistic child who was nonverbal but exhibiting symptoms of hyperlexia, emphasized Danon-Boileau's attempts to have him understand the symbolic nature of figurative drawing. Rachid was interested in lines and letters, but not figures. In Danon-Boileau's estimation, the manner in which Rachid played with toys echoed classic case studies from the works of Melanie Klein and Freud that revealed the nature of interaction for children and how disruptions in communication prevent their proper development. The clinical importance of Rachid's play was that it illustrated his struggle between abstraction of ideas and application of concepts, leaving Danon-Boileau to speculate about how Rachid did not put symbolic meaning (in a Lacanian sense) into his activities and why he was self-absorbed. After about eight months of treatment, Rachid's mother decided to reduce the amount of therapy after some growth in Rachid's communication, but Danon-Boileau was skeptical, especially of the work being done by other therapists on Rachid's team.[68] Danon-Boileau noted Rachid's progress in communication but nevertheless recognized his struggle with some abstractions (time, for example) that were "awkward." Nevertheless, for him, the growth of speech was only important in that it was a necessary condition for psychological health, even though some autistic persons might never speak.[69] While he did not articulate a specific intervention as effective, Danon-Boileau pointed to the inventive nature of psychoanalysis as necessary to give interventions an improvisational aspect that allowed the therapist to be adaptable to the specific needs of the child.

LA BAGUETTE MAGIQUE

Given the struggle with the French state to honor the Loi Chossy and the Veil circulaire, parents remained active in organizations to keep political pressure on the National Assembly and on governmental health organizations to act on recommendations set forth in 1995. With the rise of the Internet and the emergence of new theories on the origins of autism, new associations emerged, with parents seeking a magic wand to cure autism. The ability to discover new research became almost instantaneous, and parents became interested in how the latest discoveries might be brought to France. However, unlike the earlier engagement with foreign research that had been vetted through institutional channels elsewhere, many of these new theories operated on the fringe of academic research. The turn to more radical solutions undermined the legitimacy that parents had developed through their alliances with research initiatives and their emphasis on evidence-based results and caused further schisms in the parents' movement. The embrace of these ideas revealed the limits of parental expertise and how their advocacy was not always guided by the research principles that associations embraced in the 1980s.

One example of this radical solution was the turn to facilitated communication (FC). FC was developed by an Australian special educator, Rosemary Crossley, in her work with autistic children during the 1970s. The practice involved the autistic child partnering with a facilitator through a specialized keyboard device that was manipulated with the assistance of the facilitator. This intervention allowed autistic children to respond to verbal questions and communicate their desires and wishes in cases where the child was nonverbal. Crossley's method was eventually brought to the United States by Douglas Biklen, who developed a program at Syracuse University to teach FC as an effective method for autistic children to communicate and learn. Biklen's support provided additional legitimacy to Crossley's work and proved vital to introducing it to French parents' groups. In 1994, Autisme Île-de-France noted the growing acceptance of the technique in the United States and suggested that FC might be of interest to parents of autistic children because of its success in providing a method of communication. Association president Henri Doucet recognized that FC was a topic of heated debate in the United States, but nevertheless wanted to bring experts from Australia to present FC to its members that year so they could decide for themselves about its efficacy.[70]

One of the important factors driving the embrace of FC was its ability to be used with autistic persons of all ages, whereas most interventions had focused on early intervention and special education. The assumption of FC was not unlike that of psychoanalysis, which assumed that autistic individuals retreated from the world but had a rich inner life; FC would provide the tool for the autistic population to communicate with their parents, their teachers, and their therapists. Through the work of the facilitator, autistic persons could manipulate the keyboard and "speak" with their voice to express their thoughts and feelings. A French expert, Anne-Marguerite Vexiau, also gave her assessment of the merits and pitfalls of FC in a presentation to the association that year and became an important advocate for FC in France. She formed the association Ta main pour parler in 1996 to promote the use of FC, working with parents to help give speech to their children. As president of the association, Vexiau remained cautious about FC and did not want to repeat the same problems with FC that happened in the United States.[71] Nevertheless, the association recognized a surge in interest in 1995 and 1996 about the value and use of FC, including media coverage on the technique. With its emphasis on communication and allowing autistic persons to speak, FC could be a point of intersection between parents and psychoanalysts, since both parties were interested in having autistic individuals speak.

However, by 1996, there was already growing evidence of the failures of FC because of its lack of reproducible validity. Questions regarding the process of FC and the verification of the client speaking were countered with claims that skeptics did not believe in the abilities of disabled people.[72] Moreover, FC suggested an entirely new framework for autism that went against the biological research that had developed in France in the 1980s and one that increasingly put parents on the defensive, especially in light of numerous allegations of sexual abuse that appeared during FC sessions in the United States. Proponents of FC claimed that nonverbal people could communicate with the physical support of a trained assistant, who would help guide the hands of patients to use a keyboard to speak. They often relied on the same concepts that had informed psychoanalysis, namely, the image of the "child within" who had been trapped by autism, but believed that learning and understanding were happening despite the child's mutism.[73] Again, the emphasis on the connection between childhood and autism was inherent in FC, although it did not distinctly suggest that FC would work for all autistic populations. Yet the allegations by American autistic children captured headlines and made FC a legal issue in the United States by 1993, accelerating the discrediting of the practice.[74] These were the issues that Vexiau had hoped to avoid in France with a more robust effort to ensure effective techniques.

FC failed to develop broadly as a practice in France because of the turn to education and the method's abandonment as an intervention by most professionals globally by the turn of the century. Nevertheless, Ta main pour parler remained committed to promoting FC as a valuable tool for connecting autistic persons with society, suggesting its deeper connection with the patient and its recognition of the social and spiritual nature of the autistic individual, with the association having grown in numbers to reach nearly 550 members in 2003. Yet Vexiau noted how careful facilitators needed to be in their work because of the attention that

FC attracted as an alternative intervention to the primary fields of psychoanalysis and special education in France. While Ta main pour parler eventually folded into another association—Enseignement pratique et information sur la communication chez l'enfant autistique—FC remained marginalized in France, although it has continued to attract the attention of parents to the present day. Nevertheless, the interest in FC illustrates that associations were increasingly fragmented coming into the twenty-first century and willing to experiment with methods lacking rigor, one of the critiques often launched at psychoanalysis.

The transformation of the political landscape concerning autism in France during the 1990s did not provide the outcomes that parents' associations had hoped for, nor did it diminish the influence of psychoanalysis in the field. Rather, it expanded the number of entities potentially involved with the issue and put the French divergence in sharp relief with that of other European states and global norms. Analysts, for their part, emphasized the value of divergence, even as parents continued to look to foreign ideas for a solution to the challenges of autism. While these efforts had often energized the parents' movement in earlier decades, the valuing of discredited ideas revealed that parents' alliance with scientific authorities did not make them immune to pseudoscience. The new politics of autism and its emphasis on special education and behaviorist therapy through government mandate set in motion a new phase—*la bataille de l'autisme*—that has defined the rhetoric of the twenty-first century and shown that the issue of autism as a disability has not been resolved. Nevertheless, despite the cacophony of voices that emerged at the end of the twentieth century, the voices of autistic persons were still absent from the discourse and from activism, a lacuna that meant children were still the focus.

NOTES

1. Stuart Murray, *Representing Autism: Culture, Narrative, Fascination* (Liverpool, UK: Liverpool University Press, 2008), 12–13.
2. See, for example, Marie-Laure Huille, "Des silences lourds à porter," *En avant: Bulletin hebodomaire de l'armée du salut* 5880 (March 6, 2000): 1–2.
3. "Interview de France Inter," *Pro Aid Autisme: La forteresse eclatée* 4 (July 1989): 3.
4. Article 6, Loi n° 75-534 du 30 juin 1975 d'orientation en faveur des personnes handicapées, accessed March 20, 2023, https://www.legifrance.gouv.fr/loda/id/LEGIARTI000006696074/1989-01-14/.
5. "Michel Creton se bat toujours en faveur des handicapés," *Le Parisien*, January 27, 2009, https://www.leparisien.fr/societe/michel-creton-se-bat-toujours-en-faveur-des-handicapes-27-01-2009-388713.php.
6. Michel Creton, *De quoi je me mêle: Les handicapés et nous* (Paris: Plon, 1993), 58–59.
7. Ibid., 61.
8. Ibid., 70.
9. Paul Bouchet, Gérard Joinneaux, and Jean-Marc Dupeux, "Comment rester 'contre,'" *Information sociales* 90/91 (January 2001): 39.
10. Nicole Toureille, "Editorial," *Pro Aid Autisme: La forteresse eclatée* 18 (March 1993): 1.

11. "Le mot de la président," *Autisme Île de France: Bulletin de liaison* 33 (June 1990): 2.
12. "Allocution de M. Yvon Gasser, president de l'UNAFAM," *UNAFAM* 3 (1993): 7.
13. Richard Bates, *Psychoanalysis and the Family in Twentieth-Century France* (Liverpool, UK: Liverpool University Press, 2022), 210.
14. Josette Combes, "France," in *International Handbook of Child Care Policies and Programs*, ed. Moncrieff Cochran (Westport, CT: Greenwood Press, 1993), 205.
15. Beatriz Markman Rubins, *Pioneers of Child Psychoanalysis: Influential Theories and Practices in Healthy Child Development* (New York: Routledge, 2014), chap. 9.
16. Jonathyne Briggs, "Reinventing Play: Autistic Children and the Normativity of Play in Postwar France," *Historical Reflections/Réflexions historiques* 45, no. 2 (2019): 54.
17. Björn Salomonsson, "Psychodynamic Therapies with Infants and Parents: A Critical Review of Treatment Methods," in *Advances in Psychodynamic Psychiatry*, ed. César A. Alfonso, Richard C. Friedman, and Jennifer I. Downey (New York: Guilford Press, 2018), 262.
18. Claudine Geissmann and Pierre Geissmann, *A History of Child Psychoanalysis* (New York: Routledge, 1998), 294.
19. Bates, *Psychoanalysis and the Family*, 211.
20. Ibid., 214.
21. Ibid.
22. Claude Janin and Denys Ribas, "Argument," *Revue française de psychanalyse* 60 (April–June 1996): 294.
23. Bonnie Evans, *The Metamorphosis of Autism: A History of Child Development in Britain* (Manchester, UK: Manchester University Press, 2017), 234; and Frances Tustin, Autism and Childhood Psychosis (London: Hogarth Press, 1972).
24. Charles Aussilloux and Marie-Françoise Livoir-Petersen, eds., *L'autisme cinquante ans après Kanner* (Ramonville, France: Erès, 1994), 76.
25. See, for example, Jacques Touze, ed., *Meltzer in Paris* (Chicago: Phoenix Publishing House, 2017), a collection of reactions from French psychoanalysts concerning Meltzer's seminars conducted in France.
26. Bernard Golse, *Insister-exister: De l'être à la personne* (Paris: Presses Universitaires de France, 1990),28.
27. Ibid., 252.
28. Lorna Wing, "The Relationship between Asperger's Syndrome and Kanner's Autism," in *Autism and Asperger's Syndrome*, ed. Uta Frith (Cambridge: Cambridge University Press, 1991), 93-121.
29. For example, see Dominique Sauvage, "L'autisme et ses énigmes," *Le Monde*, November 18, 1992; reprinted in *Autisme Île de France: Bulletin de liaison* 42 (February 1993): 22.
30. Luiz Eduardo Prado de Oliveira, "Little Jeremy's Struggle with Autism, Schizophrenia and Paranoia," *International Forum of Psychoanalysis* 8, no. 3/4 (December 1999): 174.
31. Gilbert Lelord and Dominique Sauvage, *L'autisme de l'enfant* (Paris: Masson, 1991), 7–9.
32. Marie-Thérèse Letablier and Ingrid Jönsson, "Caring for Children: The Logics of Public Action," in *Working Mothers in Europe: A Comparison of Policies and Practices*, ed. Ute Gerhard, Trudie Knijn, and Anja Weckwert (Northampton, MA: Edward Elgar, 2005), 45–46.
33. Charlotte Faircloth, *Militant Lactivism? Attachment Parenting and Intensive Motherhood in the UK and France* (New York: Berghahn Books, 2013), 11.

34. For example, see Pamela Druckerman, *French Children Don't Throw Food* (New York: Doubleday, 2012); Catherine Crawford, *Why French Children Don't Talk Back* (London: John Murray, 2012); and Karen Le Billon, *French Kids Eat Everything: How Our Family Moved to France, Cured Picky Eating, Banned Snacking, and Discovered 10 Simple Rules for Raising Happy, Healthy Eaters* (New York: Harper Collins, 2012).
35. Jacques Hochmann, Histoire de l'autisme: De l'enfant sauvage aux troubles envahissants du développement (Paris: Odile Jacob, 2009).
36. Adam Feinstein, *A History of Autism: Conversations with the Pioneers* (New York: Wiley–Blackwell, 2011), 104.
37. Florence Vallade, "Autisme: L'écran des évidences éducatives," *Éducation et sociétés* 36, no. 2 (2015): 38.
38. Autisme France, "Rapport sur le vecu des autistes et de leurs familles en France à l'aube du XXIe siècle," *Livre blanc* (1994): 4.
39. Ibid., 37.
40. Ibid., 45.
41. Ibid., 47.
42. "Rapport moral," *Autisme Île de France: Bulletin de liaison* 38 (October 1991): 3.
43. See Fondation d'entreprise France Télécom, *Répertoire de structures accueillant des personnes autistes* (Paris: Fondation d'entreprise France Télécom, 1996).
44. "La Santé et l'Autisme," https://www.fondationorange.com/en/health-and-autism, accessed March 27, 2023.
45. Laurence Folléa, "L'IGAS dénonce les incohérences de la prise en charge des jeunes autistes," *Le Monde*, November 27–28, 1994.
46. Claude Wacjman and Olivier Douville, "La fabrication de l'«autiste handicap». Chronique d'un passage à l'acte," *Figures de la psychanalyse* 24, no. 2 (2012): 106.
47. "Circulaire AS/EN n° 95-12 du 27 avril 1995," accessed March 27, 2023, http://www.cra-champagne-ardenne.fr/uploads/pdf/Circulaire27avril1995-14-12-2017-15-11-49.pdf.
48. "Rapport moral du president," *Autisme Île de France: Bulletin de liaison* 48 (October 1996): 2.
49. Kaspar Burger, "A Social History of Ideas Pertaining to Childcare in France and in the United States," *Journal of Social History* 45, no. 4 (2012): 1014.
50. Loi n° 96-1076 du 11 décembre 1996 modifiant la loi n° 75-535 du 30 juin 1975 relative aux institutions sociales et médico-sociales et tendant à assurer une prise en charge adaptée de l'autisme, accessed March 29, 2023, https://www.legifrance.gouv.fr/jorf/id/JORFTEXT000000746537.
51. Max Artuso, "Une nouvelle letter et de vieux combats," *La lettre d'Autisme France* 1 (1999): 3.
52. Pierre Fouquet, "Autisme et psychotherapies," *La lettre d'Autisme France* 1 (1999): 5.
53. Pierre Fouquet, "Remplacer Freud par le poney," *La lettre d'Autisme France* 3 (1999): 7.
54. John G. Richardson, "Unintended Convergence: Introduction, Thesis, Central Concept and Comparative Forms," in *The Global Convergence of Vocational and Special Education: Mass Schooling and Modern Educability*, ed. John G. Richardson, Jinting Wu, and Douglas M. Judge (New York: Routledge, 2016), 3–30.
55. Serafino Malaguarnera, *Théorisations psychanalytiques sur l'autisme et psychose infantile: Et l'école du quotidien* (Paris: Publibook/Société des écrivains, 2006), 235.
56. Max Artuso, "Editorial," *La lettre d'Autisme France* 2 (November 1999): 3.

57. Jean-Pierre Stroobants, "La Belgique, refuge des autistes français," *Le Monde* (April 19, 2007): 3.
58. Geraldine Van Bueren, *Child Rights in Europe: Convergence and Divergence in Judicial Protection* (Strasbourg: Council of Europe, 2007), 25.
59. Evelyne Friedel, "Introductory Remarks on the Rights of People with Autism to Education and Employment: The Convention on the Rights of Persons with Disabilities and the European and National Perspective," in *Protecting the Rights of People with Autism in the Fields of Education and Employment: International, European, and National Perspectives*, ed. Valentina Della Fina and Rachel Cera (New York: Springer, 2015), 2.
60. No. 13/2002 International Association Autism-Europe v. France Complaint (July 27, 2002): 4 and 12, https://minorityrights.org/wp-content/uploads/old-site-downloads/download-258-AUTISM-EUROPE-v-FRANCE-complaint.pdf.
61. Dominique Lerch, "Séparer, intégrer, inclure: Enfants handicapés à l'école," *Ethnologie française* 39, no. 3 (July–September 2009): 446.
62. Decision on the merits: International Association Autism-Europe v. France, Collective Complaint No. 13/2002, https://hudoc.esc.coe.int/eng/#{%22sort%22:[%22ESCPublicationDate%20Descending%22],%22ESCDcIdentifier%22:[%22cc-13-2002-dmerits-en%22]}.
63. Resolution ResChS (2004) 1, Collective complaint no. 13/2002, Autism-Europe against France, https://hudoc.esc.coe.int/eng/#{%22sort%22:[%22ESCPublicationDate%20Descending%22],%22ESCDcIdentifier%22:[%22reschs-2004-1-en%22]}.
64. Laurent Danon-Boileau, The Silent Child: Bringing Language to Children Who Cannot Speak, trans. Kevin Windle (New York: Oxford University Press, 2001.
65. Lacan's interest in language was a reaction to his reading of the work of Ferdinand de Saussure. Lacan understood language to be a system that structures the unconscious as well as a method to engage the Other; Jacques Lacan, Écrits*: The First Complete Edition in English*, trans. Bruce Fink (New York: W. W. Norton, 2006), 300–301.
66. Danon-Boileau, *The Silent Child:*, 19–20.
67. Shuli Barzilai, *Lacan and the Matter of Origins* (Stanford, CA: Stanford University Press, 1999), 214.
68. Danon-Boileau, *Silent Child*, 98.
69. Ibid., 157.
70. Henri Doucet, "Editorial," *Autisme Île de France: Bulletin de liaison* 45 (May 1994): 1.
71. Anne-Marguerite Vexiau, "Le mot de la présidente," *La main pour parler bulletin* 1 (April 1996): 2.
72. Diane Twachtman-Cullen, *A Passion to Believe: Autism and the Facilitated Communication Phenomenon* (Boulder, CO: Westview Press, 1997), x.
73. John Donvan and Caren Zucker, *In a Different Key: The Story of Autism* (New York: Crown, 2016), 357.
74. Daniel Goldman, "New Treatments for Autism Arouse Hope and Skepticism," *New York Times*, July 13, 1993, C1.

6

The Battle and the Arrival of Self-Advocacy

The announcement by Prime Minister François Fillon in 2012 of the selection of autism as *la grande cause nationale* brought to a head the political factions that had been building around the issue of autism since the 1990s. In his speech, Fillon noted that the French response has long been criticized for its backwardness, indicating that the French state could "no longer close its eyes to the suffering this backwardness has caused," and outlined the direct role the state must play in addressing those criticisms.[1] The heightened conflict between parents' associations and psychology professionals was matched by the French state's increased effort in developing a national response to autism. While this had been the case since the 1990s, the so-called *bataille de l'autisme* had gone from a cold conflict to a hot one, with associations openly questioning the authority of professionals and seeking to eliminate the influence of psychoanalysis within French medicine. For their part, professionals doubled down on their emphasis on the value of psychoanalysis, pointing to lacuna in biological and behavioral models to explain the origins and meaning of autism and how psychoanalysis helped to understand autistic persons on an individual and subjective level while providing humane treatment. In the view of analysts, the focus on symptoms, special education, and diagnosis that motivated associational advocacy and connected parents to organizations outside France did not effectively serve autistic people because they failed to understand the nature of autism itself.

The open conflict between parents' associations and psychoanalysts expanded as a result of the government's attention to the issue of autism but also in large part because associations endeavored to alert the French public about their qualms with the practices of psychoanalysis. The antipsychoanalytic rhetoric of the 1990s was amplified after 2005 and the legal affirmation of the right to education, but psychoanalysts were able to counter most efforts through their own turn to laws and medical authority. Nowhere was their success more evident than in the case of the 2011 documentary *Le mur*, which included interviews with parents and psychoanalysts to publicize their thoughts on the proper treatment of autism and

Perpetual Children. Jonathyne Briggs, Oxford University Press. © Oxford University Press (2025).
DOI: 10.1093/9780197683002.003.0007

became a flashpoint in the history of autism in France. Psychoanalysts rejected the presentation of their ideas in the film as out of context and manipulated, suing its director, Sophie Robert, to keep the film from broader circulation. The debate around the film was a microcosm of the larger ideological conflict between parents' associations and professionals, serving as a public framework for the divergent interpretations of appropriate interventions for autistic persons. However, the conflict between the two groups still focused on issues of child psychology and special education and emphasized the viewpoints of neurotypical adults, whether parents or professionals, about what they saw as the proper approach to the growing issue of autism.

Yet in this same period, a neurodivergent movement developed in France, at times in alliance with parents' associations and professionals and sometimes in conflict with those groups. Associations of autistic persons presented their perspective of the experience of autism and advocated for their positions not as children, but as disabled people. Autistic individuals published memoirs and manifestos to position themselves as the experts on the issue, emphasizing their knowledge and their distance from both parents and professionals. The intervention of the autistic population in the French debate reframed the issue of autism from one associated primarily with children to one that was more broadly and diversely defined. Beyond associations, militant autistic persons used their voices to self-advocate and argue for the importance of recognizing and accepting neurodiversity and myriad forms of autism in France, critiquing the shape of the debate so far and offering new insights to help the French public understand how the debate impacted autistic individuals directly. The voices of the autistic community challenged assumptions concerning the meaning of autism in a new way that somewhat shifted public perspective in France, although the entrenchment of parents and professionals remained firm in the ongoing debates of the twenty-first century.

LE LIVRE NOIR DE LA PSYCHANALYSE

In September 2005, the book *Le livre noir de la psychanalyse* was released.[2] Edited by Catherine Meyer, the 830-page book outlined a series of criticisms against the practice of psychoanalysis from numerous perspectives, emphasizing its failure as an effective form of therapy while addressing the French divergence concerning psychoanalytic theory. The collection rejected the dominance of psychoanalysis in French medicine and questioned the credentials of practicing analysts who operated as experts on mental health, especially in the global context of the retreat from Freudian concepts in psychology. For Meyer, the position of psychoanalysis in France was contingent on the reverence for thinkers such as Jacques Lacan, Françoise Dolto, and Bruno Bettelheim in the media.[3] That two of those names were so closely connected to autism suggested why parents' efforts had often failed to resonate with a broader section of the French public. *Le livre noir*, however, focused on an internal debate within the psychology sector between behaviorists and psychoanalysts, with the former attempting to reform practices to end the French divergence and the latter emphasizing the need for an alternate, holistic approach in contrast to the dominant global psychological models. The publication signaled a new period of struggle for parents' associations, and the commercial success of the book exacerbated the conversation about autism during the first decade of the twenty-first century.

Jean Cottraux, a psychiatrist and academic, examined the enduring power of psychoanalysis in France in his contribution to the collection. He noted the ascent of psychoanalysis in the 1960s within the psychology profession as a result of its mystical allure and its support within the academic system. This combination established a cathexis of psychology and psychoanalysis within France and contributed to the enduring influence of psychoanalysis across the psychology sector and then the French mediascape, noting the presence of Dolto on the radio and Bettelheim on television as psychoanalysis grew in stature during the 1970s.[4] Additionally, the *Livre noir* dedicated a section of the collection to victims of psychoanalysis and contained a chapter on autism that included translations of critical works concerning Bettelheim, as well as Catherine Barthélémy's proposal for a new understanding of autism outside the parameters of psychoanalysis and based on accepted research outside France, rather than the continued concept of maternal culpability. Barthélémy pointed to research suggesting neurological origins for the developmental disorder and arguing that the behaviors associated with autism were the products of sensory and communication disorders, rather than deliberate responses.[5] The interventions promoted by parents' associations and the French government after 2005 operated from these positions, putting them in conflict with norms of French psychology.

Divisions within the psychology profession continued, especially as some professionals sided with parents' associations to promote new interventions and move away from psychoanalysis, leading to a retrenchment from other professionals. One example of this movement was the formation of the Programme de recherches et d'études sur l'autisme (PREAUT) in 1998, which sought to unify neurological research with elements of psychoanalysis and cognitive approaches to identify and diagnose autism at an early age in response to the conflicts over the lack of diagnoses during the 1990s. PREAUT also promoted professional training and the development of structural approaches to care for the most difficult cases of developmental disability in children. Yet among the group's members, there was a keen awareness of the different approaches and the value of keeping the two strands of inquiry separate. As PREAUT president Graciela C. Crespin asserted in 2006, "Psychoanalysts are wary of therapy, which they consider to be a reduction or even a derivative of their practice. The history of the psychoanalytical movement proves them right, Freud always fought for a secular psychoanalysis that escaped the influence of medicine, and we know Lacan thought 'healing comes as an added bonus' at the end of an analysis well conducted."[6] This assertion of the colonizing nature of anglophone methodology questioned the practical aspects of therapy, which often were greeted with skepticism in the psychoanalytic world.[7] While psychoanalysis had influenced French medicine, its practitioners saw themselves as operating independent of it and therefore having a philosophical resistance to pressures of integrating cognitive approaches from abroad.

Upon publication, the *Livre noir* was an immediate bestseller in France, leading to two more editions in 2010 and 2013, as well as numerous translations. Psychoanalysts responded to the text with a series of criticisms that took aim at the book's major arguments concerning the scientific value of psychoanalytic theory and its attempts to discredit the approach. Bernard Brusset gave a lengthy retort in *Revue française de psychanalyse* that largely dismissed the collection as a mere promotion of cognitive therapy and an "accumulation of all the criticisms already made of psychoanalysis" that falsely suggested to the French public a conspiratorial nature to psychoanalysis, which analysts had addressed previously.[8] Others claimed the work distorted the scholarship on psychoanalysis as part of its agenda to discredit its value.[9] An ardent defender of psychoanalysis, Élisabeth Roudinesco, published a response to the *Livre noir* in 2005, *Pourquoi tant de haine?* [*Why All the Hate?*], which echoed many of Brusset's sentiments and rejected the collection outright.[10] The responses of defenders of psychoanalysis in the French media made the conflict between the two positions more public than the efforts of parents' associations had been in the 1980s and 1990s and lent some professional credence to criticism of the psychology sector. The opening of a public debate over psychoanalysis in 2005 ultimately set the stage for the open conflict of *la bataille de l'autisme.*

THE WALL AND THE BATTLE AGAINST IT

The questioning of psychoanalysis had a prelude to the *Livre noir*—in 2004, the Institut national de la santé et de la recherche médicale (INSERM) published a report evaluating the efficacy of its interventions in clinical settings, which concluded that there was no evidence to show that three primary approaches of psychoanalysis worked in treating developmental disorders. The report had been commissioned by a group of interested parties that included the Union des familles de malades mentaux et de leurs associations (UNAFAM), and its publication became a brief scandal in France. The report recognized the French divergence in the field of psychology and attempted to evaluate how psychoanalytic interventions worked to promote mental health and well-being. Given the participation of parents' associations in the request for the report, the evaluation of methods to treat autism was highlighted in the study, and INSERM emphasized that cognitive approaches showed efficacy in improved outcomes, especially with autism, in comparison to psychoanalytic approaches.[11] Much of the report was based on a meta-analysis of research conducted outside France to be compared with specific studies done in France during 2002 and 2003. Yet in the wake of its publication, Minster of Health Philippe Douste-Blazy gave a speech to a group of analysts that criticized the report and promised to remove the entire report from the ministry's website.[12]

For parents' associations, this reaction put them on the defensive and led to the development of new associations to press for specific reforms. One such organization, Autistes sans frontières, however, wanted to continue the public debate concerning the place of psychoanalysis in French medicine considering the INSERM report. Founded in 2004, the mission of Autistes sans frontières was not dissimilar to that of other associations: promoting special education in France, pressing for the inclusion of autistic persons in society, and advocating for increased diagnosis. Another important new association was Léa pour Samy, which later became Vaincre l'autisme; the two emerged as more media-savvy organizations that transformed the conversation concerning treatment.[13] These associations argued that the failure of government interventions in the issue of autism necessitated a more radical critique of the role of psychoanalysis in French medicine because of the persistence of concepts of mental illness in understanding autism. As the public debate concerning psychoanalysis heated up after 2005, these associations hoped to take advantage of increased public interest to offer their criticisms of the status quo.

A combination of awareness campaigns and an emphasis on developing special education further through the operation of centers, these new associations operated in a manner similar to the earlier efforts of UNAFAM, the Union nationale des associations de parents et amis de personnes handicapées mentales, and the Association au service des inadaptés ayant des troubles de la personalité. However, their actions found greater resonance, perhaps because of the greater attention concerning debates about psychoanalysis and autism. Operating from the perspective of parents, much of their energies were focused on advocating for the rights of disabled children, although there was recognition of the need for autistic adults to have acceptance and integration. The framing of the issues remained tied to the treatment of children and the cessation of psychoanalysis as a result of implicit parent blaming. Working with documentarian Sophie Robert, Autistes sans frontières offered its perspective on the limitations of psychoanalysis in the form of the 2011 film *Le mur ou la Psychanalyse à l'épreuve de l'autisme* [*The Wall, or Psychoanalysis Put to the Test on Autism*], which intensified the ongoing rhetorical conflict between parents' associations and professionals.[14] The release of *Le mur* precipitated a legal response from psychoanalysts who felt that the film presented a skewed vision of their therapeutic interventions that twisted their words through editing, again showing how the struggle over the meaning of autism had become as much a legal issue as a medical one in twenty-first-century France.

Le mur opened by framing the ongoing debate in France concerning the biological and psychogenic divide as a position outside the global mainstream, pointing to the French divergence in a direct manner. In an interview with Alexandre Stevens, a psychoanalyst and member of the École de la Cause freudienne, Robert asked him directly whether he considered autism a form of psychosis caused by extreme conditions, to which Stevens replied in the affirmative. Stevens claimed his position was distorted in the film and that he did not blame parents for this psychosis.[15] Stevens, however, was not the only psychoanalyst to participate in the film, and the collective presentation emphasized the position of autism as a psychogenic response to external trauma in childhood, placing the trauma in the family by default. The documentary emphasized Lacan's continued influence on psychoanalysis to the point of including the interpretations of Genevieve Loison and her assessment of children's decision to play with a toy crocodile as part of her treatment. Rehashing the Lacanian interpretation of the mother as a threat to the child's desire, Loison noted her pleasure when her patients "fight" the toy crocodile in their play therapy because it can be interpreted as a form of resistance to their mother's destructive desire. Also present in *Le mur* was Laurent Danon-Boileau, who questioned the position of mothers as a type of unassailable authority within childhood and saw them as a potential threat to the development of language.

Le mur pivots to interviewing families about their experiences in contrast to the position of psychoanalysts, which emphasized the role of the depressive mother and her influence on the psychotic behavior of her children. Yet the scenes with Sabrina Cavret, Sandrine Guy, and other parents suggested these parents engaged with their children's practical issues, including nonverbal behavior and aggression, and lamented what they saw as limitations in terms of options for care and answers. Guy spoke of her experience working with picture communication techniques supported by parents' associations and how it helped her son Guillaume to develop speech as a result of early intervention. However, the psychoanalytic perspective in the film emphasized the theoretical import of desire and the role of the mother in failing to separate her desire from that of her children, creating the conditions of retreat at work in autism. Robert noted that the French perspective was tied to the profound influence of Lacan in defining psychoanalytic culture after the 1960s and the static nature of that influence in the contemporary discussion of parents' role in the development of autism. The parents in the film detailed their experience of their children receiving analysis despite their efforts to procure different services, with Guy rejecting the conclusions of analysts concerning the reasoning for Guillaume's behavior.

Le mur presented a narrative that highlighted enduring conceptions of parental norms tied not only to gendered concepts of sexuality rooted within Freudian and Lacanian theories but also to concepts that failed to recognize the profound transformations in the experience of parenting and the social challenges of raising disabled children in France. The emphasis on the fundamental and gendered role of parenting emphasized the culpability of mothers without the analysts in question resorting to mother blaming explicitly. There was less discussion of the direct roles of fathers; instead, there was an emphasis on their symbolic role within the dynamics of the family as expressed in Lacanian theory. Yet the composition of families has changed dramatically from the nuclear model that informed much of the work of the École des parents in the 1950s, with the rise of single parenting and blended families in France, with the former accounting for nearly a quarter of French families in 2020.[16] The continued ideation of the nuclear model suggested that the behavioral disruptions of autistic persons were an example of how important traditional concepts of the family were to defining the psychoanalytic framework, especially in light of how traditional norms had informed the work of Dolto. The impact of mother blaming also has been profound in shaping how mothers participated in their children's interventions, which at times led to depression, anxiety, and other forms of mental distress.[17]

Le mur advocated for the promotion of cognitive and behavioral interventions as an effective method to help autistic individuals participate in and integrate into society, but the psychoanalysts in the film argued that these approaches were encroaching on values that psychoanalysis provides in its less aggressive intervention with patients. Analysts positioned themselves as a defense against the mechanistic nature of educational therapies that were tied to specific outcomes and benchmarks, seeing them as antithetical to the nature of subjectivity—this philosophical divide defined the *bataille de l'autisme*. After the film was screened in September 2011, psychoanalysts quickly responded with legal action against Robert to prevent its further distribution, claiming that the filmmaker distorted their positions and conclusions through editing. The French courts initially agreed in 2012, ordering that Robert remove the interview segments of three analysts—Stevens, Eric Laurent, and Esthela Solano-Suarez—from the film before its continued distribution.[18] This decision was eventually overturned in appeals but illustrated the level of conflict that the issue of autism had reached.

Laurent and other analysts did not just take legal action to defend their position within French medicine; they also asserted their expertise by relying on their connection to the French public via publishing. Laurent, Bernard Golse, and other analysts released works that positioned their efforts as critical in the continued efforts to address the issue of autism in France, despite the pressures of parents' associations and the national government. Analysts heaped criticism on Robert's film as a work of propaganda designed to undermine the value of psychoanalysis as a valuable tool while decrying the emphasis on biological and behavioral approaches, which they felt could not answer vital questions about autism. According to this constituency, *Le mur* lacked the level of sophistication that was required to understand the nuances of psychoanalytic thought and thus warped its meaning. In their published responses, proponents of psychoanalysis emphasized their place as defenders of autistic children, at times even against the family.

Some proponents of psychoanalysis directly criticized the documentary in the press, illustrating the continued cultural capital that psychoanalysts could draw on from French audiences and media. For example, Golse asserted his long career of helping autistic children as evidence of his sincerity to help and the damage done by the documentary in undermining psychoanalysis. As a member of La coordination internationale de psychothérapeutes psychanalystes s'occupant de personnes avec autisme, another professional association that defended the position of psychoanalysis, he found that Robert's film offered a flawed perspective on how psychoanalysis had engaged with new ideas and concepts and had left behind parent blaming and worked with other professionals to provide a wide range of educational therapies.[19] Like Golse, Loriane Brunessaux dismissed the dichotomy between the different approaches presented in the documentary, instead arguing that the film ignored the efforts of collaboration between analysts and scientific researchers (such as the work being done by PREAUT) and signified the antipsychoanalytic nature of many parents' organizations and activists.[20]

Perhaps the most visible and vocal critic of *Le mur* was Laurent, a participant in the documentary and then a litigant in the defamation trial. Laurent responded with the publication of *La bataille de l'autisme*, a work that offered evidence of the vital role of psychoanalysis in understanding autism, as well as an assessment of the politicized nature that discussions of the disorder had developed in France by 2012. Laurent noted that the intervention of the French government through the declaration of *la grande cause nationale* contributed to the politicization of the disorder, but the increased media attacks against psychoanalysis revealed another new front in the conflict over autism, especially given associations' language about battle and struggle.[21] Reiterating the limitations of the biological and cognitive models in explaining autism, he positioned psychoanalysis as method of opening engagement with the challenges in thinking about autism that were more existential in nature. Much of Laurent's book detailed the various efforts of psychoanalysts to support and treat autistic persons despite the efforts of parents' groups to promote cognitive and behavioral methods; psychoanalysis became a form of resistance to their global influence, with analysts finding allies throughout the world.[22] He concluded his response by observing that associations have achieved a level of public notoriety and used that power to attack psychoanalysis, but in ways that did not undermine the validity of the ideas of psychoanalysis.[23]

Yet Laurent's diatribe illustrated a similar tendency as the associations—the location of the field of autism. The battle was about childhood, early intervention, treatment, and cures, all situated as a struggle over the proper type of care for children. This emphasis on childhood revealed how little the framework had changed with regard to understanding autism among professionals, and just like parents, they situated autistic subjects as children, even as statistically the number of autistic adults continued to climb in France. Given their accelerated conflict with associations, professionals remained focused on the treatment of children, all but ignoring the position of autistic adults who provided testimony of their experiences in a manner that challenged assumptions about autism. The *bataille de l'autisme* was very much a struggle over defining what intervention was proper in terms that often vilified the opposition, but both sides agreed that the focus should be on children, continuing assumptions that had developed since the 1950s. Laurent pointed out that the 2012 conflict was likely just another skirmish in an ongoing war, but it also was merely another iteration of a struggle that developed in the 1950s that linked autism and childhood. By the 2010s, a new group of voices spoke up to try to change the parameters of this debate and emphasize that autism was a lifelong experience that did not solely exist in childhood. Rather, its medicalization revealed that it challenged not just the norms of childhood development but also those of adult sociability and communication.

The Beginnings of Self-Advocacy

While parents, professionals, and politicians continued to spar over the meaning and treatment of autism into the twenty-first century, autistic individuals themselves began to advocate for their own position in France. The self-advocacy movement had already gained momentum in the United States following the publication of Jim Sinclair's essay "Don't Mourn for Us" in 1993, and with the expansion of the Internet into more public places and the growth of online communities, the lull that parents' associations experienced in France was not as long for autistic persons attempting to organize along the same lines.[24] The first association created by autistic individuals was Spectre autistique, troubles envahissants du développement, international (SATEDI), which formed in alliance with Autisme France in 2004. As Brigitte Chamak observed, SATEDI's links to Autisme France meant that the association "accepted the definition of autism as a neurodevelopmental disease" thanks to the persistence of psychoanalysis.[25] The position of the association was out of step with that of other self-advocacy groups in the world, which had adopted the notion of neurodivergence as an understanding of autism, but SATEDI was nevertheless critical in shifting the debates in France by positioning autism outside the exclusive realm of childhood through the organization of autistic adults. Other groups formed, some with the support of parents and others with that of professionals, revealing that the bifurcation of the *bataille de l'autisme* was not so easily divided among autistic persons themselves, who saw value and limitations in each of the models that had been championed in France. Ultimately, the increased participation in the public debate by autistic individuals illuminated how the debates thus far had not engaged with the autistic perspective as a resource to finding a pathway to social acceptance and recognition for this population through the advocacy of neurodiversity.

An early example of autistic expression in France was *Le papotin*, a publication produced by autists and professionals at the Hôpital du jour d'Antony in the Île-de-France region through the association Fenêtre sur la ville since 1990. A combination of literature, art, and interviews with political and cultural figures, *Le papotin* revealed that autistic persons were deeply engaged with French society and had opinions and insights to share with audiences. For example, in the 2002 issue, the editors interviewed President Jacques Chirac, inquiring about his favorite car, his musical preferences, his ideas of tolerance, and his thoughts on death. Chirac responded with thoughtful answers that showed his engagement and sincerity in the exchange.[26] In an editorial in the same issue, Moïse Assouline noted the potential negative reaction to the efforts of *Le papotin* to participate in political discourse but asserted that the journal played an important role in articulating the viewpoint of autistic individuals who were an equal part of society.[27] Interaction with political figures continued throughout the publication's history, with later interviews with Dominique de Villepin, Nicolas Sarkozy, Anne Hidalgo, and Emmanuel Macron, among others, revealing how *Le papotin* provided autistic persons with a method to advocate for their ideas and provided a platform for them to participate in the social discourse. Moreover, the journal illustrated the negotiation of identity that was part of a nascent neurodiversity movement in the 1990s, in which autistic individuals of all types articulated a social identity that recognized autism as a distinct culture through the inclusion of graphic art and poetry from the editorial staff, with much of the content discussing the challenges and joys of living with autism.

Originally composed of only patients from the Hôpital du jour d'Antony, the staff expanded in the 2000s to include autistic persons and other "atypicals" from throughout the region to create a network of voices that spoke of their experiences, aspirations, and frustrations. *Le papotin* operated with the assistance of directors who were psychoanalysts, revealing that the process of preparing the journal was part of a therapeutic practice that emphasized individual expression and had elements of art therapy. Each issue in the journal's history was developed by an ever-changing group of patients who were older than fifteen, reframing the discussion of autism away from one of childhood. *Le papotin* was instead the foundation for a series of forms of *action culturelle* that included theater troupes, musical groups, and television productions; these were not distinct forms of therapy but rather methods to reveal and celebrate the diverse experiences and expressions of autism, as well as to inform readers on the variety of autistic arts in contemporary France. Here, the alliance between psychoanalysts and autistic persons suggested that forms of self-expression were vital manifestations of the value of autistic voices, especially adult ones that had been lost in the debates over autism in France.

One of the major patrons of *Le papotin* was Howard Buten, an American author and clown who lived in France and became an advocate for autistic persons during the 1970s. He founded an *institut médico-éducatif* in Saint Denis during the 1990s and had supported musical and theatrical programs for autistic individuals throughout his career. As an advocate, Buten questioned the binary tendencies that framed the autism debates in France and dismissed the emphasis on normality that governed the perception of autistic behaviors and often dehumanized the autistic population. In his 2003 work, *Il y a quelqu'un là-dedans* [There is someone in there], Buten asserted the negative impact of attempts to extinguish autistic behaviors that did no harm, but instead offered a benefit to the autistic individual, insisting that much of this effort was about the rigidity of social norms and attempts to eliminate autistic identity rather than mental wellness. Although he was tangentially connected to the world of psychoanalysis, Buten did not follow the same patterns as many other analysts and did not see autism as connected to schizophrenia or psychosis.[28] Moreover, he also saw challenges for autistic persons within the education sector, especially given the notion of social conditioning that operated inherently within that system to reify notions of normality. Autistic individuals struggled to navigate that system because of its punitive nature toward their behaviors and the lack of creativity in engaging with them.[29] Buten championed a more holistic approach that permitted autistic people to be self-expressive, especially those who were deemed low functioning, which also framed his interactions with *Le papotin*.

The emphasis on the arts as a form of therapeutic expression had several supporters in the French community, which again suggested a framework for understanding autism beyond its conception within childhood and for promoting acceptance of the autistic population. Many advocates argued that the challenges of autonomy, socialization, and community could be satisfied through the arts. Given the importance of the visual and plastic arts in French culture, the intersection of the two was a logical connection to make once advocates recognized the value in autistic art and embraced the ideal of inclusion that museums purported to represent. Working with the Louvre, advocates helped develop programs that recognized the challenges of the disabled population but could assist them in accessing the museum.[30] Efforts to integrate autistic adults into social life had vocal advocates who understood it not just as a form of therapy but also as a practice of belonging to the French community. While art therapy had been embraced by psychoanalysts since the 1950s for autistic children and championed by parents' associations beginning in the 1970s, the turn in the twenty-first century was more about supporting self-expression rather than using art as a method of analysis or therapy, even among some psychoanalysts.[31] The increased recognition of the need to integrate autistic adults signaled a more sophisticated understanding of autism that was developing beyond the limited bounds of the *bataille de l'autisme* that recognized the lifetime experience of autistic persons.

The New Militancy

Perhaps one of the most significant interventions from the autistic community in France was the publication of Hugo Horiot's *Autisme: J'accuse* in 2018, a polemical work that condemned the French history of marginalizing autistic persons.[32] Ruminating on his experiences and the contours of the autism debate in France, he focused on the processes of marginalization and exclusion that operated through the enforcement of normality that impacted the social acceptance of autistic individuals. Horiot had been the subject of Françoise Lefèvre's work from the late 1980s (see Chapter 4) and had become a writer himself in adulthood. His memoir *L'empereur, c'est moi* offered a vital counterpoint to her fictionalized portrayal of his childhood, at once a work of love, frustration, and discovery that illuminated his experience and put him at the center of the story. Horiot became a central voice in the twenty-first century through his advocacy for the inclusion of autistic voices in the discussion about treatment, education, and equality for autistic persons and his questioning the emphasis on norms inherent in the *bataille de l'autisme*, arguing against archaic practices that ignored the humanity of the autistic population and defined the French divergence. His publications signified a more direct approach that autistic persons adopted and helped to elevate the autistic perspective within the French public by detailing the specific challenges facing autistic individuals in France, including the lack of social support, the continued emphasis on harmful interventions and institutionalization, and their lower life expectancy.

He saw himself as part of a constellation of militant autistic persons who included Julie Dachez and Josef Schovanec, all autistic adults who offered new insights on the limitations of the historical discussions of autism, as well as Daniel Tammet, a prominent writer and critic who refused to be reduced to his autistic identity despite embracing his diagnosis. These militants hoped to find acceptance for all autistic individuals. They were in positions of influence that allowed them to impact the debate and present new insights to the French public, all appearing in the 2010s, with significant publications addressed directly to neurotypical readers that attained a visible media presence. Offering a different example of autism than that offered by professionals and parents, these militants symbolized further evidence of autism as a spectrum of experiences and behaviors, reinforcing it as a disability that needed acceptance rather than an illness needing elimination. Although he was critical of the psychoanalytic approach, Horiot did not support the behavioralist approach either, adding nuance and complexity that took this spectrum into account in the oft-Manichean debate about autism.

Horiot observed the development of extreme positions within the French debate in the twenty-first century, exemplified by either attempts by the National Assembly to outlaw psychoanalytic interventions outright in cases of autism or the continued support for institutionalization from the perspective of psychoanalysts rooted in the continued influence of Bettelheim.[33] He rejected both of these positions and presented a different perspective to the *bataille de l'autisme* that suggested that it was much an economic struggle as an ideological one, given the increasing national budgets earmarked for autism in France. Each group was fighting for greater portions of that budget. Horiot also lamented the continued need for autistic persons and their families to seek support and care in Belgium despite the national efforts and funding from the French government to address this situation. For him, it was about French society's lack of commitment to understanding the variety of autistic experiences and the continued pressure to institutionalize autistic individuals, to put them behind walls.[34] His evocative use of the expression *ghettoization* echoed the earlier sentiments of parents' associations from the 1970s, revealing the enduring stereotypes concerning autistic individuals and how social isolation continued into the new century.

Horiot served as an example of the autistic subject and object because he was central to the story of *Le petit prince cannibale*. In that text, discussed in Chapter 4, Horiot was portrayed as angry and aggressive, struggling within the French system, while Lefèvre received blame for her son's condition. Horiot wrote a sort of response to Lefèvre's story, *L'empereur, c'est moi*, in 2013, which offered his perspective on his childhood and the treatments he endured. He explained his love of stimming with his toy car's wheels and expressed confusion at the conclusions of psychoanalysts who attempted to interpret his behaviors as a reaction to traumas within his household.[35] Horiot's skepticism of professionals and their grasp of the situation illustrated their limits in comprehending his condition, while his reflections on his family's responses also pointed to their inability to understand him. The two factions within the politics of autism, for him, lacked the information that autistic people could provide. For example, Horiot recounted a visit to the therapist in which his frustration in the office, symbolized by his decision to kick the plastic castle there, was interpreted as an attack on his father, whereas for Horiot it was an expression of his displeasure with the therapist.[36] His voice and humor, combined with the bitterness concerning his treatment by professionals, pointed to the needed contribution that the autistic population could bring to the ongoing conversation about how French society should treat autistic people, both medically and socially.

Horiot's work served as an example of what Vivienne Orchard termed life-writing, an expression of narrative that presented a "contribution to the politics of knowledge," in this case autism, which had so far ignored the input of autistic individuals in France. For Orchard, Horiot's memoir itself was an expression of the politics of autism that also served as its context, while at the same time offering a counternarrative to the powerful myths surrounding autism.[37] In the same sense, *L'empereur* put the parents' memoir, such an important cornerstone of the autism debates, into a conversation that questioned the limits of how much parents spoke for their disabled children.[38] Horiot built on the commercial success of his memoir by becoming a critical figure in the autism debate as a public expert in autism rooted in his life-writing. He leaned more heavily into direct political engagement during the 2010s, culminating in the publication of *L'autisme: j'accuse* in 2018 and has continued since.

Along with Horiot, the myriad of autistic life stories demanded a reformulation of the conception of autism that moved it away from its emphasis on childhood while detailing the specific experiences of autistic childhood. For example, Joffrey Bouissac, an autistic individual from Strasbourg, published his biography in 2002 detailing his life in various facilities until he was eighteen. His memoir, drawn from a journal that he kept in 1998 as part of his therapy, was edited and published as an early manifestation of autistic literary self-expression in France, echoing works in anglophone countries by autistic authors such as Temple Grandin and Donna Williams, both of whom had been translated into French by the late 1990s.[39] Bouissac lived with his parents while receiving services at various *instituts medico-pédagogiques* (IMPs) in his region, enjoying his collection of Playmobil figures and sets and spending time with his parents. Recounting moments in his childhood, he explained his struggles with his disability and his emotional states, revealing anxieties about his fixations and repetitive behaviors as well as his struggles with depression.[40] Bouissac communicated his comfort within the familial space and his connection to his father and his frustrations with having to abandon his stimming behaviors and toys in adulthood. The book followed literary patterns that were similar to the narrative style of parent-centered works but offered the new perspective of an autistic child and their reflections on their treatment in highly emotive language that showed a young man who was not detached from the world or his family, but anxious about his place in the world because of his disability. His memoir offered insights into the human impact of the struggle over the meaning of autism and how he navigated IMPs, schools, and day hospitals as a teenager quickly approaching adulthood.

The work of Julie Dachez, who was not diagnosed until her twenties, signified another important intervention in the interpretation of autism in France, as she shared her thoughts and experiences in her blogs and her celebrated graphic novel, *La différence invisible*.[41] Her advocacy was significant not only because of its continued intervention in the autism debate in France but also because of her emphasis on the importance of recognizing the female experience of autism. The overwhelming image within the conception of autism in France (and elsewhere) was that of a young boy, and many prominent researchers had postulated autism as an expression of an extreme male brain because of social and behavioral characteristics associated with male behaviors.[42] The common association of autism with men has often obscured the population of autistic women, although some of the first self-advocates to publish their views were women. Dachez was one of the first autistic women in France to be vocal about her experience through her publications and her advocacy work.

Dachez's 2018 *Dans ta bulle! Les autistes ont la parole: Écoutons-les!* [In your bubble: Autistic people have the floor: Let's listen to them!] expanded the conversation that Horiot had started in his work as she argued for the "emancipation of autists" by telling her life story as well as those of fellow autistic adults.[43] She noted that she was uninterested in the origins of autism, which had taken up so much of the discussion, and instead wanted to question the notion of normativity and its cultural subjectivity, extolling autistic persons and their allies to follow the path that homosexual activists took in challenging psychology to end the pathologizing of sexual orientation.[44] She also pointed out how the word autistic had become a slur within certain cultures (including French culture), showing another challenge to equality outside medical pathologies via social discrimination. While much of the debate that has been discussed in France hinged on medical issues, Dachez argued that autism should be understood as a social question rather than a medical one, identifying the direction that militant autistic individuals wanted the debate to take in the twenty-first century. From her perspective, the expansion of the parameters of the debate demanded the inclusion of autistic persons as participants. She observed that the process of defining normativity has been dominated by neurotypical individuals, following earlier historical patterns of minority subjugation, and autistic persons challenged neurotypical behaviors and beliefs.

As a social psychology researcher, Dachez straddled the line between the medical field and the social world of autism, especially after receiving her diagnosis at the age of twenty-seven. While understanding the struggles autistic people faced from a personal perspective, she wanted to incorporate her knowledge of social psychology to articulate the shared challenges that autistic individuals experienced in France through a series of interviews with other autistic adults in her book *Dans ta bulle*. Interspersed with her assessment of these interviews was Dachez's recounting of her own experiences and how they led her to her current militancy and political position in her quest to be herself within French society, something she wanted for all of the autistic population in France. While often aligning with parents' associations efforts, such as increased support for education and services as well as the emphasis on improved diagnosis, Dachez, along with the other militants, articulated a new perspective that accounted for the experience of autism, including the social treatment of the autistic population, in a broad manner that included all kinds of autistic persons, even as many militants considered themselves *aspergers*, a term that had fallen out of use in anglophone countries.[45]

Dachez also published a celebrated graphic novel detailing her struggles as an autistic adult to work, live, and interact socially while being judged as different by her peers. *La différence invisible* [*Invisible Differences*] showed how Marguerite (the character who represented Dachez) attempted to understand social norms such as the dress code at work while navigating her challenges with sounds and smells in the office, much to the chagrin of her coworkers. The artist, Mademoiselle Caroline, provided visual representations of ritualized behaviors associated with autism through the replication of panels in the opening portion of the story.[46]

Marguerite sought answers to explain her behaviors, especially given that the rigidity she needed impacted relationships with her neurotypical boyfriend and colleagues. She researched her behaviors online and found a community that shared many of her struggles, which was not very well known in France, and wondered if she was autistic despite never receiving a diagnosis.[47] In her attempt to engage with professionals to explore her autism, she encountered a psychologist who dismissed her self-diagnosis and instead inquired about her childhood.[48] Marguerite eventually was able to secure an appointment with the Centre de ressources autisme after a long wait and received a diagnosis of autism (Asperger syndrome).

Her life was transformed afterward because she had a new understanding of her habits and behaviors and why she felt different. Marguerite had a sense of peace, but found her interactions with others still a challenge because of their own misconceptions about autism, based on stereotypes and media presentations such as *Rain Man*.[49] Like other self-advocates, Dachez found a community online and eventually joined by publishing her own blog about her experiences.[50] She studied the literature on autism and Asperger syndrome but found it wanting, so she eventually returned to school for graduate studies in psychology, where she conducted research on autism. Her diagnosis was the catalyst for her embrace of her identity, and she finally accepted herself and rejected the notion of changing her behaviors. The appendix of the book gave a brief synopsis of autism and how the divergence had created much of the misunderstanding that was prevalent in French society. Perhaps one of the more pertinent elements of her story was her recognition of other invisible disabilities in her environment and the need to accommodate rather than alter nonnormative behaviors. Dachez articulated much of the philosophy of neurodivergence without referencing the term explicitly, and her work attracted the attention of audiences beyond France, especially in her portrayal of the gendered experience of disability that would influence other autistic women to share their stories.

Another vocal militant from the autistic community in the twenty-first century was Josef Schovanec, whose *Je suis à l'est* [I am in the east] appeared in 2012 during the *grande cause nationale* focused on autism. Schovanec, who identifies as an *aspergers*, met with parents' groups and other stakeholders to present to them an autistic perspective and hoped to have interested parties rethink their entrenched perspectives on autism. Much like Horiot and Dachez, Schovanec decided against defining autism in his book, instead choosing to tell his life story as a method of providing one possible definition. He became a media figure and public presence in the autism debates, participating in multiple conferences, appearing in television programs, and continuing to publish about autism while supporting other autistic voices. In *Je suis à l'est*, he chronicled his experiences as a mute and how he and his parents navigated the French system, which diagnosed him as psychotic. His parents, like many of those in associations, fought against authorities in the 1980s and 1990s to have Schovanec educated within French schools, which he recounted in his experiences of alienation and marginalization there and the methods of regimentation that did not align with his autistic views.[51] Moreover, like Dachez, he spoke of the pressures of conformity and his awareness of his disconnection from his classmates, which perpetuated their stereotypes when he failed to conform.

Schovanec's memoir emphasized his experience of exclusion and how that shaped his mental state, always seeking to understand how to align his behaviors with social norms. While he understood that he did not think like his classmates, he lacked the language to articulate this difference until 2001, when he met with a psychiatrist who prescribed medications. Although that did not profoundly transform his experience, it introduced him to the world of psychology and its history, leading him to study the works of Louis Althusser and Michel Foucault, as well as the history of Antonin Artaud during his incarceration in asylums. Schovanec became interested in the classification of disorders and antipsychotic medicines, which he understood through his interactions with various professionals.[52] After working with a series of psychologists and psychoanalysts, he received the diagnosis of Asperger syndrome. Although he wished to continue to take various medications, he was eventually cut off from his prescriptions and struggled with withdrawal.

Schovanec embraced his new identity and sought to understanding its meaning, turning again to the history of autism to try to articulate what it meant to be autistic in French society. He likened the social treatment of autistic persons to that of other marginalized groups, including immigrants and the disabled, as a result of the autistic struggles against prejudice in social situations.[53] Reflecting on his own identity, he noted that his autism was constructed socially by neurotypical populations based on their beliefs concerning proper behaviors. Trained as a philosopher, Schovanec released several works engaging with his experience as a new form of subjectivity and argued for the social acceptance of neurodiversity. Moreover, Schovanec became a critical media figure, contributing to numerous books that emphasized the autistic perspective, participating in several television series and conferences discussing the situation of autism in France, hosting his own popular travel show on Europe 1, and acting as a public representative for autistic persons and the greater disabled community.

Unlike Schovanec, Daniel Tammet was reluctant to engage with the autism debate, despite his social status. His response suggested that the approach of the more visible militants was not the only possibility open to the new wave of autistic writers. Although he was quite renowned for his powerful mnemonic abilities, Tammet migrated to France in the early 2010s and became a celebrated writer and thinker, thanks largely to his works about religion. He was not interested in his autistic identity to the same degree as his fellow militants, seeking instead to downplay its importance to his work while not denigrating or denying it.[54] Tammet's celebrity made him a significant figure in the militant movement, even if he did not actively engage in it. Tammet's approach was to show that his autism was but one part of his identity. But the visibility and acceptance of the militants signaled the beginning of a new conversation about autism that was led by autistic individuals.

In the wake of Dachez, other autistic females spoke up in celebrating their autistic identity, most notably the visual artist and writer Nathalie Fougeras, who published her *La marquise aux pieds nus* in 2019, a combination of biography and her social observations in the form of a glossary in the second half of the book. *La marquise* detailed Fougeras's childhood and growing up within a religious sect that her mother had joined in the south of France during the late 1970s.[55] By the early 1980s, Fougeras had been taken out of school and struggled at times with communication, although she rejected her mother's efforts to have her join the religious community and become a wife. Fougeras's idiosyncrasies and struggles were not diagnosed, however, and she left home in her late teens to pursue studies in art history. She provided little discussion of her condition during the narrative, which was not surprising given that she did not receive her diagnosis until she was forty-seven but did not retroactively attempt to assess her childhood through the prism of autism once she was aware. "It [autism] did not change the person I have always been, it explained on the other hand in a detailed fashion why am I that way."[56]

In her book's second part, Fougeras offered her reflections on what she saw as aspects of her autistic experience, while at the same time avoiding defining autism. For her, there was a simple reason: autism was an individual thing, an interiority that was little understood by professionals. She noted that most French professionals were operating within an outdated framework that did little to help autistic persons in an effective manner.[57] Her view echoed that of the militants of the neurodiversity moment, and while she was less confrontational than the other militants, she nevertheless saw *La marquise* as a didactic work to teaching others about difference and acceptance. She used a public exhibition of her paintings in 2019 to announce her condition months before the publication of her book.[58] Like the other vocal advocates, Fougeras shifted the discussion of autism definitively away from childhood, arguing instead for acceptance and accommodation of new forms of thinking rather than its continued pathologization.

The emergence of autistic militant voices in the 2010s added a corrective to the ongoing debates concerning autism through their examples of autistic contributions to French society. While they often self-identified as *aspergers*, they all recognized the variety of experiences of autism—often emphasizing that the concept of a spectrum implied the existence of autisms—and argued for the importance of inclusion and acceptance of adults and children, speaking and nonspeaking, high-functioning and otherwise. Their stories shared the frustration and alienation they encountered as young people as well as their struggles within families, but these challenges did not define their autistic lives. Rejecting the narrative of illness for autism, these voices revealed how the lack of participation from the autistic community had shaped the public awareness of autism as well as the medical position that had been so entrenched since the 1950s. Yet even with the increased vocal presence of autistic individuals in the discussion, the debates continued between parents and professionals because of ongoing practices and increased government attention that raised the stakes. The individual voices were not enough to end the debate, leading autistic persons to organize into associations that could engage the debate at a practical level using the organizational structures that had defined so much of the history of autism in France to this point to address the French divergence and potentially end the *bataille*.

Organizations for Autistic Identity

While the individual activists were crucial to the emergence of a new discourse on autism in France, new associations also played a key role, especially given that associations and political lobbying had become so central to the autism debate in the twenty-first century. Several associations formed as a result of inspiration from the wave of militants—for example, the Collectif pour la liberté d'expression des autistes (CLE Autistes) was established in 2018 following criticism against Horiot's book from parents' associations.[59] CLE Autistes, organized and run by autistic individuals, criticized the privileged position of parents in discussions of autism policy and advocated for greater input from the autistic population on both social and medical policies. It was not alone: several other self-advocacy associations were founded to take up the ideas of the militants and put them into practice. The increased engagement of the autistic population revealed that autistic persons hoped to take a leadership role in the discussion of autism after decades of being silent and conceding the discussion to parents and professionals.

CLE Autistes published its manifesto, "Nous, autistes, ne nous tairons plus [We autists will no longer be silent]," in 2019, outlining its critique of the expertise of parents and professionals and how that expertise has been used as a method to silence autistic persons from public expression or to control the discourse.[60] The manifesto highlighted the aspirations of the association and its embrace of the ideas of the neurodiversity movement, seeking inclusion, deinstitutionalization, equality, and the medicalization of disability. CLE Autistes questioned the push to abandon psychoanalysis completely in the treatment of autism in France as an overcorrection to the criticisms put forth by parents' associations and the emergence of private care subsidized by the French government. These approaches limited the options for autistic persons to receive care and gave parents overwhelming authority to dictate care without input from those affected by the decisions. For the association, it was a method of privatizing care that should be available to all autistic persons in France in a manner that serves the population equitably. The collective believed that the efforts to serve parents' associations had exacerbated the inherent inequities that disabled people already faced in France, despite the government's efforts to address the issues.

Other associations, such as the Collectif des 39, developed alliances between autistic persons and analysts with the hope of psychoanalysis serving as a method of liberation and understanding, building on the revolutionary aspirations that developed after the Events of 1968 in France. Rejecting state efforts to limit psychoanalysis in the treatment of autism, the Collectif emphasized its value in connecting thought, speech, and the subject as complex individuals who could not be defined by a diagnosis.[61] The Collectif revealed the influence of another international movement that developed outside France but connected with many of the cultural ideas operant in the late twentieth century: Mad Pride. The Mad Pride movement developed in the United States and Great Britain in the late 1960s as part of the larger phenomena of antipsychiatry and deinstitutionalization and their connection to the emergence of a New Left movement there.[62] The Collectif took the ideas of the Mad Pride movement and applied them to challenge the ascent of cognitive psychology and the notion of operant conditioning of autistic individuals, which were interpreted as methods of control. For the group, psychoanalysis offered a humane method of recognizing the individual nature of autism, and therefore the Collectif rejected government efforts to limit its use by legislative fiat.[63] A grouping of analysts and autistic individuals, the association was challenging the authority of parents' associations to dictate national policy and undermine psychoanalysis.

One of the impetuses for the continued press against psychoanalysis was the practice of *le packing*, which involves wrapping the autist person in cold, wet towels and then binding them in blankets to help keep the body warm. The goal of the approach was to help integrate sensory disorders and make the patient more aware of their own body using extreme temperatures in a controlled environment, although there were psychodynamic elements that constituted parts of the rationale of *le packing* that tangentially linked the practice to psychoanalysis. The method had been used to treat other disorders, including catatonia, anorexia, and self-injury, but its use in cases of autism elicited controversy beginning in the early 2000s in France with its denouncement from parents' associations.[64] Proponents saw the technique as a last resort in cases that would otherwise require heavy doses of neuroleptics and its efficacy was being studied carefully.[65] Nevertheless, parents' associations launched public campaigns against *le packing*, combining political lobbying with short public service announcements to increase awareness about the practice. For example, in a short film from Vaincre l'autisme, *le packing* was presented in the manner of a horror film in which disabled children were tortured by professionals, equating the technique to waterboarding.[66] Yet parents' associations found allies among the militants in seeking a moratorium on the practice in France despite the efforts of proponents to maintain it as a possible intervention. Horiot, for example, equated *le packing* to other forms of marginalization that led to the shorter life expectancy of autistic persons in France.[67] In challenging *le packing*, many autistic individuals found common cause in pressing for government intervention and the state's alleged favoritism toward psychoanalysis despite its limited connection to the practice.

Other associations were alliances of parents and autistic persons, such as Autism'Aide 35, founded in 2013 in Ille-et-Vilaine to promote inclusion and recognize the perspective of autistic individuals. Inspired by the ideas of Schovanec and Tammet, the collective emphasized the importance of the acceptance of autism and the right to be different. This association, however, did not see parents' associations as problematic in the same way; rather, they were another resource to help autistic persons obtain financial and political support for education, job training, and housing. Autism'Aide 35 rejected the idea of psychogenic origins of autism, favoring the organic theory instead.[68] The association's mission was to inform parents of the most current information on autism and to promote acceptance in the classroom, in the workspace, and in social settings. Although a regional association, Autism'Aide 35 worked with national networks to advocate for policies to improve the social treatment of autistic persons by working with other parents' associations and the associational methods they had developed since the 1960s by demanding the recognition of the educational and labor rights of the autistic population.

Still others, such as *Le papotin*, continued to operate and support autistic expression. The development of organizations with roles for autistic persons blurred many of the boundaries that the conflict between parents' associations and professionals had formed since the 1950s. Autistic individuals aligned with both sides yet also offered insights on the impact of each approach. The visibility of autistic persons in the French media provided new models of understanding autism as a lifelong disability that impacted an increasing number of French people. The appearance of adults engaged with their autistic identity challenged the entrenched stereotypes that had developed out of the French reliance on psychoanalysis, and while many autistic persons found value with the ideas of analysis as a method of expressing holistic care, others saw common ground with parents' associations and the lobbying model they developed in the 2000s as a method of advocating for autistic rights. While the twenty-first century saw the continued expansion of the state into the autism debates, it also was a period in which autistic people could freely provide testimony of their experiences and opinions on how they were marginalized medically and socially.

Their self-expression demanded a reconsideration of autism outside the parameters established by professionals and parents, and the impact of militants speaking loudly within the French discourse was to inspire other autistic persons to organize, publish, protest, and express themselves as a challenge to normativity and the social order that had marginalized and exiled them. With greater representation, autistic individuals influenced the discussion of treatment and inclusion in a direct way that also contested the expertise of parents and professionals, each group struggling against the other to reify their position of the proper treatment of autism (and, by extension, autistic persons). The militants' stories also focused on their adulthood and how autism shaped their identity and success, focusing attention away from childhood and reminding audiences of the lifelong experience of the disorder. The belated appearance of the autistic population forced a rethinking of expertise that would reshape the politics of autism and throw into question the persistence of the French divergence as they explained the impact of those politics on all ages of their population.

NOTES

1. "Déclaration de M. François Fillon, Premier ministre, sur la reconnaissance de l'autisme comme grande cause nationale et les grandes orientations d'un nouveau plan autisme, à Paris le 9 février 2012," https://www.vie-publique.fr/discours/184371-declaration-de-m-francois-fillon-premier-ministre-sur-la-reconnaissan.
2. Le livre noir de la psychanalyse: Vivre, penser et aller mieux sans Freud, Catherine Meyer, ed. (Paris: Éditions des Arènes, 2005).

3. Catherine Meyer, "Pourquoi un livre noir de la psychanalyse?" in *Le livre noir de la psychanalyse: Vivre, penser et aller mieux sans Freud*, Catherine Meyer, ed. (Paris: Éditions des Arènes, 2005), 8.
4. Jean Cottraux, "Chronique d'une génération: Comment la psychanalyse a pris le pouvoir en France," in *Le livre noir*, 250 and 253.
5. Catherine Barthélémy, "Comprendre et soigner autrement: À propos de l'autisme," in *Le livre noir*, 552.
6. Graciela C. Crespin, "Introduction," in *Autismes: Etat des lieux du soin*, ed. Graciela C. Crespin (Paris: L'Harmattan, 2006), 9.
7. Émile Jalley, *La psychanalyse et la psychologie: Aujourd'hui en France* (Paris: Vuibert, 2006), 11.
8. Bernard Brusset, "Une lecture du *Livre noir de la psychanalyse*," *Revue française de psychanalyse* 70, no. 2 (2006): 571.
9. Serge Tisseron, "'*Livre noir de la psychanalyse*,' la main dans le sac," *Le Monde*, October 5, 2005.
10. Élisabeth Roudinesco, *Pourquoi tant de haine? Anatomie du* Le livre noir de la psychanalyse (Paris: Narvarin, 2005).
11. INSERM, *Psychothérapie: Trois approaches évaluées* (Paris: Éditions INSERM, 2004), 237.
12. "'Psys': L'inserm se dit 'choqué' par le désaveu du minister," *Le Monde*, February 9, 2005.
13. Céline Borelle, "The Paradoxical Place of Psychiatry in the Administration of Disability: Dealing with the Reframing of Autism from a Psychiatric to an Educative Issue in the Concrete Making of a Target Public," in *Creating Target Publics for Welfare Policies: A Comparative and Multi-level Approach*, ed. Lorenzo Barrault-Stella and Pierre-Edouard Weill (Germany: Springer International Publishing, 2018), 116.
14. *Le mur: La psychanalyse à l'épreuve de l'autisme*, directed by Sophie Robert (Lille, France: Ocean Invisible Productions, 2011).
15. Jean-François Marmion, "Alexandre Stevens: Pourquoi j'ai porté plainte contre Sophie Robert," *Sciences humaines*, March 7, 2012, https://www.scienceshumaines.com/alexandre-stevens-pourquoi-j-ai-porte-plainte-contre-sophie-robert_fr_28636.html.
16. Élisabeth Algava, Kilian Bloch, and Isabelle Robert-Bobée, "Families in France in 2020: 25% Single-Parent Families, 21% Large Families," *INSEE Focus* 249, September 12, 2021, https://www.insee.fr/en/statistiques/5428547#:~:text=n%C2%B0%20249-,Families%20in%20France%20in%202020%3A%2025%25%20single%2D,parent%20families%2C%2021%25%20large%20families&text=In%20France%2C%20in%202020%2C%208.0,one%20minor%20child%20at%20home.
17. Isabelle Courcy and Catherine des Rivières, "'From Cause to Cure': A Qualitative Study on Contemporary Forms of Mother Blaming Experienced by Mothers of Young Children with Autism Spectrum Disorder," *Journal of Family Social Work* 20, no. 3 (2017): 245.
18. Laure Mentzel, "Autisme: La psychanalyse au pied du mur," *Le Monde*, January 13, 2012.
19. "Autisme: Trois psys répondent aux accusations du film «*Le mur*»," https://www.collectifpsychiatric.fr/?p=2832.

20. Loriane Brunessaux, "À propos du documentaire «*Le mur*»," *L'information psychiatrique* 88 (2012): 177.
21. Eric Laurent, *La bataille de l'autisme: De la clinique à la politique* (Paris: Navarin/Le champ freudien, 2012), 9.
22. Ibid., 110.
23. Ibid., 198.
24. Sarah Pripas-Kapit, "Historicizing Jim Sinclair's 'Don't Mourn for Us': A Cultural and Intellectual History of Neurodiversity's First Manifesto," in *Autistic Community and the Neurodiversity Movement*, ed. Steven K. Kapp (New York: Palgrave Macmillan, 2020), 23–29.
25. Brigitte Chamak, "Autism and Social Movements in France: A Comparative Perspective," in *Worlds of Autism: Across the Spectrum of Neurological Difference*, ed. Joyce Davidson and Michael Orsini (Minneapolis: University of Minnesota Press, 2013), 247.
26. "Notre visite à l'Élysée," *Le papotin* 21 (March–April 2002): 3–5.
27. Moïse Assouline, "*Le papotin* et les politiques," *Le papotin* 21 (March–April 2002): 2.
28. Howard Buten, *Il y a quelqu'un là-dedans* (Paris: Odile Jacob, 203), 13.
29. Ibid., 133–34.
30. Catherine Treese-Daquin, *Autisme et culture: Balades au Musée du Louvre* (Grasse, France: Autisme diffusion, 2016), 32.
31. For example, see Jean-Pierre Royol, *La cause de l'autiste* (Paris: L'Harmattan, 2019), 27.
32. Hugo Horiot, Autisme: J'accuse (Saint-Amand-Montrond, France: L'Iconoclaste, 2018).
33. Ibid., 28–30.
34. Ibid., 41–43.
35. Hugo Horiot, *The Emperor, c'est moi*, trans. Linda Coverdale (New York: Seven Stories Press, 2015).
36. Ibid., 50–51.
37. Vivienne Orchard, "*Autisme, j'accuse!* Life-writing, Autism and Politics in the Work of Hugo Horiot," *French Cultural Studies* 30, no. 3 (2019): 258–59.
38. Jonathyne Briggs, "From Collaboration to Resistance: The Family Dynamic in Autism Literature in Contemporary France," *Contemporary European History* 32 (2023): 268.
39. Temple Grandin, *Penser en images: Et autre témoignages sur l'autisme*, trans. Virginie Schaefer (Paris: Grand livre du mois, 1997); and Donna Williams, *Si on me touche je n'existe plus: Le témoignage exceptionnel d'une jeune autiste*, trans. Fabienne Gérard (Paris: Grand livre du mois, 1992). Similarly, Katia Rohde's *L'enfant hérisson* was a work produced through facilitated communication (FC) that detailed her thoughts about her life and her condition, but Bouissac's was the first to have confirmed authorship, given the continued controversies surrounding FC; see Katia Rohde, *L'enfant hérisson: Autobiographie d'une autiste* (Paris: Imago, 1999). Another example of a biography told through FC is Claire B.'s *Ouvrir la nuit pour te dire*, which shares many similar themes to Rohde's work. See Claire B., *Ouvrir la nuit pour te dire* (La Chapelle Gonaguet, France: Paroles de vie, 2003).
40. Joffrey Bouissac, *Qui j'aurai été: Journal d'un adolescent autiste* (Colmar, France: Autisme Alsace, 2002), 45.

41. Julie Dachez and Mademoiselle Caroline, Invisible Differences" A Story of Aspergers, Adulting, and Living a Life in Full Color, translated by Edward Gauvin (Portland, OR: Oni Press, 2020).
42. Simon Baron-Cohen, "The Extreme Male Brain Theory," *Trends in Cognitive Science* 6, no. 6 (2002): 248–54. Baron-Cohen's theory is that male brains are designed to operate systematically while female brains operate empathetically, with autistic persons having more pronounced male behavioral traits. His thesis came under greater scrutiny in the 2010s among researchers questioning the framework that divided male and female behavioral traits and the alleged lack of empathy in autistic individuals. See, for example, Liza van Eijk and Brendan P. Zietsch, "Testing the Extreme Male Brain Hypothesis: Is Autism Spectrum Disorder Associated with a More Male-Typical Brain?" *Autism Research: Official Journal of the International Society for Autism Research* 14, no. 8 (2021): 1597–608, which suggests that brain size might be a more significant explanation than the expression of male behaviors.
43. Julie Dachez, *Dans ta bulle! Les autistes ont la parole: Écoutons-les!* (Vanves, France: Marabout/Hachette, 2018), 19.
44. Ibid., 24.
45. The *DSM-5* eliminated the diagnosis of Asperger syndrome, replacing it with autism spectrum disorder, in 2013.
46. Dachez and Caroline, *Invisible Differences*, 64.
47. Ibid., 95.
48. Ibid., 102–3.
49. Ibid., 131–32.
50. http://emoiemoietmoi.over-blog.com/.
51. Josef Schovanec, *Je suis à l'est: Savant et autiste un témonage unique* (Paris: Plon, 2012), 32.
52. Ibid., 86.
53. Ibid., 181–82.
54. Daniel Tammet, *Born on a Blue Day: Inside the Extraordinary Mind of an Autistic Savant* (New York: Free Press, 2007).
55. Nathalie Fougeras, *La marquise aux pieds nus* (Saint-Etienne, France: Faralonn, 2019).
56. Ibid., 100.
57. Ibid., 134.
58. "Nathalie Fougeras, artiste peintre contemporain: «Nos differences méritent d'être reconnues comme des valeurs ajoutées»," *Le havre*, January 11, 2019, https://www.lehavre.fr/actualites/nathalie-fougeras-artiste-peintre-contemporain-nos-differences-meritent-detre-reconnues.
59. "CLE Autistes: Qui sommes nous," CLE Autistes, accessed May 17, 2023, https://asso.cle-autistes.fr/qui-sommes-nous/.
60. CLE Autistes, "Nous, autistes, ne nous tairons plus," *Médiapart*, April 2, 2019, reprinted at https://cle-autistes.fr/nous-autistes/.
61. Collectif des 39, "Un mouvement pour la psychiatrie," Collectif Psychiatrie, accessed May 18, 2023, https://www.collectifpsychiatrie.fr/?cat=13.
62. Nick Crossley, *Contesting Psychiatry: Social Movements in Mental Health* (New York: Routledge, 2006), 182.
63. Collectif des 39. "Vers un solstice d'hiver pour l'autisme en France?," Collectif Psychiatrie, accessed May 23, 2023, https://www.collectifpsychiatrie.fr/?p=8495.

64. Brigitte Chamak, "Lobbying by Association: The Case of Autism and the Controversy over Packing Therapy in France," *Social Science and Medicine* 230 (2019): 258.
65. Catherine Vincent, "Autisme: La technique du 'packing', enjeu d'un violent conflit," *Le Monde*, February 16, 2012, https://www.lemonde.fr/societe/article/2012/02/16/autisme-la-technique-du-packing-enjeu-d-un-violent-conflit_1644322_3224.html; and Stéphany Gardier, "Le packing, une méthode contestée pour traiter l'autisme ou des psychoses," *Le figaro*, January 12, 2015, https://sante.lefigaro.fr/actualite/2015/01/12/23248-packing-methode-contestee-pour-traiter-lautisme-psychoses.
66. Vaincre l'autisme, "Packing … le film," https://www.youtube.com/watch?v=4ghYPnXiETQ. See also Vaincre l'autisme, *Position scientifique contre la psychanalyse appliquée à l'autisme* (Paris: Vaincre l'autisme, 2016), 6.
67. Horiot, *L'autisme*, xx.
68. Autism'Aide 35, "L'association," Autism'Aide 35, accessed May 18, 2023, https://www.autismaide35.com/qui-sommes-nous-.

CONCLUSION

A New Age of Autism?

The French prime minister Édouard Philippe announced France's fourth autism plan in April 2018, accompanied by the slogan "Change the situation." One of the commitments of the plan was "to put science back at the heart of public policy concerning autism by endowing France with research excellence."[1] The plan earmarked 334 million euros to address the issue and established a collaborative group drawn from several ministries to assess needs from numerous perspectives. However, like previous plans, the strategy focused primarily on early interventions for children, special education, and the recognition of the important role of parental expertise, which threw into question how much the situation would change in France. Despite all the efforts to respond to autism that the French state had enacted, the struggles of autistic persons remained profound, especially in terms of diagnoses and long-term care; Sophie Cluzel, the minister of state for disabled people, observed in the introduction to the plan that the situation had led to social isolation and discrimination against this population.[2] The sentiments of militants were that many autistic persons were still undiagnosed thanks to the stereotypical perceptions of autism that had calcified during the nearly seventy-year debate about its origins and meaning, which did not capture the variety of experiences and situations that each autistic individual had. In France, that debate was framed by psychoanalysis for the entire span, thanks to its significance in French intellectual culture and its continued ability to defend its privileged position in French psychology.

However, even as many children lacked adequate treatment for decades, the continued need to recognize adult populations was the challenge facing autistic persons in the twenty-first century, in particular those who remained undiagnosed. A France 24 report in 2023 noted the ongoing delay of diagnosis for many autistic adults, keeping them from accessing important resources to aid in their social integration; some experienced waits of years before receiving access to a diagnosis, despite rhetoric to address this shortfall from the French government.[3] While the 2018 plan recognized the need to support adults, the primary energy was still directed at children and attuned to the needs of their families, despite the overwhelming majority of autistic population being adults; the Haute authorité de santé suggested that the total number of autistic individuals in France was seven

Perpetual Children. Jonathyne Briggs, Oxford University Press. © Oxford University Press (2025).
DOI: 10.1093/9780197683002.003.0008

hundred thousand, with nearly six hundred thousand over the age of twenty.[4] These estimates also reveal that the lack of diagnosis remained a barrier to addressing the reality of the size and nature of the population in France. Many self-advocates stressed the importance of diagnosis in helping them to understand their experiences better and get access to aid, although this was not without complications. In an analysis of a survey of French autistic individuals in the early 2020s who had received a diagnosis, Raven Bureau and Céline Clément noted that reactions to the process included little support for patients due to the reality of the psychological environment and the stigma of disability. Bureau and Clément's observations revealed how the French divergence impacted this experience in contrast to anglophone examples they used for comparison, especially regarding attitudes toward disability in France.[5] Even with attention given to the situation, the variation of resources available to autistic persons illuminated the arrested transition between psychoanalytically oriented services and cognitive and behavioral approaches in contemporary France and how that gulf impacted the delivery of services to the autistic population.

Moreover, international news coverage of autism in France emphasized how the French had fallen behind the rest of the world in terms of its treatment and understanding of the disorder, pointing to the negative consequences of the divergence, which were echoed in the sentiments of the Fourth Autism Plan. The rhetoric of state efforts signaled an acceptance of the French divergence as a digression from the forms of intervention and acceptance that had defined other nations' efforts and indicated that it was vital that the French state help the nation catch up with others. This type of language suggested that the influence of psychoanalysis on conceptions of autism might have been on the wane in the twenty-first century, but proponents remained steadfast in their beliefs of the value and need for thinking outside the orthodoxy of behavioral psychology, which had made inroads in French academic and research centers. The emphasis on children and parents in the outline of the plan pointed to the fact that parents' associations had been somewhat successful in shifting the conversation after years of struggling against the influence of psychoanalysts dominating the discourse and now had a seat at the policy table. However, the continued emphasis on families and children also revealed that the foundations of defining autism established by analysts in the 1950s remained in place, with family as the site of intervention. Autism was something primarily found in childhood, and while increasing numbers of autistic adults were identified, services remained primarily directed at autistic children and their caregivers. This emphasis on childhood served to further marginalize the autistic community and diminished the role of autistic persons in social engagement by undermining a complex understanding of autism.

Associations welcomed the new plan with their usual apprehension, noting the failure of the French government to deliver on earlier promises built into previous plans and legal victories by autistic individuals. The Union nationale des associations de parents et amis de personnes handicapées mentales, still a powerful lobbying organization, offered a critique of Philippe's proclamation by reminding members of the lack of progress in fulfilling the requirements from earlier efforts such as the Veil Plan in 1994 or the outcome of the Autism-Europe case from 2004. Associations did not see the newest iteration of the French plan as anything other than more of the status quo, despite the changed language that recognized the issues associations had been pressing for since the 1980s. Other groups such as Autisme France argued that the newest plan failed to address the diagnosis gap that made services difficult to access, never mind the hopes for autistic persons to validate their own experiences. SOS Autisme noted the lack of support in the plan for job training to provide adults with labor skills that would allow them to enter the workforce as part of their integration and acceptance in society. As many autistic self-advocates experienced, diagnosis was transformational in helping them navigate social challenges by providing a framework to understand themselves. Autism had become as much a social identity embraced by autistic people as one imposed on them by professionals, thanks to the growing stature of advocates and the continued presence of associations in the debate.

The parameters of the debate continued to shift as a result of the increasing activism of autistic persons and the global perspective of nongovernmental organizations that were critical of France's divergence. The globalization of the issue of autism and the ongoing situation with Belgian facilities being an option for treatment placed the French situation in transnational terms. The medical exodus to southern Belgium for many French families led to the development of new facilities that have been subsidized by the French state while governed by Belgian norms. The environment of discrimination has led some autistic adults, including Josef Schovanec and Hugo Horiot, to leave France for Belgium; in Schovanec's opinion, Belgium provided a more inclusive and accepting society for disabled people.[6] The opportunity for exile provided an option for French individuals with the financial means and ability to leave. However, the COVID-19 pandemic of 2020 presented a challenge to this situation and the need to receive medical care abroad, with limitations to movement leading to further pressure on the French government to solve the issue domestically.[7] However, movement on addressing the autism situation saw little change, despite the promises of the national plan. The United Nations' Committee on the Rights of Persons with Disabilities and the Council of Europe ruled against France in 2021 and 2023, respectively, for its failure to recognize the human rights of disabled people and for not providing the services promised in past intervention plans.[8] These legal decisions echoed previous ones concerning France's treatment of autistic populations, and earlier responses to them suggested the limits of such findings on changing the situation and willingness of the French state to respond to these concerns.

In the Fourth Plan, much of the policy change and rhetoric remained embedded in the notion of the family as the logical driver of autistic care, which illustrates that continuities throughout the debates in the latter half of the twentieth century did not fully turn the conversation away from the role of the family in the treatment of autism. While mother blaming had waned as a social practice, autistic individuals were still primarily and culturally understood as children and autism as a disorder of childhood development. Even with more adults in the autistic population in France, the state persisted in its focus on children. The link between autism and childhood persisted in policymaking and medical practice despite the demographic reality of adulthood and autism as a lifelong disorder that affected people in different ways, again suggesting the influence of psychoanalysis in establishing this tendency through its enduring cultural power in France. Moreover, by keeping the issue focused on families and children, the French state downplayed the individual rights of autistic adults to receive proper care and social support to allow for their inclusion.

Yet families still faced frustrations in terms of care, despite the national attention given to autism. One example was in the case of Georgio Loiseau, the mayor of Poses who launched a hunger strike in May 2023 to protest the inability of his son Eyles to attend school because he had aged out of the special education program. Instead, the only option was for Eyles to continue his education through a distance education program that kept him at home. Loiseau pointed to promises the state had made about the situation and how the reality facing autistic individuals, even the children the plan focused on, illustrated how far the French still had to go to address the shortcomings in the system.[9] His nine-day protest and the attention it received through social media again reified the role of parents as primary advocates, no doubt reinforced by Loiseau's success in getting Eyles placed in a program in September 2023 and addressing members of National Assembly to discuss the issues.[10] While Loiseau succeeded in guaranteeing the creation of 135 adult spaces in programs in Eure, the situation required a dramatic intervention of parents and associations to pressure authorities despite the changes in the rhetoric and the efforts of self-advocates to change the conversation.

Another important element of the Fourth Plan was reintroducing the issues that had led to the Accoyer Amendment in 2003, basically establishing a legal contrast between the scientific elements of cognitive, behavioral, and neuropsychology and the philosophical and rhetorical aspects of psychoanalysis. The emphasis on science as part of the state's research harkened back to the earlier debates over psychoanalysis that dominated the *bataille de l'autisme* in the 1990s and 2000s, with analysts successfully pushing back against it then. Proponents saw the support of science as evidence of the assertion of medical power and classification as norms and the ascent of human management, all in contrast to the exploratory, philosophical, and oppositional nature of psychoanalysis and its humanist approach.[11] Others argued for the clinical efficacy of psychoanalysis, rejecting the earlier conclusions of the Accoyer Amendment in the language of scientific methodology.[12] The durability of psychoanalysis in France contributed to the ongoing tensions around diagnosis, so critical to behavioral approaches and special education, and isolation as treatment, even with French politicians taking a more vocal stance against it.[13] There were also efforts to reduce the influence of psychoanalysis within the French legal system in another attempt to curtail its relationship with the treatment of autism.[14]

Yet proponents of psychoanalysis remained steadfast in their assertion of the important role it played in the understanding of autism, even as public support became more subdued in the twenty-first century. Analysts steeped in the Lacanian tradition have emphasized their relevance in the light of the continued emphasis on changing perceivable behaviors as a method of treatment favored by practitioners of applied behavior analysis and other behavioral-based approaches.

According to analysts, this approach forces autistic persons to mimic normative behaviors—masking—which can be harmful to them and a threat to their own subjectivity.[15] Drawing on the critical element that gave psychoanalysis attention after 1968, proponents asserted that conformity operated counter to the individual approach that characterized psychoanalytically informed intervention. Echoing earlier sentiments concerning psychoanalysis as a form of manifesting negative social influences from thinkers such as Maud Mannoni, Françoise Dolto, and Bruno Bettelheim, French analysts positioned themselves as fighting against a global hegemony of behavioralism.[16] The Lacanian approach, while under fire in France, has found supporters in Brazil, Argentina, and Italy in the twenty-first century, especially with the interest in psychoanalysis and criticisms of the appropriateness of anglophone approaches in those national contexts and the different understandings of autism in these states. Like the situation in France, the influence of psychoanalysis within the university system provided a method of projecting influence within the medical fields in these different countries. Despite the efforts of parents' associations throughout the twentieth and twenty-first centuries to undermine the connection of psychoanalysis to autism, it was still a vocal part of the conversation and finding new avenues of support, even outside France, and gave a level of credence to the value of the French divergence in offering a different path for others to follow.

Self-advocacy groups saw the tensions of the *bataille de l'autisme* as a limitation to developing an effective method of recognizing the equality and humanity of autistic persons, with each side of the conflict failing to address the true challenges they faced throughout their lifetime and continuing to medicalize autism. The French state's shift toward more biological approaches and research into genetics led to concerns about eugenics from CLE Autistes in response to the Cohorte Marianne project. Launched in 2023, Cohorte Marianne purported interest in identifying biological and environmental determinants of autism, but the association saw these outcomes as an effort to eliminate autistic populations, revealing skepticism about an emphasis on science as the necessary pathway to helping autistic individuals. For CLE Autistes, Cohorte Marianne operated in a similar fashion as psychiatry had done before—to legitimize the social inequality of autistic people.[17] Perhaps summed up best by Peter Crosbie, the issue in France was not whether autism was "a psychosis or psychopathology," but rather "who gets to fix them [autists]."[18] The shared concept that linked the various sides of the *bataille* was that autistic persons needed to be fixed to fit into French society, and while the issues of neurodiversity are not unique to France, Crosbie saw the hostility toward disability as part of the assimilation demand of modern French political culture. Autistic self-advocates saw that the shift toward science was merely a new iteration of the ongoing *bataille* and something that would not transform their lives in a way that recognized their individuality.

All of these social actors—parents, politicians, professionals, and autistic persons—operated within the contours of the French divergence that helped to define the meaning of autism as rooted in childhood, even with the vast growth of adult populations. Socially, culturally, medically, and politically, autistic individuals lived as perpetual children thanks to the forces that dictated their experiences through specific lenses that had little to do with their individual lives or the other challenges they faced. This situation meant that ideas about the origin of and response to autism lay squarely in the field of child psychology. And as children, autistic individuals had little agency to assert themselves and their identities. Although the rhetoric of childhood was combined with understandings of autism, autism still was perceived as outside childhood: different, alien, children but not children. This paradox played out in various forms of treatment, debates about those treatments, and questions about origins and social responsibilities concerning autism. In the intersection of disability and childhood, autistic persons were often marginalized, isolated, and ignored, and even with the succession of national attempts to address the situation, the French state could not break away from its emphasis on understanding autism through the lens of childhood and directed its economic power toward children.

The family was socially responsible for the care of children, which played out in the treatment of autism. While society had a role, it was culturally within the family where action had to happen, where autistic persons found advocates, and where political action was energized. The parents' associations, however, often reified the equivocation of autism and childhood, at times by design and at times passively. Using the social power of children's issues to attempt to address the problems facing autistic French individuals during the twentieth century, the image of the child was inscribed as the exemplar of autism, limiting the social imagination to all the varieties of autism and making debates as much about parental rights as individual ones. This connection did contribute to the growth of associations into a national force, but also confounded similar growth in self-advocacy groups. National associations were part of policy discussions, but the inclusion of autistic individuals in such plans was minor at best. Again, the lacuna pointed toward autism's connection to childhood undermined the ability of autistic adults to lead a self-advocacy movement to change this equation. The chosen exile of highly visible self-advocates to Belgium suggested that the French divergence was rooted in deeper issues than psychoanalysis against behavioralism or parents against professionals. As adults, autistic individuals had to be exceptional to be heard, leaving many more without a voice, save for parents, whose continued presence in debates only made the childhood connection easier to assert. With the debate about the French position on autism ongoing, the durable notion of autistic persons as perpetual children has impacted the ability of French society to fully address the needs of the autism community and reckon with the rights and inclusion of the entirety of that community, despite the promises not only of national plans, but also of those of the French Republic.

NOTES

1. Édouard Philippe, "Stratégie nationale pour l'autisme 2018–2022: Changeons la donne! [April 6, 2018]", Gouvernement français, accessed December 20, 2024, https://www.info.gouv.fr/actualite/10095-strategie-nationale-pour-l-autisme.

2. Ministère des Solidarités, de l'Autonomie et de l'Egalité entre les femmes et les hommes, *Stratégie nationale pour l'autisme au sein des troubles du neuro-développement*, 3, https://handicap.gouv.fr/IMG/pdf/strategie_nationale_autisme_2018.pdf. The Ministry of Disabled People was formed in 1969, but autistic populations had long had an unclear relationship with the organization because of the question of whether autism was a disability or an illness.
3. Stéphanie Cheval, "Autism Diagnosis: An Uphill Battle," *France in Focus*, April 18, 2023, https://www.france24.com/en/tv-shows/france-in-focus/20230418-autism-diagnosis-an-uphill-battle.
4. "La stratégie nationale autisme et troubles du neuro-développement," Ministère des solidarités et des familles, August 1, 2023, https://handicap.gouv.fr/la-strategie-nationale-autisme-et-troubles-du-neuro-developpement#:~:text=Les%20chiffres&text=La%20Haute%20Autorit%C3%A9%20de%20sant%C3%A9%20estime%20donc%20qu'environ%20100,adultes%20sont%20autistes%20en%20France.
5. Raven Bureau and Céline Clément, "'Survival Classes for a Neurotypical World': What French Autistic Adults Want and Need after Receiving an Autism Diagnosis," *Autism* 28, no. 4 (April 2024): 846.
6. "Interview de Josef Schovanec, «Etre malheureux comme un autiste en France»," *Le magazine de la différence*, April 27, 2021, https://lemagazinedeladifference.com/interview-de-josef-schovanec-etre-malheureux-comme-un-autiste-en-france/.
7. Jérémy Mandin, "When Universal Health Care Falls Short, French People with Disabilities Move to Belgium," *The Conversation*, January 17, 2023, https://theconversation.com/when-universal-health-care-falls-short-french-people-with-disabilities-move-to-belgium-194963.
8. "France Has Violated the Rights of People with Disabilities, Rules Council of Europe," *The Local* France, April 17, 2023, https://www.thelocal.fr/20230417/france-has-violated-the-rights-of-people-with-disabilities-rules-council-of-europe.
9. Apolline Convain, "Autisme: Georgio Loiseau, un maire et un père en grève de la faim," *Le Monde*, June 2, 2023, https://www.lemonde.fr/societe/article/2023/06/02/handicap-georgio-loiseau-un-maire-et-un-pere-en-greve-de-la-faim_6175880_3224.html.
10. Sandrine Etoa-Andegue, "Le maire de Poses, dans l'Eure, revient sur son combat entamé en mai dernier afin d'alerter sur la situation de son fils autiste," *France info*, August 21, 2023, https://www.francetvinfo.fr/replay-radio/ils-ont-fait-l-actu/ils-ont-fait-l-actu-georgio-loiseau-maire-de-l-eure-a-fait-une-greve-de-la-faim-pour-aider-son-enfant-autiste_5945708.html.
11. Agnès Aflalo, *The Failed Assassination of Psychoanalysis: The Rise and Fall of Cognitivism*, trans. A. R. Price (New York: Routledge, 2015), 128.
12. Guénaël Visentini, "Fifteen Years after the INSERM Report: Psychoanalysis's Efficacy Reevaluated," *L'évolution psychiatrique* 86, no. 3 (September 2021): 1–17.
13. Sarah Mackel, "On Neglect for Those Impacted by Autism in France," *The Roosevelt Group*, June 14, 2022, https://www.roosevelt-group.org/quick-takes/on-neglect-for-those-impacted-by-autism-in-france.
14. Cécile Thibert, "Des psychiatres et des psychologues appellent à exclure la psychanalyse des tribunaux," *Le figaro*, October 30, 2019, https://sante.lefigaro.fr/article/des-psychiatres-et-des-psychologues-appellent-a-exclure-la-psychanalyse-des-tribunaux/.

15. Eric Garcia, *We're Not Broken: Changing the Autism Conversation* (New York: Houghton Mifflin Harcourt, 2021), 178–80.
16. Laura Tarsia and Kristina Valendiova, "Introduction," in *Treating Autism Today: Lacanian Perspectives*, ed. Laura Tarsia and Kristina Valendiova (New York: Routledge, 2022), 6.
17. CLE Autistes, "#StopCohorteMarianne—Contre l'eugénisme gouvernmental," CLE Autistes, May 16, 2023, https://cle-autistes.fr/stop-cohorte-marianne-eugenisme-gouvernemental/.
18. Peter Crosbie, "Autism in France," The Autism Advantage (2018), accessed December 20, 2024, https://autism-advantage.com/autism-in-france.html.

BIBLIOGRAPHY

Serials

A.S.I.T.P. Île-de-France: Bulletin de liaison
Autisme Île-de-France: Bulletin de liaison
En avant: Bulletin hebodomaire de l'armée du salut
Epanouir
Esprit
Express
Le figaro
Le havre
L'impartial
Journal officiel de la République française: Débats parlementaires
La lettre de l'ARAPI
La lettre d'autisme France
Le Monde
The New York Times
Nos enfants inadaptés
Le nouvel observateur
Papillons blancs ADAPEI
Papillons blancs des Côtes du Nord
Le papotin
Le parisien
Pro Aid Autisme: La forteresse éclatée
Sésame: Bulletin de l'ASITP
Sud-Ouest
Ta main pour parler bulletin
UNAFAM
Vie et bonté: Nouvelles de la Croix-Rouge française

Unpublished and other sources

Archives Nationales (hereafter AN) 19840763/1
Circulaire AS/EN n° 95-12 du 27 avril 1995
Literature on the Orthogenic School, n.d., Orthogenic School Archives, University of Chicago Special Collections
Loi n° 75 534 du 30 juin 1975 d'orientation en faveur des personnes handicapées

Loi n° 96-1076 du 11 décembre 1996 modifiant la loi n° 75-535 du 30 juin 1975 relative aux institutions sociales et médico-sociales et tendant à assurer une prise en charge adaptée de l'autisme

No. 13/2002 International Association Autism-Europe v. France Complaint (July 27, 2002): Decision on the merits: International Association Autism-Europe v. France, Collective Complaint No. 13/2002

Resolution ResChS (2004) 1, Collective complaint no. 13/2002, Autism-Europe against France

Published Sources

Accampo, Elinor Ann, Rachel G. Fuchs, and Mary Lynn Stewart. *Gender and the Politics of Social Reform in France, 1870–1914.* Baltimore: Johns Hopkins University Press, 1995.

Aflalo, Agnès. *The Failed Assassination of Psychoanalysis: The Rise and Fall of Cognitivism.* Translated by A. R. Price. New York: Routledge, 2015.

Amouroux, Rémy, and Nicholas Zaslawski. "Beyond Indifference and Aversion: The Critical Reception and Belated Acceptance of Behavior Theory in France." *History of Psychology* 20, no. 3 (2017): 313–29.

Amouroux, Rémy, and Nicholas Zaslawski. "'The Damned Behaviorist' versus French Phenomenologists: Pierre Naville and the French Indigenization of Watson's Behaviorism." *History of Psychology* 23, no. 1 (2020): 77–98.

Apgar, Amanda. *The Disabled Child: Memoirs of a Normal Future.* Ann Arbor: University of Michigan Press, 2023.

Apple, Rima Dombrow. *Perfect Motherhood: Science and Childrearing in America.* New Brunswick, NJ: Rutgers University Press, 2006.

Assouline, Moïse "Autisme: Adolescence, sexualité et vie sociale." *L'information psychiatrique* 89, no. 7 (2013): 559–70.

Asperger, Hans. "Autistic Psychopathy in Childhood." In *Autism and Asperger's Syndrome,* edited by Uta Frith, 37–92. New York: Cambridge University Press, 1991.

Asperger, Hans. *Les psychopathes autistiques pendant l'enfance.* LePlessis-Robinson, France: Inst. synthélabo pour le progrès de la connaissance, 1998.

Aussilloux, Charles, and Marie-Françoise Livoir-Petersen, eds. *L'autisme cinquante ans après Kanner.* Ramonville, France: Erès, 1994.

Autisme France. *Livre blanc: Rapport sur le vecu des autistes et de leurs familles en France à l'aube du XXIe siècle.* Paris: Autisme France, 1993.

B., Claire. *Ouvrir la nuit pour te dire.* La Chapelle Gonaguet, France: Paroles de vie, 2003.

Badinter, Élisabeth. *Mother Love: Myth and Reality, Motherhood in Modern History.* New York: Macmillan, 1981.

Barnartt, Sharon, and Richard Scotch. *Disability Protests: Contentious Politics, 1970–1999.* Washington, DC: Gallaudet University Press, 2001.

Baron-Cohen, Simon. "The Extreme Male Brain Theory." *Trends in Cognitive Science* 6, no. 6 (2002): 248–54.

Barzilai, Shuli. *Lacan and the Matter of Origins.* Stanford, CA: Stanford University Press, 1999.

Bates, Richard. "Democratic Babies? Françoise Dolto, Benjamin Spock, and the Ideology of Post-war Parenting Advice." In *Ideologies in Action: Morphological Adaption and Political Ideas,* edited by David Laycock, Maiken Umbach, and Mathew Humphrey, 201–19. New York: Routledge, 2020.

Bates, Richard. "Mediating Trauma and Anxiety: Letters to Françoise Dolto, 1976–1978." *Journal of Medical Humanities* 42, no. 2 (2021): 269–76.

Bates, Richard. *Psychoanalysis and the Family in Twentieth-Century France*. Manchester, UK: Manchester University Press, 2022.

Bélanger, Natalie, and Nicolas Garant. "Educational Opportunities and Polysemic Notions of Equality in France." In *Disability, Human Rights and Education*, edited by Felicity Armstrong and Len Barton, 132–48. Philadelphia: Open University Press, 1999.

Béliard, Aude, and Jean-Sébastien Eideliman. "Familles et handicaps mentaux ou psychiques." *Savoir/Agir* 47, no. 1 (2019): 73–82.

Berquez, Gérard. *L'autisme infantile: Introduction à une clinique relationnelle selon Kanner*. Paris: PUF, 1983.

Bettelheim, Bruno, and Daniel Karlin. *Un autre regard sur la folie*. Paris: Club français du livre, 1975.

Bettelheim, Bruno. *La forteresse vide: L'autisme infantile et la naissance du soi*. Translated by Roland Humery. Paris: Gallimard, 1969.

Bettelheim, Bruno, and Emmy Sylvester. "A Therapeutic Milieu." *American Journal of Orthopsychiatry* 18, no. 2 (1948): 191–206.

Birns, Beverly, and Niza Ben-Ner. "Psychoanalysis Constructs Motherhood." In *The Different Faces of Motherhood*, edited by Beverly Birns and D. F. Hay, 47–72. Boston: Springer, 1988.

Bishop, D. V. M., and Joel Swendsen. "Psychoanalysis in the Treatment of Autism: Why Is France a Cultural Outlier?" *BJPsych Bulletin* 45, no. 2 (2021): 89–93.

Bishop, Michael. "Review of Le Petit Prince cannibale by Françoise Lefèvre." World Literature Today 65, no. 3 (1991): 457.

Bode, Ingo. "A New Agenda for European Charity: Catholic Welfare and Organizational Change in France and Germany." *Voluntas: International Journal of Voluntary and Nonprofit Organizations* 14, no. 2 (June 2003): 205–25.

Borelle, Céline. "The Paradoxical Place of Psychiatry in the Administration of Disability: Dealing with the Reframing of Autism from a Psychiatric to an Educative Issue in the Concrete Making of a Target Public." In *Creating Target Publics for Welfare Policies: A Comparative and Multi-level Approach*, edited by Lorenzo Barrault-Stella and Pierre-Edouard Weill, 111–30. Cham, Switzerland: Springer International, 2018.

Borsay, Anne, and Pamela Dale, eds. *Disabled Children: Contested Caring, 1850–1979*. New York: Routledge, 2016.

Botbol, Michel, and Adeline Gourbil. "The Place of Psychoanalysis in French Psychiatry." *BJPsych International* 15, no. 1 (February 2018): 3–5.

Bouchet, Paul, Gérard Joinneaux, and Jean-Marc Dupeux. "Comment rester 'contre.'" *Information sociales* 90/91 (January 2001): 34–45.

Bouissac, Joffrey. *Qui j'aurai été: Journal d'un adolescent autiste*. Colmar, France: Autisme Alsace, 2002.

Bourg, Julian. "You Can't Always Get What You Want: The Psychoanalytic Ambivalence of Michel Foucault." In *The Politics of Desire: Foucault, Deleuze, and Psychoanalysis*, edited by Agustin Colombo, Edward McGushin, and Geoff Pfeifer, 123–44. Lanham, MD: Rowman & Littlefield, 2022.

Brauner, Alfred, and Françoise Brauner. *L'enfant déréel: Histoire des autismes depuis les contes de fées fictions littéraires et réalités clinques*. Toulouse, France: Privat, 1986.

Brauner, Alfred, and Françoise Brauner. *Vivre avec un enfant autistique*. Paris: Presses universitaires de France, 1978.

Brenner, Leon S. "The Autistic Mirror in the Real: Autism in Lacan's Mirror State." *Theory & Psychology* 31, no. 6 (2021): 950–72.

Brenner, Leon S. *The Autistic Subject: On the Threshold of Language*. New York: Springer, 2020.

Briggs, Jonathyne. "The Enduring Fortress: The Influence of Bruno Bettelheim in the Politics of Autism in France." *Modern Intellectual History* 17, no. 4 (2020): 1163–91.

Briggs, Jonathyne. "Les enfants perdus: Asylum Reform, Parents' Groups, and Disability Rights in France, 1968–1975." *French Politics, Culture & Society* 39, no. 3 (2021): 26–45.

Briggs, Jonathyne. "From Collaboration to Resistance: The Family Dynamic in Autism Literature in Contemporary France." *Contemporary European History* 32, no. 2 (2023): 254–69.

Briggs, Jonathyne. "Reinventing Play: Autistic Children and the Normativity of Play in Postwar France." *Historical Reflections/Réflexions historiques* 45, no. 2 (2019): 47–64.

Briggs, Jonathyne. *Sounds French: Globalization, Cultural Communities, and Pop Music, 1958–1980*. New York: Oxford University Press, 2015.

Brisenden, Simon. "Independent Living and the Medical Model of Disability." *Disability, Handicap & Society* 1, no. 2 (1986): 173–78.

Brunessaux, Loriane. "À propos du documentaire «*Le mur*»." *L'information psychiatrique* 88 (2012): 177–79.

Brusset, Bernard. "Une lecture du *Livre noir de la psychanalyse*." *Revue française de psychanalyse* 70, no. 2 (2006): 571–82.

Bureau, Raven, and Céline Clément. "'Survival Classes for a Neurotypical World': What French Autistic Adults Want and Need after Receiving an Autism Diagnosis." *Autism* 28, no. 4 (April 2024): 843–53.

Burger, Kaspar. "A Social History of Ideas Pertaining to Childcare in France and in the United States," *Journal of Social History* 45, no. 4 (2012): 1005–25.

Buten, Howard. *Il y a quelqu'un là-dedans*. Paris: Odile Jacob, 2003.

Carey, Allison C., Pamela Block, and Richard K. Scotch. *Allies and Obstacles: Disability Activism and Parents of Children with Disabilities*. Philadelphia: Temple University Press, 2020.

Carey, Allison C. *On the Margins of Citizenship: Intellectual Disability and Civil Rights in Twentieth-Century America*. Philadelphia: Temple University Press, 2009.

Chamak, Brigitte. "Autism and Social Movements: French Parents' Associations and International Autistic Individuals' Organisations." *Sociology of Health & Illness* 30, no. 1 (2008): 76–96.

Chamak, Brigitte. "Autism and Social Movements in France: A Comparative Perspective." In *Worlds of Autism: Across the Spectrum of Neurological Difference*, edited by Joyce Davidson and Michael Orsini, 239–58. Minneapolis: University of Minnesota Press, 2013.

Chamak, Brigitte. "Lobbying by Association: The Case of Autism and the Controversy over Packing Therapy in France." *Social Science and Medicine* 230 (2019): 256–63.

Cheval, Stéphanie. "Autism Diagnosis: An Uphill Battle." France in Focus, April 18, 2023, https://www.france24.com/en/tv-shows/france-in-focus/20230418-autism-diagnosis-an-uphill-battle.

Chodorow, Nancy. *The Reproduction of Mothering: Psychoanalysis and the Sociology of Gender*. Berkeley: University of California Press, 1978.

Coblence, Françoise. *Serge Lebovici*. Paris: Presses universitaires de France, 1996.

Coldefy, Magali, and Sarah E. Curtis. "The Geography of Institutional Psychiatric Care in France 1800–2000: Historical Analysis of the Spatial Diffusion of Specialised Facilities for Institutional Care of Mental Illness." *Social Science & Medicine* 71 (2010): 2117–29.

Colvin, Kelly Riccardi. *Gender and French Identity after the Second World War, 1944–1956: Engendering Frenchness*. New York: Bloomsbury, 2017.

Combes, Josette. "France." In *International Handbook of Child Care Policies and Programs*, edited by Moncrieff Cochran, 187–210. Westport, CT: Greenwood Press, 1993.

Constant, Paule. "Review of Sans histoire, plus de mots, by Frédéric Bonhomme, Caroline Tiné, Françoise Lefèvre, and Anne Garréta," *Revue des deux mondes* (1990): 168.

Courcy, Isabelle, and Catherine des Rivières. "'From Cause to Cure': A Qualitative Study on Contemporary Forms of Mother Blaming Experienced by Mothers of Young Children with Autism Spectrum Disorder." *Journal of Family Social Work* 20, no. 3 (2017): 233–50.

Crawford, Catherine. *Why French Children Don't Talk Back*. London: John Murray, 2012.

Crespin, Graciela C., ed. *Autismes: Etat des lieux du soin*. Paris: L'Harmattan, 2006.

Creton, Michel. *De quoi je me mêle: Les handicapés et nous*. Paris: Plon, 1993.

Crossley, Nick. *Contesting Psychiatry: Social Movements in Mental Health*. New York: Routledge, 2006.

Dachez, Julie. *Dans ta bulle! Les autistes ont la parole: Écoutons-les!* Vanves, France: Marabout/Hachette, 2018.

Dachez, Julie, and Mademoiselle Caroline. *Invisible Differences: A Story of Asperger's, Adulting, and Living a Life in Full Color*. Translated by Edward Gauvin. Portland, OR: Oni Press, 2020.

Danon-Boileau, Laurent. *The Silent Child: Bringing Language to Children Who Cannot Speak*. Translated by Kevin Windle. New York: Oxford University Press, 2001.

Debray-Ritzen, Pierre. *La scholastique freudienne*. Paris: Fayard, 1972.

Debray-Ritzen, Pierre. *L'usure de l'ame*. Paris: Albin Michel, 1980.

Delville, Jacqueline, Joseph Duchêne, and M. Mattys, eds. *Éthique et handicap mental*. Namur, Belgium: Presses universitaires de Namur, 1997.

Denis, Philippe. "Le couple et la famille au prisme d'une revue: Histoire des feuilles familiales (1938–1975)." *Revue d'histoire ecclésiastique* 84, no. 2 (1989): 390–403.

De Oliveira, Luiz Eduardo Prado. "Little Jeremy's Struggle with Autism, Schizophrenia and Paranoia." *International Forum of Psychoanalysis* 8, no. 3/4 (December 1999): 172-188

Dolnick, Edward. *Madness on the Couch: Blaming the Victim in the Heyday of Psychoanalysis*. New York: Simon & Schuster, 1998.

Dolto, Françoise. *Le cas Dominique*. Paris: Seuil, 1971.

Dolto, Françoise. *Lorsque l'enfant paraît, Tome 1*. Paris: Seuil, 1977.

Dolto, Françoise. *Lorsque l'enfant paraît, Tome 2*. Paris: Seuil, 1978.

Dolto, Françoise. *Lorsque l'enfant paraît, Tome 3*. Paris: Seuil, 1979.

Dolto, Françoise. *Lorsque l'enfant paraît—integrale*, France Inter FA5222, 2008. CD-ROM, nine compact discs.

Dolto, Françoise. *Séminaire de psychanalyse d'enfants*. Paris: Seuil, 1982.

Donvan, John, and Caren Zucker. *In a Different Key: The Story of Autism*. New York: Crown, 2016.

Doussinet, Pierre. "La recuperation professionnelle et sociale des déficients sensoriels et des inadaptés psychiques." *Ligue française pour la santé mentale: L'hygiène mentale*, no. 2 (1950): 35–50.

Druckerman, Pamela. *French Children Don't Throw Food*. New York: Doubleday, 2012.

Duchen, Claire. *Women's Rights and Women's Lives in France, 1944–1968*. New York: Routledge, 2003.

Duffy, John, and Rebecca Dormer. "'The Pathos of 'Mindblindness'': Autism, Science, and Sadness in 'Theory of Mind' Narratives." *Journal of Literary and Cultural Disability Studies* 5, no. 2 (2011): 201–15.

Durham, Charles. "Evolution of Services for People with Autism and Their Families in France: Influence of the TEACCH Program." *International Journal of Mental Health* 29, no. 1 (2000): 22–34.

Evans, Bonnie. *The Metamorphosis of Autism: A History of Child Development in Britain*. Manchester, UK: Manchester University Press, 2017.

Eyal, Gil, Brendan Hart, Emine Oncular, Neta Oren, and Natasha Rossi. *The Autism Matrix: The Social Origins of the Autism Epidemic*. New York: Polity Books, 2010.

Faircloth, Charlotte. *Militant Lactivism? Attachment Parenting and Intensive Motherhood in the UK and France*. New York: Berghahn Books, 2013.

Falisse, Gaston, and Marie-Françoise Falisse. *Nos enfants handicapés*. Paris: Editions universitaires, 1962.

Feinstein, Adam. *A History of Autism: Conversations with the Pioneers*. New York: Wiley-Blackwell, 2011.

Fessaguet, Dominique. "De Sophie Morgenstern l'oubliée à Françoise Dolto la tapageuse." *Topique* 2, no. 115 (2011): 79–82.

Fisher, James T. "No Search, No Subject? Autism and the American Conversion Narrative." In *Autism and Representation*, edited by Mark Osteen, 51–64. New York: Routledge, 2008.

Fishman, Sarah. *The Battle for Children: World War II, Youth Crime, and Juvenile Justice in Twentieth-Century France*. Cambridge, MA: Harvard University Press, 2002.

Fishman, Sarah. *From Vichy to the Sexual Revolution: Gender and Family Life in Postwar France*. New York: Oxford University Press, 2017.

Fondation d'entreprise France Télécom. *Répertoire de structures accueillant des personnes autistes*. Paris: Fondation d'entreprise France Télécom, 1996.

Fougeras, Nathalie. *La marquise aux pieds nus*. Saint-Etienne, France: Faralonn, 2019.

Fredet, Françine. *Mais, Madame, vous êtes la mère*. Paris: La Centurion, 1979.

Friedel, Evelyne. "Introductory Remarks on the Rights of People with Autism to Education and Employment: The Convention on the Rights of Persons with Disabilities and the European and National Perspective." In *Protecting the Rights of People with Autism in the Fields of Education and Employment: International, European, and National Perspectives*, edited by Valentina Della Fina and Rachel Cera, 1–10. New York: Springer, 2015.

Garcia, Eric. *We're Not Broken: Changing the Autism Conversation*. New York: Houghton Mifflin Harcourt, 2021.

Geissmann, Claudine, and Pierre Geissmann. *A History of Child Psychoanalysis*. New York: Routledge, 1998.

Genigar, Yizchak. "Fourth Congress of the League of International Societies for the Mentally Handicapped." *Journal of Learning Disabilities* 3, no. 3 (1970): 180–82.

Gentis, Roger. *Les murs de l'asile*. Paris: François Maspero, 1970.

Gentis, Roger. *N'être*. Paris: Flammarion, 1977.

Gitter, L. L. "From Charity to Rights." *Academic Therapy* 4, no. 3 (1969): 189–90.

Golse, Bernard. *Insister-exister: De l'être à la personne*. Paris: Presses universitaires de France, 1990.

Gomez, Jean François. *Le temps des rites: Handicaps et handicapés*. Quebec City: Presses de l'Université Laval, 2005.

Graber, Abraham, and Jessica Graber. "Applied Behavior Analysis and the Abolitionist Neurodiversity Critique: An Ethical Analysis." *Behavior Analysis in Practice* 2 (March 2023): 1–17.

Grandin, Temple. *Penser en images: Et autre témoignages sur l'autisme*. Translated by Virginie Schaefer. Paris: Grand livre du mois, 1997.

Grinker, Roy Richard. *Unstrange Minds: Remapping the Worlds of Autism*. New York: Basic Books, 2008.

Hacking, Ian. "Humans, Aliens & Autism." *Daedalus* 138, no. 3 (2009): 44–59.

Hampton, Jameel. *Disability and the Welfare State in Britain: Changes in Perception and Policy, 1948–79*. Bristol, UK: Policy Press, 2016.

Hénault, Marcelle. *Mon fils Emmanuel*. Tours, France: Mame, 1973.

Henckes, Nicolas. "Entre maladie et handicap: Repenser la critique psychiatrique de la loi du 30 juin 1975 d'orientation faveur des personnes handicapées." *ALTER, European Journal of Disability Research* 6 (2012): 242–54.

Henckes, Nicolas. "French Deinstitutionalization or the Irony of Success. Psychiatrists, the State and the Transformation of the French Psychiatric System, 1945–2010." In *Deinstitutionalisation and After. Post-war Psychiatry in the Western World*, edited by Despo Kritsotaki, Victoria Long, and Matthew Smith, 115–33. London: Palgrave Macmillan, 2016.

Herzog, Dagmar. *Cold War Freud: Psychoanalysis in the Age of Catastrophe*. New York: Cambridge University Press, 2017.

Hewitt, Jessie. *Institutionalizing Gender: Madness, the Family, and Psychiatric Power in Nineteenth-Century France*. Ithaca, NY: Cornell University Press, 2020.

Hochmann, Jacques. "Autism in the Neoliberal Age: Some Reflections." In *Treating Autism Today: Lacanian Perspectives*, edited by Laura Tarsia and Kristina Valendinova, 1–10. New York: Routledge, 2022.

Hochmann, Jacques. *Histoire de l'autisme: De l'enfant sauvage aux troubles envahissants du développement*. Paris: Odile Jacob, 2009.

Horiot, Hugo. *Autisme: j'accuse*. Paris: L'Iconoclaste, 2018.

Horiot, Hugo. *The Emperor, c'est moi*. Translated by Linda Coverdale. New York: Seven Stories Press, 2015.

Houzel, Didier. "The Psychoanalysis of Infantile Autism." *Journal of Child Psychology* 30, no. 2 (2004): 225–37.

Husson, Thérèse-Adèle, Catherine J. Kudlick, and Zina Weygand. *Reflections: The Life and Writings of a Young Blind Woman in Post-revolutionary France*. New York: New York University Press, 2001.

INSERM. *Autisme infantile: Colloque international INSERM-CNRS à l'initiative de l'ARAPI*. Paris: Editions INSERM, 1987.

INSERM. *Psychothérapie: Trois approaches évaluées*. Paris: Éditions INSERM, 2004.

Jack, Jordynn. *Autism and Gender: From Refrigerator Mothers to Computer Geeks*. Urbana: University of Illinois Press, 2014.

Jalley, Émile. *La psychanalyse et la psychologie: Aujourd'hui en France*. Paris: Vuibert, 2006.

Janin, Claude, and Denys Ribas. "Argument." *Revue française de psychanalyse* 60 (April–June 1996): 293-295.

Jarrett, Simon. "'Belief,' 'Opinion,' and 'Knowledge': The Idiot in Law in the Long Eighteenth Century." In *Intellectual Disability: A Conceptual History, 1200–1900*, edited by Patrick McDonagh, C. F. Goodley, and Tim Stainton, 162–89. Manchester, UK: Manchester University Press, 2018.

Jobs, Richard I. *Riding the New Wave: Youth and the Rejuvenation of France after the Second World War*. Stanford, CA: Stanford University Press, 2007.

Jurgensen, Geneviève. *La folie des autres: L'expérience d'une jeune éducatrice française à l'École orthogénique de Bruno Bettelheim*. Paris: Robert Laffont, 1973.

Kallivayalil, Roy Abraham. "The Burgholzli Hospital: Its History and Legacy." *Indian Journal of Psychiatry* 58, no. 2 (Spring 2016): 226–28.

Kanner, Leo. "Problems of Nosology and Psychodynamics of Early Infantile Autism." *American Journal of Orthopsychiatry* 19, no. 3 (July 1949): 416–26.

Kapp, Steven K., ed. *Autistic Community and the Neurodiversity Movement: Stories from the Frontline*. New York: Palgrave Macmillan, 2020.

Karlin, Daniel and Tony Lainé. La raison de plus fou. Paris: Editions sociales, 1977.

Kelly, Michael. "French Intellectuals: The Legendary Exception." In *The French Exception*, edited by Emmanuel Godin and Tony Chafer, 193–207. New York: Berghahn Books, 2005.

Klein, Melanie. "Early Stages of the Oedipus Conflict (1928)." In *The Selected Melanie Klein*, edited by Juliet Mitchell, 69–83. New York: Free Press, 1987.

Knibiehler, Yvonne. *La révolution maternelle: Femmes, maternité, citoyenneté depuis 1945*. Paris: Perrin, 1997.

Kolvin, I., C. Ounsted, M. Humphrey, and A. McNay. "Studies in the Childhood Psychoses. II. The Phenomenology of Childhood Psychoses." *The British Journal of Psychiatry: The Journal of Mental Science* 118 (April 1971): 385–95.

Kugelmann, Robert, and Jacob A. Belzen. "Historical Intersections of Psychology, Religion, and Politics in National Contexts." *History of Psychology* 12, no. 3 (2009): 125–31.

Kuisel, Richard. *Seducing the French: The Dilemma of Americanization*. Berkeley: University of California Press, 1993.

Lacan, Jacques. Écrits*: The First Complete Edition in English*. Translated by Bruce Fink. New York: W. W. Norton, 2006.

Laurent, Eric. *La bataille de l'autisme: De la clinique à la politique*. Paris: Navarin/Le champ freudien, 2012.

Le Billon, Karen. *French Kids Eat Everything: How Our Family Moved to France, Cured Picky Eating, Banned Snacking, and Discovered 10 Simple Rules for Raising Happy, Healthy Eaters*. New York: Harper Collins, 2012.

Lebovici, Serge. *Un cas de psychose infantile: Étude psychanalytique*. Paris: Presses universitaires de France, 1960.

Lebovici, Serge. "Contribution à l'étude nosologique et psychopathologique de la schizphrenie infantile." *Evolution psychiatrique* 1949:329–52.

Lefèvre, Françoise. *Le petit prince cannibale*. Paris: J'ai Lu, 1990.

Lelord, Gilbert, and Dominique Sauvage. *L'autisme de l'enfant*. Paris: Masson, 1991.

Lemarchand, M. "International League of Societies for the Mentally Handicapped, 3rd International Congress." *Occupational Therapy* 29, no. 9 (September 1966): 21–22.

Leon, Sharon M. An Image of God: The Catholic Struggle with Eugenics. Chicago: University of Chicago Press, 2013.

Lerch, Dominique. "Séparer, intégrer, inclure: Enfants handicapés à l'école." *Ethnology française* 39, no. 3 (July–September 2009): 443–51.

Letablier, Marie-Thérèse, and Ingrid Jönsson. "Caring for Children: The Logics of Public Action." In *Working Mothers in Europe: A Comparison of Policies and Practices*, edited by Ute Gerhard, Trudie Knijn, and Anja Weckwert, 41–57. Northampton, MA: Edward Elgar, 2005.

Ligue française de l'enseignement et de l'éducation permanente. *Le drame de Froissy: La presse découvre l'enfance inadaptée*. Paris: Ligue française de l'enseignement et de l'éducation permanente, 1969.

Longmore, Paul K. "'Heaven's Special Child': The Making of Poster Children." In *The Disability Studies Reader*, edited by Lennard J. Davis, 34–41. New York: Routledge, 2013.

Longmore, Paul K. *Telethons: Spectacle, Disability, and the Business of Charity*. New York: Oxford University Press, 2016.

Losserand, Jean. "La psychanalyse d'enfant: L'histoire de la psychanalyse d'enfants en France." *Le coq-héron* 119 (February 1991): 3–65.

Lovaas, Ivar, R. Koegel, J. Q. Simmons, and J. S. Long. "Some Generalization and Follow-Up Measures on Autistic Children in Behavior Therapy." *Journal of Applied Behavior Analysis* 6, no. 1 (1973): 131–65.

Malaguarnera, Serafino. *Théorisations psychanalytiques sur l'autisme et psychose infantile: Et l'école du quotidien*. Paris: Publibook/Société des écrivains, 2006.

Malson, Lucien. *Les enfants sauvages: Mythe et réalité*. Paris: 10/18, 1964.

Mannoni, Maud. *The Backward Child and His Mother: A Psychoanalytic Study*. Translated by A. M. Sheridan. New York: Pantheon Books, 1972.

Mannoni, Maud. *The Child, His "Illness" and the Others*. New York: Pantheon Books, 1970.

Mannoni, Maud. *Education impossible*. Paris: Seuil, 1973.

Mannoni, Maud. *Un lieu pour vivre: Les enfants de Bonneuil, leurs parents et l'équipe des "soignants."* Paris: Seuil, 1976.

McDougall, Joyce, and Serge Lebovici. *Dialogue with Sammy: A Psycho-analytical Contribution to the Understanding of Child Psychosis*. New York: Avon Books, 1969.

McGuire, Anne. *War on Autism: On the Cultural Logic of Normative Violence*. Ann Arbor: University of Michigan Press, 2016.

McLaughlin, Janice, Edmund Coleman-Fountain, and Emma Claverling. *Disabled Childhoods: Monitoring Differences and Emerging Identities*. New York: Routledge, 2016.

Mehahem, Ruth. *Joyce McDougall*. Paris: Presses universitaires de France, 1997.

Menechal, Jean. *Psychanalyse et politique: Le complexe de thésée*. Paris: Erès, 2008.

Mesibov, Gary B., Victoria Shea, and Eric Schopler. *The TEACCH Approach to Autism Spectrum Disorders*. New York: Springer, 2004.

Meyer, Catherine, and Mikkel Borch-Jacobsen, eds. Le livre noir de la psychanalyse*: Vivre, penser et aller mieux sans Freud*. Paris: Arènes, 2005.

Middleton, Laura. *Disabled Children: Challenging Social Exclusion*. New York: Wiley, 1999.

Milcent, Catherine. *L'autisme au quotidien*. Paris: Odile Jacob, 1991.

Misès, Roger, Nicole Garret-Gloanec, and Yvonne Coinçon. "Classification de l'autisme et des psychoses précoces, plaidoyer pour des convergences." *L'information psychiatrique* 86, no. 3 (2010): 223–26.

Misès, Roger, Nicole Garret-Gloanec, and Yvonne Coinçon. *L'enfant déficient mental: Approche dynamique*. Paris: PUF, 1975.

Misès, Roger, Nicole Garret-Gloanec, Yvonne Coinçon, Jacques Fortineau, Philippe Jeammet, et al. "A French Classification of Mental Disorders in Children and Adolescents." *La psychiatrie de l'enfant* 31, no. 1 (1988): 67–134.

Mitchell, David, and Sharon Snyder. "The Eugenic Atlantic: Race, Disability, and the Making of an International Eugenic Science, 1800–1945." *Disability and Society* 18, no. 7 (2003): 843–64.

Mitchell, David, and Sharon Snyder. *Cultural Locations of Disability*. Chicago: University of Chicago Press, 2006.

Morgan, Sian. "Childhood Psychosis." In *Theory and Practice in Child Psychoanalysis: An Introduction to the Work of Françoise Dolto*, edited by Guy Hall, Françoise Hivernel, and Sian Morgan, 39–62. New York: Routledge, 2009.

Morgenstern, Sophie. "Un cas de mutisme psychogène." *Revue française de psychanalyse* 1, no. 3 (1927): 492–504.

Morgenstern, Sophie. "La psychanalyse infantile et son rôle dans l'hygiène mentale," *Revue française de psychanalyse* 4, no. 1 (1930): 136–62.

Moro, Marie Rose. "Entretien avec Joyce McDougall," *Le carnet PSY* 67 (July 2001): 20–27.

Murray, Stuart. *Representing Autism: Culture, Narrative, Fascination*. Liverpool, UK: Liverpool University Press, 2008.

Nadesan, Majia Holmer. *Constructing Autism: Unraveling the "Truth" and Understanding the Social*. New York: Routledge, 2005.

Ohayon, Annick. *L'impossible rencontre: Psychologie et psychanalyse en France 1919–1969*. Paris: La découverte, 1999.

Orchard, Vivienne. "*Autisme, j'accuse!* Life-Writing, Autism and Politics in the Work of Hugo Horiot." *French Cultural Studies* 30, no. 3 (2019): 256–65.

Park, Clara Claiborne. *The Siege: The First Eight Years of an Autistic Child*. New York: Harcourt, Brace, and World, 1967.

Parnas, Josef, Pierre Bovet, and Dan Zahavi, "Schizophrenic Autism: Clinical Phenomenology and Pathogenic Implications." *World Psychiatry: Official Journal of the World Psychiatric Association* 1, no. 3 (October 2002): 131–36.

Peeters, Théo. *Autism: From Theoretical Understanding to Educational Intervention*. San Diego, CA: Singular, 1997.

Peeters, Théo. *Autisme: La forteresse éclatée*. Paris: Pro Aid Autisme, 1988.

Pelka, Fred. *What We Have Done: An Oral History of the Disability Rights Movement*. Amherst, MA: University of Massachusetts Press, 2012.

Perrin, Burt. "The Original 'Scandinavian' Normalization Principle and Its Continuing Relevance for the 1990s." In *A Quarter-Century of Normalization and Social Role Valorization: Evolution and Impact*, edited by Robert J. Flynn and Raymond A. Lemay, 181–96. Ottawa, ON: University of Ottawa Press, 1999.

Pierret, Janine. "The Social Meanings of Health: Paris, the Essonne, the Herault." In *Le sens du mal: Anthropologie, histoire, sociologie de la maladie*, edited by Marc Augé and Claudine Herzlich, 175–206. Paris: Éditions des archives contemporaines, 1983.

Porret, Philippe. *Joyce McDougall: Une écoute lumineuse*. Clamency, France: Campagne Première, 2006.

Pripas-Kapit, Sarah. "Historicizing Jim Sinclair's 'Don't Mourn for Us': A Cultural and Intellectual History of Neurodiversity's First Manifesto." In *Autistic Community and the Neurodiversity Movement*, edited by Steven K. Kapp, 23–39. New York: Palgrave Macmillan, 2020.

Razon, Laure, Olivier Putois, and Alain Vanier. "The Lacanian Concept of Cut in Light of Lacan's Interactions with Maud Mannoni." *Frontiers in Psychology* 8 (December 2017): 1–10.

Richardson, John G. "Unintended Convergence: Introduction, Thesis, Central Concept and Comparative Forms." In *The Global Convergence of Vocational and Special Education: Mass Schooling and Modern Educability*, edited by John G. Richardson, Jinting Wu, and Douglas M. Judge, 3–30. New York: Routledge, 2016.

Rimmerman, Arie. *Family Policy and Disability*. New York: Cambridge University Press, 2015.

Ritvo, Edward R., and Gloria Laxer. *Autisme: La vérité refuse*. Paris: SIMEP, 1983.

Robcis, Camille. *Disalienation: Politics, Philosophy, and Radical Psychiatry in Postwar France*. Chicago: University of Chicago Press, 2021.

Robcis, Camille. *The Law of Kinship: Anthropology, Psychoanalysis, and the Family in France*. Ithaca, NY: Cornell University Press, 2013.

Robert, Sophie, dir. *Le mur: La psychanalyse à l'épreuve de l'autisme*. Lille, France: Ocean Invisible Productions, 2011.

Rohde, Katia. *L'enfant hérisson: Autobiographie d'une autiste*. Paris: Imago, 1999.

Roos, Philip. "Parents of Mentally Retarded People." *International Journal of Mental Health* 6, no. 1 (Spring 1977): 96–119.

Rosental, Paul-André. *A Human Garden: French Policy and the Transatlantic Legacies of Eugenic Experimentation*. Translated by Carolyn Avery. New York: Berghahn Books, 2020.

Rosen, Nicole E., Catherine Lord, and Fred R. Volkmar. "The Diagnosis of Autism: From Kanner to *DSM-III* to *DSM-5* and Beyond." *Journal of Autism and Developmental Disorders* 51 (2021): 4253–70.

Ross, Kristin. *Fast Cars, Clean Bodies: Decolonization and the Reordering of French Culture*. Cambridge, MA: MIT Press, 1996.

Roudinesco, Élisabeth. *Jacques Lacan & Co.: A History of Psychoanalysis in France, 1925–1985*. Translated by Jeffrey Mehlman. Chicago: University of Chicago Press, 1990.

Roudinesco, Élisabeth. *Pourquoi tant de haine? Anatomie du* Le livre noir de la psychanalyse. Paris: Narvarin, 2005.

Roudinesco, Élisabeth. "Psychoanalysis." In *The Columbia History of Twentieth-Century French Thought*, edited by Lawrence D. Kritzman, 100–101. New York: Columbia University Press, 2006.

Roudinesco, Élisabeth. *Why Psychoanalysis?* Translated by Rachel Bowlby. New York: Columbia University Press, 2001.

Royol, Jean-Pierre. *La cause de l'autiste*. Paris: L'Harmattan, 2019.

Rubins, Beatriz Markman. *Pioneers of Child Psychoanalysis: Influential Theories and Practices in Healthy Child Development*. New York: Routledge, 2014.

Salomonsson, Björn. "Psychodynamic Therapies with Infants and Parents: A Critical Review of Treatment Methods." In *Advances in Psychodynamic Psychiatry*, edited by César A. Alfonso, Richard C. Friedman, and Jennifer I. Downey, 247–68. New York: Guilford Press, 2018.

Schaefer, Joy C. "Truffaut's *L'enfant sauvage* (The Wild Child, 1970): Evoking Autism and the Nascent 'Eugenic Atlantic.'" *Ought: The Journal of Autistic Culture* 1 (2019): 10–41.

Schafer, Roy. "Narration in the Psychoanalytic Dialogue." *Critical Inquiry* 7, no. 1 (Autumn 1980): 29–53.

Schopler, Eric, and Gary B. Mesibov. "Guest Editor's Introduction: Cross-cultural Priorities in Developing Autism Services." *International Journal of Mental Health* 29, no. 1 (2000): 11–12.

Schopler, Eric, and Gary B. Mesibov. "Parent Essays." In *High-Functioning Individuals with Autism*, edited by Eric Schopler and Gary B. Mesibov, 275–81. New York: Plenum Press, 1992.

Schovanec, Josef. *Je suis à l'est: Savant et autiste un témonage unique*. Paris: Plon, 2012.

Schreibman, Laura. *The Science and Fiction of Autism*. Cambridge MA: Harvard University Press, 2005.

Seligmann, Guy, dir. *Vivre à Bonneuil*. Paris: Office de radiodiffusion-télévision française, 1975.

Shakespeare, Tom. "The Social Model of Disability." *The Disability Studies Reader* 2, no. 3 (2006): 197–204.

Shapira, Michal. *The War Inside: Psychoanalysis, Total War, and the Making of the Democratic Self in Postwar Britain*. Cambridge: Cambridge University Press, 2013.

Sheffer, Edith. *Asperger's Children: The Origins of Autism in Nazi Vienna*. New York: W. W. Norton, 2018.

Silberman, Steve. *NeuroTribes: The Legacy of Autism and the Future of Neurodiversity*. New York: Avery Books, 2015.

Silverman, Chloe. *Understanding Autism: Parents, Doctors, and the History of a Disorder*. Princeton, NJ: Princeton University Press, 2012.

Stevenson, Jennifer L., Bev Harp, and Morton Ann Gernsbacher. "Infantilizing Autism." *Disability Studies Quarterly* 31, no. 3 (2011): 1–17.

Stiker, Henri-Jacques. *A History of Disability*. Translated by William Sayers. Ann Arbor: University of Michigan Press, 2019.

Sufian, Sandra M. *Familial Fitness: Disability, Adoption, and Family in Modern America*. Chicago: University of Chicago Press, 2022.

Synodinou, Claire. *Autisme infantile: Approche thérapeutique*. Paris: Aubier, 1985.

Tammet, Daniel. *Born on a Blue Day: Inside the Extraordinary Mind of an Autistic Savant*. New York: Free Press, 2007.

Tarsia, Laura and Kristina Valendiova, eds. Treating Autism Today: Lacanian Perspectives. New York: Routledge, 2022.

Tendlarz, Silvia Elena. *Childhood Psychosis: A Lacanian Perspective*. Milton Park, UK: Karnac, 2003.

Thomas, Carol. *Sociologies of Disability and Illness: Contested Ideas in Disability Studies and Medical Sociology*. New York: Palgrave Macmillan, 2017.

Togman, Richard. *Nationalizing Sex: Fertility, Fear, and Power*. New York: Oxford University Press, 2019.

Touze, Jacques, ed. *Meltzer in Paris*. Chicago: Phoenix, 2017.

Treese-Daquin, Catherine. *Autisme et culture: Balades au Musée du Louvre*. Grasse, France: Autisme Diffusion, 2016.

Turkle, Sherry. *Psychoanalytic Politics: Jacques Lacan and Freud's French Revolution*. New York: Basic Books, 1978.

Tustin, Frances. "Thoughts on Autism with Special Reference to a Paper by Melanie Klein." *Journal of Child Psychotherapy* 9 (1983): 119–31.

Tustin, Frances.Autism and Childhood Psychosis. London: Hogarth Press, 1972.

Twachtman-Cullen, Diane. *A Passion to Believe: Autism and the Facilitated Communication Phenomenon*. Boulder, CO: Westview Press, 1997.

UNESCO. *International Yearbook of Education*. Vol. 28. Geneva: International Bureau of Education and UNESCO, 1967.

Union national des associations des parents d'enfants inadaptés, *Rencontres de Vichy (2e): Autisme et psychose* (21–22 mars 1981). Paris: UNAPEI, 1981.

Urfer, Annick. "Phenomenology and Psychopathology of Schizophrenia: The Views of Eugene Minkowski." *Philosophy, Psychiatry, and Psychology* 8, no. 4 (December 2001): 279–89.

Vallade, Florence. "Autisme: L'écran des évidences éducatives." *Éducation et sociétés* 36, no. 2 (2015): 35–49.

Vaincre l'autisme. *Position scientifique contre la psychanalyse appliquée à l'autisme*. Paris: Vaincre l'autisme, 2016.

Van Bueren, Geraldine. *Child Rights in Europe: Convergence and Divergence in Judicial Protection*. Strasbourg: Council of Europe, 2007.

Van Eijk, Liza, and Brendan P. Zietsch. "Testing the Extreme Male Brain Hypothesis: Is Autism Spectrum Disorder Associated with a More Male-Typical Brain?" *Autism Research: Official Journal of the International Society for Autism Research* 14, no. 8 (2021): 1597–608.

Vanheule, Stijn. *The Subject of Psychosis: A Lacanian Perspective*. New York: Palgrave Macmillan, 2011.

Vanier, Catherine, and Kareen Malone. "The Experimental School in Bonneuil-sur-Marne . . . with Commentary from a North American Context." *Frontiers in Psychology* 8 (October 2017): 1–7.

Vattier, G. "Experimental Pedagogy in France," *Journal of Educational Psychology* 1, no. 7 (1910): 389–403.

Verdier, Pierre. "Les décrets d'application de la loi rénovant l'action sociale et medico-sociale." *Journal du droit des jeunes* 6, no. 226 (2003): 23–34.

Vicedo, Marga. *Intelligent Love: The Story of Clara Park, Her Autistic Daughter, and the Myth of the Refrigerator Mother*. Boston: Beacon Press, 2020.

Visentini, Guénaël. "Fifteen Years after the INSERM Report: Psychoanalysis's Efficacy Reevaluated." *L'évolution psychiatrique* 86, no. 3 (September 2021): 1–17.

Wacjman, Claude, and Olivier Douville. "La fabrication de l'«autiste handicapé». Chronique d'un passage à l'acte." *Figures de la psychanalyse* 24, no. 2 (2012): 99–129.

Waltz, Mitzi. *Autism: A Social and Medical History*. New York: Palgrave Macmillan, 2013.

Watters, Ethan. *Crazy Like Us: The Globalization of the American Psyche*. New York: Free Press, 2010.

Webb, Eugene. *The Self Between: From Freud to the New Social Psychology of France*. Seattle: University of Washington Press, 1993.

Williams, Donna. *Si on me touche je n'existe plus: Le témoignage exceptionnel d'une jeune autiste*. Translated by Fabienne Gérard. Paris: Grand livre du mois, 1992.

Winance, Myriam, Isabelle Ville, and Jean-François Ravaud. "Disability Policies in France: Changes and Tensions between the Category-Based, Universalist, and Personalized Approaches." *Scandinavian Journal of Disability Research* 9, no. 3–4 (2007): 160–81.

Windebank, Jan. "Family." In *Encyclopedia of Contemporary French Culture*, edited by Alex Hughes, Alexandra Hughes, and Keith A. Reader, 198. New York: Routledge, 1998.

Wing, Lorna. "The Relationship between Asperger's Syndrome and Kanner's Autism." In *Autism and Asperger's Syndrome*, edited by Uta Firth, 93–121. Cambridge: Cambridge University Press, 1991.

Winzer, Margaret A. *The History of Special Education: From Isolation to Integration.* Washington, DC: Gallaudet University Press, 1993.

Wustefeld, Sophie, and Timothy Scott Johnson. "Maud Mannoni and Piera Aulagnier on Mental Illness and Disability: Parents at the Boundary between Society and Childhood (France 1960–1980)." *Psychoanalysis and History* 21, no. 2 (2019): 193–209.

INDEX

For the benefit of digital users, indexed terms that span two pages (e.g., 52–53) may, on occasion, appear on only one of those pages.